THE TRAINING OF TEACHERS
IN ENGLAND AND WALES DURING THE
NINETEENTH CENTURY

THE TRAINING OF TEACHERS
IN ENGLAND AND WALES
DURING THE NINETEENTH CENTURY

by

R. W. RICH

Professor of Education, University College
Hull

CAMBRIDGE
AT THE UNIVERSITY PRESS
1933

CAMBRIDGE
UNIVERSITY PRESS

University Printing House, Cambridge CB2 8BS, United Kingdom

Cambridge University Press is part of the University of Cambridge.

It furthers the University's mission by disseminating knowledge in the pursuit of education, learning and research at the highest international levels of excellence.

www.cambridge.org
Information on this title: www.cambridge.org/9781107594265

First published 1933
First paperback edition 2015

A catalogue record for this publication is available from the British Library

ISBN 978-1-107-59426-5 Paperback

CONTENTS

FOREWORD

THE TEACHER is the most vital factor in any educational system, and it is hoped that this study will prove a useful addition to the already considerable body of historical work dealing with English education in the nineteenth century by describing and discussing the development of teachers' training during that period. Whilst considerable attention is necessarily devoted to administrative measures, which after 1846 came increasingly to dominate the field of popular education, the book is more particularly concerned with the evolution of the technique of training from the first experiments in the early monitorial training centres to the work of the Training Colleges and Universities at the close of the century.

My sincere thanks are due to Sir T. Percy Nunn, Director of the University of London Institute of Education, and Professor Frank Smith, Professor of Education at Armstrong College, Newcastle-upon-Tyne, for their kindness in reading and commenting upon the manuscript, to my colleague Mr R. K. Robertson for valuable help in reading the proofs, and to the Senate of the University of London for a grant towards the cost of publication.

R. W. RICH

Hull
March 1933

CHAPTER I

THE TRAINING OF TEACHERS UNDER THE MONITORIAL SYSTEMS

A T the commencement of the nineteenth century England was notoriously behind her Continental neighbours in the matter of popular education. The enthusiasm which characterised certain sections of the community during the latter years of the previous century was largely promiscuous and ill informed, and the realisation came only very gradually that the first step in the education of the people was the education of the teachers of the people. The development of popular education under the monitorial systems of the National Society and the British and Foreign School Society is typical of the spirit of the age. The philanthropic educational enthusiast wished for an instrument that should have the great merit of being cheap, whilst at the same time it had all the appearance of efficiency. Readers of Carlyle will remember his chapter in *Past and Present* on "Morrison's Pill". The monitorial system was the "Morrison's Pill" in education. After the manner of patent medicines, it wrought apparently great benefit at first, but its after-effects did much to hinder natural progress. The early publications of Bell and Lancaster, and of the two great societies at first associated with their names, are full of glowing accounts of the miracles wrought by the monitorial system. It is even thought worth while to wrangle at great length as to whether Anglican Dr Bell or Quaker Joseph Lancaster was the first to make the stupendous discovery that elder boys might be set to instruct younger boys in a school. Monitorial schools sprang up all over the country, and the cause of popular education seemed to be progressing magnificently.

It took nearly forty years for the country to realise that a system which deposes the schoolmaster from the post of teacher, and makes him merely a supervisor, can never be an instrument of true education. Gradually it came to be understood that true education can arise only from the interaction between immature and mature minds, and that the monitor might be an instructor, but never an educator. At first this conception was looked upon as just another "system", associated particularly with the name of David Stow, but the "Simultaneous System" was more than a system, it was a gospel, and as the light of this gospel spread, the monitorial system was doomed. It died hard, however, and it left its mark on the English system of teachers' training in the pupil teacher system, which was a characteristically English compromise. The combination of apprenticeship with a system of residential training colleges was an endeavour to preserve whatever excellences there may have been in the "training" of teachers under the monitorial *régime,* whilst realising the unquestioned advantages of the Continental type of training, which meant the education of the prospective teacher in a residential seminary.

The most significant element in the victory of the "simultaneous" over the "monitorial" method was the realisation that the culture and skill of the teacher were of supreme importance in a national system of education. In the monitorial school it was the system that mattered, and not the teacher. Under the National Society, masters who had been trained in the society's central schools were forbidden, when appointed to schools of their own, to depart from "the beautiful and efficient simplicity of the system".[1] In the Lancasterian school, "the master should be a silent by-stander and inspector. What a master says should be done, but if he teaches on this system he will find the authority is not personal, that when *the pupils,* as well as the schoolmaster,

[1] National School Society, *Report,* 1814, p. 14.

understand how to act and learn on this system, *the system*, not the master's vague, discretionary, uncertain judgment will be in practice".[1] It was the mechanism that mattered, and not the personnel responsible for the working of the mechanism. Nevertheless, it was impossible to ignore the question of personnel altogether. The successful tending of any machine calls for some little experience in the minding of it, if possible under the supervision of an expert, and the educational machines "invented" by Lancaster and Bell were not so simple that the first man picked up in the street could successfully supervise their working without some previous experience. Thus arose the beginnings of the training of teachers. But here was no question of educating the teacher, or of making him an intelligent master of his craft through a theoretical and practical study of teaching; it was merely a question of "teaching the system", and the early years in the development of teachers' training are marked by the gradual discovery that it is an impossible task merely to "teach the system" without taking thought for the real education of those who are being trained.

In a letter from Dr Bell to Mrs Sarah Trimmer dated January 13th, 1806, there is an interesting passage which shows that at so early a date both Bell and Lancaster had turned their energies to the training of teachers to carry out their respective systems. The writer is describing his meeting with his great educational opponent.

"He also interrogated me about my mode of training teachers, and seemed not disposed on this point to copy, as he did in every other. My teachers were trained as every other boy in the school was, and selected according to their abilities. Every child in the school witnessed every process in the mode of conducting matters, and understood it well. Nothing was ever so burlesque as his forming his teachers by lectures on the passions. Let his teachers, created by his

[1] J. Lancaster, *Improvements in Education*, 1808, Appendix.

Promethean fire in one year, enter upon their task—what can they do? Or what would my little teachers have done without a man of age, authority, influence and ascendancy to direct their operations and to keep them steady to their purpose? It is by attending the school, seeing what is going on there, and taking a share in the office of tuition, that teachers are to be formed, and not by lectures and abstract instruction."[1]

One would give much to have some record of Joseph Lancaster's "lectures on the passions". Here we have an outstanding problem in the training of the teacher explicitly set forth: are we merely to train through practice, or should we add a rational study of the business of the teacher? Lancaster appears to have attempted some rudimentary psychology in connection with his training work, if we may trust the impression given in his opponent's account of the meeting. There is no explicit mention made of such instruction as a part of the training given in early days at the Borough Road, but it is likely that a man of so wayward and flamboyant a genius as Joseph Lancaster would not rest content with so humdrum a business as merely putting his "family" through the mill in his great school. With his well-developed faculty for enlarging grandiloquently upon the obvious, there is no doubt that he was capable of giving the most abstruse justifications of the simplest manœuvres in his system. We may, however, be fairly sure that, as Bell suspected, such lectures on the passions were not of very great practical assistance to the youths in training, and that they gave infinitely more satisfaction to the lecturer than to his audience. We must wait for a good many years before we find mental philosophy utilised intelligently in the training of teachers.

The "teachers" mentioned by Bell were the monitors, i.e. the senior pupils whose business it was to instruct their

[1] R. and C. C. Southey, *Life of Dr Bell*, 1844, vol. II, p. 127.

juniors, and it was to the senior of such monitors that a good deal of the missionary work connected with both the Madras and Lancasterian systems fell. One of the earliest of Lancaster's projects was the establishment of a department attached to his school at the Borough Road for the training of senior monitors in order that they in their turn might take charge of monitorial schools. In 1805 about £400 was raised in donations as a capital sum to help pay for the board of a certain number of youths, and on the strength of this a number of the leading monitors in the school were duly apprenticed to Lancaster, who undertook to board, clothe and train them as schoolmasters after his own system.[1] This was the beginning of what was consistently referred to by Lancaster as his "family", which was to prove a bone of contention in the quarrels that ensued later between the eccentric schoolmaster and the Royal Lancasterian Institution; for when the break at last definitely came, Lancaster carried off nearly the whole number of his apprentices to the private school he established at Tooting, leaving the Institution to carry on the work of training at the Borough Road.

In 1806 Lancaster formed an ambitious scheme, which, in his own words, was "A Plan for Educating 10,000 Poor Children by establishing Schools in Towns and Villages and for uniting Works of Industry with Useful Knowledge".[2] The centre of this experiment was to be the village of Maiden Bradley in Somerset, and it was Lancaster's purpose to establish as many schools as possible in the locality for the training of rural schoolmasters who were to take charge of schools of industry of this particular type. The experiment was, however, abandoned in 1809, but the idea of rural training centres remained a favourite with the British and Foreign School

[1] J. Lancaster, *Report of Joseph Lancaster's Progress*, 1811, p. 4.
[2] For particulars see pamphlet by Lancaster, *Outline of a Plan for Educating*, etc., 1806.

Society, only realised long afterwards by the establishment of the training college at Bangor.

Meanwhile the "family" at the Borough Road flourished, and in 1808 there were twenty-four persons in residence. Originally the idea had been to confine the training to monitors of the school, but soon there came a steady flow of outsiders who were desirous of learning the system in order to introduce it into their own schools. Of these, some were admitted to residence, whilst others provided themselves with private lodgings. In 1811 fifty persons in all were trained at the Royal Lancasterian Institution, and in 1812 the need was strongly felt for a similar institution for school-mistresses. This need was met soon after the foundation of the British and Foreign School Society. The period of time spent by visitors learning the system at the institution was extremely brief, and three months was looked upon as the outside limit. Lancaster and his supporters pushed the system far and wide, and as their enterprise abroad increased, so foreigners were sent with increasing frequency to Southwark. In 1809 "Tapahoe" of Otaheite was a student, in 1810 a West Indian negro came to study the system, and in 1811 the foreign element was represented by one Isaac Tolling, a Danish prisoner-of-war from Copenhagen, together with "George" and "Billy" from Sierra Leone.[1]

In spite of the loss of so many apprentices arising out of the secession of Lancaster in 1812, the newly formed British and Foreign School Society set themselves vigorously to the task of training teachers, and the scope of the training department was clearly set forth in the "Rules and Regulations for the Government of the Institution".

"3. . . . It shall support and train up young persons of both sexes for supplying properly instructed Teachers to the in-habitants of such places in the British dominions, at home and abroad, as shall be desirous of establishing schools on

[1] H. B. Binns, *A Century of Education*, 1908, p. 54.

the British system. It shall instruct all persons, whether natives or foreigners, who may be sent from time to time, for the purpose of being qualified as Teachers in this or any other country."[1]

The training was definitely training in the "system", and was carried out exclusively in the school at the Borough Road. Here was, in the strictest sense of the term, the Model School of the Plan, organised by the founder himself, and exhibiting the system at work in its most perfect form. Those in training worked in this school as monitors, and their sole business was to become familiar with as much of the routine as was possible during the short time at their disposal. They had not come there to educate themselves, nor even to learn the art of teaching in general, but had come to master the particular tricks devised by Lancaster to facilitate the drilling of a very large number of children in the mechanical rudiments of learning. It was essentially a method of "learning by doing".

Meanwhile similar activity was being manifested by the Church party in education, under the vigorous leadership of Dr Bell. The inventor of the "Madras Plan" soon realised the extreme importance of the development of some kind of training for teachers, if his cherished "Plan" was to be disseminated successfully throughout England. In a letter previous to the formation of the National Society he wrote:

"We shall never thrive as we ought, till we have one school in perfect order in the metropolis, where masters may be trained and to which they may be referred".[2]

A start was made by the instruction in the system of two beginners at the school in Gower's Walk, but it was felt that a real model school was needed, that might worthily correspond to the Lancasterian central school in the Borough. When the "Metropolitan Society for promoting the Educa-

[1] British and Foreign School Society, *Annual Report*, 1814, p. 3.
[2] R. and C. C. Southey, *op. cit.* vol. II, p. 343.

tion of the Poor in the Principles of the Established Church"
was formed in 1811, one of the earliest resolutions of this
body was

"That for the purpose of supplying masters wherever they
may be wanted, a central institution be established in the
metropolis, at which the present masters of the parochial and
charity schools, as also any other masters who are members
of the Church of England, if they are willing to learn the
new method of instruction, shall receive every encouragement and assistance".[1]

It was this resolution that led to the foundation of the
school at Baldwin's Gardens, which was to be the centre of
the teachers' training activities of the National Society for
the thirty years that preceded the institution of residential
colleges aided by grant from the Committee of Council on
Education. It was originally designed to accommodate 600
boys and 400 girls. This institution was to perform a large
number of functions. Besides being a school for the poor of
the locality, it was to be a centre of training, and also the
headquarters of the missionary activity of the society. The
duties of the Superintendent, the Rev. W. Johnson, illustrate
this clearly. In addition to his duties in organising the work
of the school, he had to direct and supervise the work of
those who came to the school to be trained in the Madras
Plan, to deal with applications that arrived from all parts for
masters to set up or carry on schools, to send out travelling
organisers to carry on missionary work in the provinces, to
act as Secretary to the Committee, and to act as Chaplain.[2]

There were at the school ten organisers whose main duty
was to travel about the country giving advice on the founding
or remodelling of schools. It was their duty to know the
Madras Plan with the greatest accuracy and in minutest detail, and they were in the main young schoolmasters who had

[1] R. and C. C. Southey, *op. cit.* vol. II, pp. 344, 345.
[2] *Ibid.* pp. 363, 398–9

caught the eye of Bell or his colleagues as showing particular skill in working the system.[1]

Then there were an indefinite number of probationers, who were definitely employed by the society in its schools when vacancies occurred. These were mostly young people who were instructed, in general subjects and in the system, gratuitously at the central establishment, on the under- standing that they might be sent off to schools as need arose. They were chosen with some care, particular regard being paid to qualifications of character, which had to be attested by adequate testimonials.

In addition to these probationers, masters and mistresses attended the central institution, having been sent up by patrons to learn the Madras Plan so that they might apply it in the schools to which they were already appointed. These, as might be expected, were the most difficult to deal with. Many of them had been teaching for years, and had no desire to get out of the rut which they had worn for themselves, looking upon the system they were supposed to be learning with the customary suspicion of the experienced pedagogue for new-fangled innovations in method.

Thus in most respects the National Society developed at Baldwin's Gardens a training institution very similar to that in existence at the Borough, except that the "students" made their own arrangements for board and lodging.

Whilst this progress was being made in London, an ex- tremely interesting experiment was carried out at Bishop Auckland under the inspiration of the Bishop of Durham.[2] This was the foundation of the Barrington School, which was to serve the dual function of charity school for the town and residential "training college" for "masters and ushers". The foundation stone was laid in 1808, and the master of the Grammar School in the town was engaged as its first prin-

[1] National Society, Minute, March 11th, 1812.
[2] Sir T. Bernard, *The Barrington School*, 1812.

cipal. So far as training was concerned, the project was that there were to be nine "foundation boys" who were to act as monitors in the school under the direction of an assistant master, and in return were to be clothed, maintained and educated at the Bishop's expense. The age of admission as a foundation boy was fourteen, and the length of time spent in that capacity depended largely upon the demand for teachers in the north of England. These "students" were accommodated in a dormitory at the top of the school, and there was a garden at the back where much of their leisure time might be spent.

The school was opened on May 26th, 1810, with due celebrations. Dr Bell himself condescended to come and preach a sermon, and the prospective scholars enjoyed a "feast" provided by the Bishop. There were 70 children at the opening of the school, but later this number increased to 140. The late mistress of a girls' school which had been superseded by the Barrington School, the widow of a former curate of the town, was installed as matron to supervise the domestic economy of the institution.

There was a very brisk demand for schoolmasters, and the duration of training as a foundation boy was commonly brief. The first of the foundationers to go out into the world left the school in October, 1810, being appointed usher at a new school in Gateshead at a salary of £40 a year. When later he went elsewhere, his place was taken by another Barrington boy. Another went to Holy Island. Thus the institution began to make a name for itself, for the general opinion was that the Barrington teachers, in spite of the very short period of training, were immensely superior to the old type of teacher. So we find a clergyman writing to the Bishop of Durham:

"Your Lordship's monitor, young Mills, has effected wonders. He has read to our village schoolmaster such a lecture on pedagogy as, I hope, will not soon be forgotten".

(This was a reference to a boy sent out to assist in the re-organisation of a school already in existence, not sent out to take a permanent post.)

In addition to the foundationers, acting schoolmasters attended to learn the system in exactly the same way as at Baldwin's Gardens.

The course of training was largely a matter of "learning by doing". However, it began with a study of books that explained the system, "manuals of method" in the narrowest sense of the term. When some mastery of these works had been manifested, the pupil was placed either as "teacher" (i.e. monitor) or assistant in a class, starting at the bottom in the "sand class", and working up through the school in a period of six or eight weeks. In addition to this "teaching practice" all those in training, both foundationers and school-masters, were subjected to periodic examinations. On these occasions they formed themselves into a class just like those in the school, and worked through the school text-books, commencing with the "mono-syllabic spelling book", and taking their places in class according to proficiency, just as if they were children. The authorised method was strictly adhered to. Thus, in reading, there was no departure from the "syllabic method", which consisted in reading round the class each syllable in each word, the complete word then being repeated all round. In this way two objects were attained: those in training were prepared at one and the same time both in matter and in method, learning simultaneously how to spell and how to teach spelling. This, after all, is something like what is aimed at by the ordinary training college at the present day, although this particular method is no longer necessary. However, this plan of giving students an insight into teaching by turning them into an elementary class was one which found a definite place in training college method for a large number of years, gradually giving place to the "criticism lesson" as we know it to-day.

The rules laid down for the foundation scholars indicate well the nature of their life at the Barrington School.

"1. Cleanliness, propriety of conduct, and regularity of attendance are essentially requisites for the admission or continuance of any scholar on the foundation.

"2. The foundation scholars shall be educated and instructed for masters or ushers of public schools.

"3. The foundation scholars are to keep a daily register of their lessons and studies, their writing and cyphering, and also of what they have taught others, and to show it the master every Saturday.

"4. In case any of the foundation scholars do not, at the quarterly examination, appear to have made an adequate progress, they are to be dismissed the school and sent home to their relations or friends.

"5. The master shall in the month of July, make a report to the Lord Bishop of Durham, of such of the foundation, or other scholars, as are prepared to attend in the chapel at Auckland Castle to receive the Holy Communion."[1]

A certain amount of progress was made by the monitorial training institutions in the face of very great difficulties, but the type of training was to remain substantially unchanged until the work of David Stow at the Glasgow Normal Seminary and Kay-Shuttleworth at Battersea was to suggest a new approach to the whole question of teachers' training, which arose from a realisation that the monitorial school could never claim to be more than a stop-gap, and that the only hope of developing a sound system of popular education, as distinct from popular schooling, was to be found in the "simultaneous" method which demanded that every child in a school should be directly instructed by an adult teacher.

The great difficulty that faced the monitorial training centres was the ignorance and general low quality of the

[1] Sir T. Bernard, *op. cit.* p. 189.

material upon which they had to work. In 1814 the newly formed British and Foreign School Society appointed a "Subcommittee on Schoolmasters", consisting of Joseph Hume, James Mill and J. F. Vandercrom, to deal with this question, and in their report they indicated as the root failing of the training given at the Borough Road the fact that it was the teaching of a mechanical method and nothing more.

"The system has hitherto been very defective, as no attempt has been made to teach the youths intended for schoolmasters anything beyond the general routine of school training for children in general. That hence the greater part of the time, which might have been employed to increase their knowledge and improve their minds, has been lost, and habits of idleness rather encouraged. That the degree of ignorance, in which many of the youths have been sent out to form and conduct Schools in the Country, has been such as to reflect discredit on the Institution."[1]

Accordingly they recommended that students should receive special instruction in school subjects, apart from what they picked up in their practice in the school, and particularly in English grammar, "to qualify them to speak and write their own language with correctness and propriety", handwriting, arithmetic, geography and history. For this purpose a Mr Daniel was appointed, and a permanent committee was established to superintend the work of training.[2] Thenceforward there was steady effort to improve the intellectual equipment of the students. From time to time in the minutes of the General Committee there appears a note indicating their realisation of deficiencies in this direction, and remedial measures are suggested. In 1816 they expressed their thanks to the Surrey Institution for admitting some of the students to lectures that had been given there during the session.

[1] British and Foreign School Society, General Committee, May 7th, 1814.
[2] *Ibid.*

Originally the superintendent of the Borough Road establishment had been the chief official of the British and Foreign
Society as well, but as time went on he was less and less able
to attend to the actual work of training teachers, so that in
1825 the following minute appears:

"The time and attention of the Superintendent being so
much occupied by the general business of the Society, your
committee have engaged a respectable Teacher to attend the
Central School four evenings a week in order to instruct
youths on the establishment in the most important branches
of useful knowledge".

That there was a steady improvement in the range, if not
the quality, of attainment, is proved by an inspection carried
out in 1828, when the subjects included in the examination
were ancient and modern history, geography, mathematics,
English composition, penmanship and linear drawing.

It is the same tale at Baldwin's Gardens. Almost as soon
as training commenced at the central school the necessity
was found to set a definite standard for students entering.
One of the committee of the society, writing to Bell,
says,

"We came to a resolution, on account of Grover's[1] reporting that the masters and mistresses were, in many instances, unable to write, and in some even to read, that either
a certificate of their having these qualifications must be required, or an examination by us take place, before they are
admitted to be trained; and, when found incompetent, that
they be sent to an adult school first".[2]

It is recorded in the Minutes of the School Committee of
the National Society for 1821 that Dr Bell, on account of
some dissatisfaction that had been expressed as to arrangements for training, read a paper entitled "Prospectus of an
arrangement for training masters at the Central School of the

---

[1] The official in charge of the "training masters".
[2] R. and C. C. Southey, *op. cit.* p. 438.

National Society", and this is worth reproducing, both as a specimen of Dr Bell's prose style, and as an indication of the standard of the training that was given.

"Practice and experience have been the guides in all that has been done in the National Schools. And the methods of instruction in them seem to have reached the natural limits of the principle on which they were founded and are conducted. Nothing now seems wanting but such an administration of the National System as may render these schools uniformly progressive, till they have reached the desired result; and especially that in the training of Masters the expectations which were previously entertained may not be disappointed. The failures, which amidst general success have been too often experienced in this department, and the impediments which have thence arisen in the advancement and progress of the National System, have, for a long time, attracted my attention; and after much experience and mature reflection, I have deemed it incumbent on me to submit to the consideration of the School Committee the following Outline of an arrangement, chiefly with a view to the more effectual training, at the Central School, of competent Masters (and of course Mistresses) in the National System, taking blame to myself for not having, at an earlier period, produced a digested proposal to remedy the defects which I have long felt and deplored.

"My suggestion is

"That certain classes be set apart for the instruction of masters; for example

" 1. The lowest class in the first Book of cards of Alphabet and of the combinations of vowels and consonants.

" 2. One of the classes in the second Book which is taught by previous and syllabic reading.

" 3. A class in one of the subsequent tracts, viz. Our Saviour's Sermon on the Mount (Parables or Miracles or Discourses).

"These three classes comprise the whole of the methods of instruction in the National System.

"It is proposed that each master in succession shall remain in charge of one of these classes for a given time (say one week or a fortnight) at the end of which the summary of his report of its comparative progress and present state be read, and that a brief examination take place, in the presence of all the masters which, (if the primary law of perfect instruction has been observed) will require only a very few minutes; and that, according to the conduct of the master and the progress of the class, he be ranked in the list of candidates for pay and for an appointment to a school, due attention however being paid to any other pretensions.

"It is above all essentially requisite that the Master be also well exercised in the examination of the higher as well as lower classes in the meaning of what they read, and in their knowledge of the religious principles, the great articles of the Christian Faith and Doctrines in which they are instructed.

"The advantages are—Emulation between classes taught by boys and those taught by masters; actual practice for master, and promotion on manifest practical merit; school work improved, particularly lower classes."[1]

This reveals very clearly the meagre quality of the "training" that it was even hoped could be given at Baldwin's Gardens. There was no idea of cultivating the teacher, or leading him to approach his craft from a rational standpoint. There was no need for him to learn about human nature; a knowledge of the "system" was all that was needful, and the educational value of the system can be judged from Bell's own avowal in the above passage that the three classes mentioned "comprise the whole of the methods of instruction in the National System". Moreover, any departure from the system was regarded as the most dangerous of heresies.

It should be noticed that the training masters had no prac-

[1] National Society, Minutes of School Committee, July 20th, 1821.

tice in the organisation and direction of a monitorial school. Their practice consisted in acting as monitors in the central school, and the standard of their knowledge and skill was evidently low enough to make competition between classes taught by them and those taught by boy monitors quite a sporting event. There were just three elements in their training. They went right through the school as pupils; they went through it as monitors; and they formed a class among themselves for the study of the manuals of the system.

The time spent in training was extremely short, and the two societies concerned with the training of teachers made many efforts to remedy this deficiency. In the early stages three months was an outside figure, and in general the duration was much less. In 1817 the "training masters" at Baldwin's Gardens were supposed to spend at least three half-days in each class in the school, and the course was to be repeated two or three times if possible.[1] There was no minimum time of training specified, certificates being issued by the National Society at any time to a candidate who showed himself proficient in the "system". In the *Rules and Regulations for Training Masters*, 1813, it is laid down "that no Master be on any account allowed to take charge of any class, or be placed in any responsible situation until he has been examined as to his competency and pronounced sufficiently acquainted with the Madras System to be qualified for such charge, and that none be entitled to receive his certificate until he has been at least a week in such charge, and conducted himself therein to the satisfaction of the Superintendent".[2]

The plan of taking in persons of mature years for a few weeks of training became very soon the only method employed at the Borough as well as at Baldwin's Gardens, although originally it was to have been combined with another method which, could it have been persisted in, would have

[1] National Society, *Annual Report*, 1817, p. 12.
[2] *Ibid.* 1813, p. 198.

proved much more successful. It had at first been intended that a number of promising boys from the school should be kept on for two or three years to be educated as school-masters, but this project had to be abandoned because of its expense, and because its results tended to be disappointing in that boys would profit by the extra education and then take up occupations other than teaching. It was never suggested that this method could take the place of the "short course" method for adults because the demand for teachers was too pressing to allow of it, but it is much to be regretted that the British and Foreign School Society was forced to abandon it altogether.

During the first twenty years of experiment with teachers' training, whilst little can be reported in the way of progress in actual methods of training, there was a steady expansion of the training institutions, and very considerable missionary zeal was manifested. In 1813, thirty-seven masters, including one Persian, were trained at Baldwin's Gardens, besides forty-five masters who were sent up for short periods from various dioceses. In the same year a certain amount of training was carried out at central schools in the dioceses, e.g. twelve masters and one mistress at Norwich, and twenty masters and five mistresses at Winchester.[1] These diocesan training schools are important in so far as some of them later developed into diocesan training colleges when the "boom" in such institutions commenced in the early days of the Committee of Council and its liberal grants. In 1815 the numbers at Baldwin's Gardens had increased to forty-two probationers and fifty-two men sent from the dioceses, together with eighty-six mistresses who were trained in the girls' school, although there were no mistresses directly in the pay of the society.[2] A considerable number of these trained masters were appointed to schools abroad, and one can sympathise

[1] National Society, *Annual Report*, 1813, pp. 13, 14.
[2] *Ibid.* 1815, p. 13.

with the hero of the following Minute of the School Committee: "Robert Hoddle, intended to be sent out as Schoolmaster to Van Diemen's Land, having been ordered in consequence of irregularity in his attendance to come before the Committee this day, it appears that he is no where to be found; ordered that the Secretary acquaint Mr Barnard, of Lord Bathurst's Office with this circumstance".[1]

There was never an attempt at Baldwin's Gardens to institute anything like a collegiate life as at the Borough Road. Students lived in rooms and attended for instruction during the ordinary school hours. A good deal of interest, however, was taken in their behaviour, and there appears to have been a certain amount of supervision. Amid the arid pages of a book of minutes it is pleasant to discover a human entry like the following: "Read the report of the School Committee respecting some of the training masters having been at a dance, and also on a water party, accompanied on the latter occasion by some of the training mistresses. Mr Davis, teacher of the masters' class, was called in and reprimanded by the Bishop of London, and it was recommended to the School Committee to take such measures as may prevent a recurrence of such conduct".[2]

In the earliest stages of the training institution at the Borough Road the students had resided on the premises, but there was a temporary dissolution of the boarding establishment in 1815, when students were boarded out.[3] The women students had been moved to King's Road, Chelsea, in 1814, and in this connection we get a pleasing indication of what was considered seemly apparel for the woman teacher in training, in a Minute of the Ladies' Committee, dated July

[1] National Society, Minute of School Committee, March 3rd, 1820.
[2] National Society, Minute of General Committee, October 2nd, 1816.
[3] H. B. Binns, *op. cit.* 1908, p. 83.

11th, 1814: "That it be expedient that the young women about to be removed to the King's Road, Chelsea, should be habited in cotton or queen stuffs—plain muslin handkerchiefs—plain caps without work or lace—and plain straw bonnets at a low price.—That the cloathes (*sic*) they have at present should be made neat and suitable to appear in the schoolroom. That under the new arrangement no white petticoats should be allowed".[1] New buildings, to which both men and women returned, were completed at the Borough in 1817, and the college occupied this site until its removal to Isleworth in 1890.

The British and Foreign Society was fired with missionary zeal, and the influence of the Borough Road Institution spread far beyond the bounds of Great Britain. Lancaster was closely connected with the foundation of the Kildare Place Society in December, 1811, and in November, 1812, he sent over to Ireland as a pioneer in the work of that society a young man of twenty-three, John Veevers, accompanied by a letter of recommendation which said, "He is not only fitted to organise schools, but to train schoolmasters, which he has already done in a way equal to my highest expectation.... I rejoice in being able to convey this information. I joy for Ireland and for the friends of it. You will have in him a practical Joseph Lancaster, who will carry on the work in glory".[2] It was proposed to establish a model school in Dublin, and in 1814 public advertisements were displayed in "sixteen of the most respectable provincial prints" inviting candidates for training. The work commenced early in 1814, Protestants and Roman Catholics being trained together. A house for boarding was hired, and eventually the training centre became attached to the model school in Kildare Place in 1819.

[1] British and Foreign School Society, Minute of Ladies' Committee, July 11th, 1814.
[2] H. Kingsmill Moore, *An Unwritten Chapter in the History of Education*, 1904, p. 165.

Here work was carried on along lines similar to those at the Borough Road. The training of mistresses began in 1824, and 1908 masters and nearly 500 mistresses had been trained by 1831.[1] The society did especially good work in the publication of a number of manuals of the various school subjects, which remained some of the most enlightened school text-books for many years, and had a considerable vogue in Great Britain as well as in Ireland.

The British and Foreign Society also extended its activities as far as the Continent, and there were some sporadic attempts to set up monitorial training centres. Thus in 1817 a training institution was set up in Weimar by a Borough man, and in 1818 a Captain Kearney, who had been trained at the Borough, set up a Lancasterian model school in Madrid, which later failed because of clerical opposition.[2] At the same time students from all over the world came to the Borough to learn the system.

It is easy to belittle the work of the two great educational societies during what may be called the "monitorial" period of elementary education in England, but its importance can scarcely be overestimated, nor is least merit due to their work in connection with the training of teachers. At least they showed some realisation of the fact that it was impossible to improve education without at the same time improving the teachers, and the later training college system largely developed out of their efforts. One of the leading training colleges of to-day, the "Borough Road College", enshrines in its rather puzzling name its descent from Joseph Lancaster's "family". The central school in London of the National Society has left no direct descendants, but many of the provincial colleges arose from the ruins of older diocesan model schools.

---

[1] H. Kingsmill Moore, *op. cit.* p. 204.
[2] H. B. Binns, *op. cit.* p. 89.

Moreover, and this is a most important consideration, the work of the monitorial training institutions emphasised the importance of technique in teaching, and in this respect their influence has been continuously exercised upon the development of the English training system. England was far behind her Continental neighbours in the establishment of training colleges, and her earliest efforts were almost uninfluenced by what was taking place abroad. The result was that whilst on the Continent they were busy instructing their teachers, rather than showing them how to teach, in England the main emphasis was laid on the actual method of instruction. It is true that the technique inculcated was mechanical in the extreme, and in many ways unsound fundamentally, yet the particular direction taken in those early attempts at training had the result that the training colleges never became merely places of higher education.

It is true that the method failed very largely because that higher culture, which was provided to some extent by the normal schools on the Continent, was lacking in England, and the next phase in the history of training is concerned very largely with efforts to provide the intending teacher with that culture, and in this phase Continental influence is very prominent. The great hindrance to progress all along was the lack of secondary education for the lower and middle classes, and until that deficiency had been supplied, the training college was bound to be a somewhat anomalous institution, being turned aside from its main business to do the work that properly belonged to an institution of another type. Now that the intending teacher is able to equip himself on the academic side at the secondary school and the University, we are coming back to the point of view of the old monitorial training centres, that the main business of the trainer of teachers is to train them in the technique of their craft. In the English elementary school it has always been held a heresy that provided a man knows his subject he can teach it, and the soundness of this attitude has been amply vindicated by the victory of those who have fought the battle for the training of teachers for secondary schools. We may yet see the time when even the Universities will demand that their teachers also shall have some rudimentary knowledge of the technique of their own particular type of teaching, realising that matter without method is not enough.

Nor must we underestimate the sordid material difficulties against which the early pioneers had to struggle. The low quality of the early training establishments was due more to the empty pocket than to the unenlightened mind. Good buildings, good books, good instructors, all demand adequate funds, and those funds were not forthcoming. The training of teachers was only a side-line with the societies, whose main business was the establishment of schools. Their very zeal in this latter direction militated against sound training, for so urgent was the demand for teachers that schools perforce had to be manned with a scholastic "Kitchener's Army". Again, lack of funds meant that the teaching profession was financially unattractive, "a field", in the words of a witness to Mr Slaney's Committee in 1838, "which experience has shown will never be long cultivated by the enterprising, the ambitious or the sordid", so that candidates for the profession were too often drawn from the ranks of the failures in other walks of life. Probably nothing has done more to raise the quality of the teaching personnel of the country than the improvements that have taken place in the teacher's prospects.

It is important, also, to realise that the pioneers had no tradition to guide them. They were indeed breaking new ground. The fact that the journey was over a strange country meant that the course was bound to be tortuous, and much vain expenditure of energy inevitable. Books directly bearing on the business in hand were few, educational psychology was unknown, aims and methods had yet to be thought out.

Yet a start was made, and when once a journey is begun, there is at least a chance that the destination may be reached.

BIBLIOGRAPHY

JOSEPH LANCASTER. *Improvements in Education as it Respects the Industrious Classes*, London. Numerous editions from 1805 onward. Gives an account of the Borough Road Institution, and outlines the "system", in considerable detail.
—— *Outline of a Plan for Educating* 10,000 *Poor Children by establishing Schools in Towns and Villages and for the uniting Works of Industry with Useful Knowledge*, London, 1806.
—— *The British System of Education*, London, 1810.
—— *Report of Joseph Lancaster's Progress*, London, 1811.
—— *Epitome of some of the chief Events and Transactions in the Life of Joseph Lancaster*, by Himself, 1833.
D. SALMON. *Joseph Lancaster*, London, 1904.
SIR J. G. FITCH. Article on Joseph Lancaster in *Educational Aims and Methods*, Cambridge, 1900.
BRITISH AND FOREIGN SCHOOL SOCIETY. *Annual Reports*.
—— Minutes of various Committees (in MS. at Society's Offices).
H. B. BINNS. *A Century of Education*. London, 1908. (A history of the work of the British and Foreign School Society.)
H. KINGSMILL MOORE. *An Unwritten Chapter in the History of Education*. (Account of the work of the Kildare Place Society.)
A. BELL expounded the Madras System in many pamphlets and books, most fully from the standpoint of method in *Elements of Tuition*, numerous editions, e.g. London, 1813–15: Part 1, "The Madras School" (report on his work in India); Part 2, "The English School" (application of the system in England); Part 3, "Ludus Literarius" (application of the system to higher schools).
—— *Mutual Tuition and Moral Discipline*, London, 1823, is a later manual of method.

NATIONAL SCHOOL SOCIETY. *Annual Reports.*
—— Minutes of various Committees (in MS. at Society's Offices).
R. and C. C. SOUTHEY. *Life of Rev. Andrew Bell,* 3 vols. London, 1844.
J. M. D. MEIKLEJOHN. *An Old Educational Reformer—Dr Andrew Bell,* Edinburgh and London, 1881.

CHAPTER II

A PERIOD OF TRANSITION, 1830–1840

THE period of ten years that precedes the Battersea experiment of Kay-Shuttleworth is one of great importance in connection with the training of teachers, not so much because actual tangible progress was made in the matter of training, though such progress there was, but because it was one of those "incubation" periods which occur from time to time in the history of ideas. By the end of this period the monitorial system was to all intents and purposes doomed, and with it was doomed the unambitious type of training that had been its accompaniment. The leader of the anti-monitorial movement was David Stow, whose "simultaneous system" was in time to revolutionise the work of the schools, and whose Glasgow Normal Seminary was to point the way to better things in the matter of training. Men were becoming increasingly interested in the work of the Continental normal schools, and were making invidious comparisons between these and the monitorial training institutions. Brougham, in his speech on popular education in the House of Lords in 1835, referred in a very complimentary fashion to the Continental systems of teachers' training,[1] and in the interesting discussions that took place during the taking of evidence before the Select Committees of 1834 and 1838 several speakers had some foreign method to advocate or to criticise. It is impossible to understand the form taken in the next decade by the training college unless one realises the extent to which reformers like Kay-Shuttleworth were influenced by foreign ideas

[1] Henry, Lord Brougham, *Speech in the House of Lords on the Education of the People*, London, 1835, pp. 21, 22.

In Germany, France, Holland and Switzerland there were well-developed systems of institutions for the training of teachers.[1] In Germany great progress had been made during the eighteenth century. A training seminary was founded by Franke at Halle in 1704, whilst Steinmetz set up a similar school at Klosterbergen about 1730. In 1748 a seminary for teachers was attached to the Realschule in Berlin, but little success attended attempts to "graft" training institutions upon existing universities or schools. Throughout the eighteenth century a good deal of attention had been paid to the teaching of languages, and by 1730 lectures in this connection were common in the universities. The first regular seminary for this purpose was set up at Göttingen, and this was widely imitated.

The training so far described was intended mainly for teachers in the higher types of school. The first seminary for primary teachers was instituted at Stettin in Pomerania in 1735, and similar centres were established at Berlin in 1748 and at Münster in 1757. Pestalozzi's connection with Basedow's "Philanthropinum" at Dessau was destined to bear fruit, for at the beginning of the nineteenth century a number of German students were sent to Yverdun to study his methods, and Zeller was invited to set up at Königsberg a normal seminary for inculcating Pestalozzian principles. So great was the progress made that by the middle of the century there were in existence in Germany 156 normal seminaries and 206 preparatory schools in connection with them. The work of the German training colleges is summed up in the following report made by an American investigator in 1838:

"The Seminaries produce a strong *esprit de corps* among teachers, which tends powerfully to interest them in their profession, to attach them to it, to elevate it in their eyes, and to stimulate them to improve constantly upon the attain-

[1] For a summary account of the development of foreign normal schools see H. Barnard, *Normal Schools*, 1851, Part 2.

ments with which they have commenced its exercise. By their aid a standard of examination in the theory and practice of instruction is furnished, which may fairly be expected of candidates who have chosen a different way to obtain access to the profession".[1]

In Holland the first step in the establishment of a training system had been the apprenticing of candidates for the profession between the ages of fourteen and eighteen years to act as assistants in the schools. These apprentices taught during the day and received instruction during the evening. Later this system was supplemented by the setting up of normal seminaries, the most famous of which, that at Haarlem, was founded in 1816. A series of Education Laws was passed in 1806 setting up a State qualifying examination for all teachers in the primary schools. There were four grades of certificate, and the examination included both academic subjects and the practice of teaching. Candidates were examined in reading, spelling, grammar, writing, arithmetic, theory of singing, together with history, geography, natural philosophy and mathematics if these subjects were professed by the intending teacher. An acquaintance was to be shown with French or some other foreign language. Questions were set on methods of teaching and general principles of education, and there was a practical test of teaching ability. The successful candidate received a certificate stating in what subjects he was qualified to instruct, and the class in which he had been placed as a result of the examination. These certificates were standardised throughout the country, and the class obtained determined the type of school in which the candidate might find employment. Teachers in the first two classes might teach in any type of elementary school, but those in the two lower classes were eligible only for smaller and less important schools.

[1] A. D. Bache, Report to Trustees of Girard College of Orphans, Philadelphia, 1838. Quoted in Barnard, *op. cit.* Part 2, p. 39.

At the normal school at Haarlem the regular course was for four years, students normally leaving at the age of twenty-two years, having obtained the Second Class Certificate. The school was not residential, but pupils boarded out in the town.

The French system was widely influenced by the Prussian, especially after the report on the German educational system made by Cousin in 1831. As early as 1794 the Convention had set up in Paris an institution to provide teachers of secondary schools, but this had been suppressed in the following year. When the Imperial University of France was founded in 1808, there was a strong demand that it should concern itself with the training of teachers. The Ecole Normale was set up in Paris, and the "aggrégation" instituted, but the main business of the college was academic, and what practice in teaching there was, was entirely voluntary. It was not till 1811 that the first French seminary for primary teachers was opened at Strasbourg, designed to take sixty students through a course of four years, the age for entry ranging between sixteen and thirty years. The movement was taken up vigorously. In 1820 normal schools were established in the Moselle and Meuse Departments; by 1829 there were thirteen such schools in operation throughout France; whilst between 1830 and 1833 thirty-four new normal schools were set up in the country. In general the schools gave a two-year course, students entering at sixteen years, and the regular curriculum included moral and religious instruction, reading, grammar, arithmetic, linear drawing, elements of physical science, music, gymnastics, geography, history, gardening, and the drawing up of legal documents.[1]

Stimulating as these achievements were to effort in Great Britain, the greatest influence was exercised by the work of two outstanding figures in Switzerland, De Fellenberg and

[1] J. Pillans, "Seminaries for Teachers", *Edinburgh Review*, July, 1834, vol. LIX, pp. 492–4.

Vehrli. The former of these established at the beginning of the nineteenth century a school designed for the education of children of the upper classes at Hofwyl, and proposed to incorporate with it a school for poor children. With this purpose in view he took Vehrli into his own family to train him to take up the post of master to this lower school. Very soon Hofwyl became a veritable educational centre, for in 1808 an agricultural school and a normal school were added. During the first year of the latter's existence forty-two teachers of the canton of Berne were trained, the students lodging in tents because of the lack of proper accommodation. The whole of the work of training was carried out by Vehrli, who taught the students the subjects they were to teach, gave lessons as models, supervised their practice as monitors and instructors in the school, and presided at frequent familiar discussions on all topics connected with the work in hand.

When Kay-Shuttleworth made his European tour with Tufnell in 1839, Vehrli's training school had been moved to Kreuzlingen, and he was so impressed by the life and work of the students there that in many ways he tried to reproduce them at Battersea. The whole spirit of the enterprise is well expressed in Vehrli's remark: "I am a peasant's son. I wish to be no other than I am, the teacher of the sons of the peasantry".[1] His main purpose was to equip his pupils adequately as schoolmasters, whilst at the same time training them for the inevitable simplicity and poverty of the village schoolmaster's life. Inapplicable to Kreuzlingen would have been the French mayor's remark made some years later to Tufnell, "L'orgueil est devenu le fléau des écoles normales primaires".[2]

Kay-Shuttleworth found ninety students, with ages ranging from eighteen to twenty-six years, engaged upon a course

[1] J. Kay-Shuttleworth, *Four Periods of Public Education*, 1862, p. 304.
[2] F. Smith, *Life of Sir James Kay-Shuttleworth*, 1923, p. 124.

of three years that included academic instruction, professional training, and manual occupations, much attention being paid to the "education of the heart and feelings as distinct from the cultivation of the intellect".[1] There were three distinct elements in the life of the student: life in the home circle, life in the schoolroom and life beyond the walls in the cultivation of the soil. The students rose at four or five o'clock, according to the season, and retired at nine. There were three meals in the day, and the rest of the time was spent in strenuous labour in the fields or in the schoolroom. The students wore the coarsest of clothes, wooden shoes and no stockings, but, in spite of the simplicity and hardship of their lives, they reached a comparatively high standard of academic attainment. Vehrli's school was the model for a number of similar institutions in Switzerland, all of them labouring to produce a race of educated and yet simple-minded teachers of the peasantry.

Before considering the discussion on teachers' training, contained in the reports of evidence before the Select Committees of 1834 and 1838, it will be advisable to describe the foundation of two new training institutions which took place during the ten years now under discussion, viz. the Glasgow Normal Training Seminary and the training establishment of the Home and Colonial Society, both of which are of considerable significance in connection with the history of the training of teachers in Great Britain.

David Stow's contribution to the development of popular education has received ample recognition at the hands of the educational historian, and it is unnecessary here to give any account of the general characteristics of his "training system". It is important to realise, however, that this title has nothing to do with the training of teachers, since some confusion is likely to arise from the fact of Stow's experiments in teachers' training. The "training system" was a system of general

[1] J. Kay-Shuttleworth, *op. cit.* p. 305.

education, and the name was coined by its originator to emphasise that he regarded training of character, as distinct from mere instruction, as the true foundation of popular education. The Glasgow Normal Seminary was set up in order to train teachers to carry out this "training system", and the certificate it issued was one of proficiency in the "theory and practice of training".[1]

Like the monitorial training centres, the Glasgow Normal Seminary grew up in connection with a school run on a system. If a system is to survive, successive generations of teachers must be brought up to the understanding and practice of it. If Stow was to "train up the child in the way he should go", it was essential that he should also "train up the teacher in the way he should go", so that he might not depart from it. Accordingly he trained teachers at his school in Glasgow from its inception in 1826,[2] and at first the training consisted in little more than attending at the school and picking up its methods. There was, however, this great advantage, that on the whole the candidates that came were better educated than those that attended the monitorial centres. During the following eight years 300 teachers were "trained" in his infant school, and it came to be felt that a special building devoted to the business of training was essential. Voluntary effort raised the funds, and the Glasgow Educational Society was founded, an inaugural lecture being given to the society on November 6th, 1834, by Dr Welsh. This lecture was on "Prussian Education",[3] and did much to foster enthusiasm in the society for the projected training seminary. The foundation stone of the seminary was laid on November 14th,

[1] *Third Report of the Glasgow Education Society's Normal Seminary*, 1836, p. 18.

[2] For a discussion of this date, see R. R. Rusk, *The Training of Teachers in Scotland*, 1928, p. 27 et seq., and cf. D. Stow, *The Training System and Normal Seminary*, 1854, p. 343.

[3] See copious quotations in R. R. Rusk, *op. cit.* p. 66.

1836, and the college was formally opened in 1837.[1] The post of rector, for which Thomas Carlyle thought of applying,[2] was given to John M'Crie, with a salary of £300 a year. The duties of the rector were "to superintend the practical working of the system pursued in the Model Schools, and to superintend and train the Normal Students both in the theory and in the art of teaching and training".[3] Before taking up his appointment he was to spend several months investigating the methods of training in vogue in Germany and France.[4] The new buildings housed four separate schools besides the students in training: the Infant School, the Juvenile School, the Commercial School and the Female School of Industry. There were thirteen classrooms for the use of the students, mainly for practice and criticism lessons, together with the Rector's Hall, the Museum, Library and Committee Rooms.[5] The seminary was not planned as a residential college. "Moral and intellectual training during the day in school, and separate houses in the evening," said Stow, "we find to be decidedly the safer mode for both students and scholars."[6]

Students were supposed to have equipped themselves on the academic side before entering the seminary, which did not profess to teach ordinary school subjects, and they had to be provided with a certificate of moral character. They all had to serve an apprenticeship in the infant school, and must be prepared to remain in the seminary for at least three months, otherwise they received no certificate at the end of their period of training. The students varied greatly in quality, the upper limit being represented by students from

[1] W. Fraser, *Memoir of David Stow*, 1868, pp. 137–9, 143.

[2] J. A. Froude, *Thomas Carlyle: a History of his Life in London*, vol. I, p. 24, and R. R. Rusk, *op. cit.* p. 78.

[3] Glasgow Education Society, *Third Report*, 1836, p. 15.

[4] *Ibid.* p. 15.   [5] *Ibid.* p. 22.

[6] D. Stow, *The Training System and Normal Seminary*, 1846, p. 500.

the University who attended the seminary in order to have an additional qualification for teaching in the academies.[1]

It was found impossible to limit the work of the seminary purely to professional training, and almost from the first the students received some instruction in school subjects. At first it was comparatively little, consisting of one hour daily devoted to the study of grammar, roots of words, scripture history and geography. Later the study of "sacred music" was introduced, with practice in "marching airs" three times a week.[2]

The work at Glasgow is best described by an outside observer, Mr J. Gibson, one of the earliest of Her Majesty's Inspectors, in his Report to the Committee of Council on Education in 1841, the first Government Report on the institution.[3]

By this time the minimum length of attendance at the seminary had been increased to six months, whilst the average duration of training was eight or nine months. The time devoted to academic instruction had increased from the original one hour daily to $16\frac{1}{4}$ hours a week, the rest of the time being devoted to training the students "to skill in the art of teaching, and in communicating to them enlarged and enlightened views on the general subject of education".[4]

The professional part of the course was far in advance of anything existing in any other training institution in Great Britain. Part of the time was spent in teaching and observation in the model schools, but in addition a number of lessons were delivered to drafts of the children in the seminary proper. Sometimes use was made of the "gallery"[5] in the

[1] Glasgow Education Society, *Third Report*, pp. 16, 17.

[2] *Ibid.* p. 17.

[3] Committee of Council on Education, Minutes, 1840–1, pp. 412–21.

[4] *Ibid.* p. 413.

[5] For some account of the "gallery lesson" see C. Birchenough, *History of Elementary Education*, 1914, pp. 239–42.

hall, sometimes students taught classes in the miniature class-rooms that opened off from it. When teaching was going on in the seminary the regular arrangement was for half of the students to be in the hall, where one of their number would give a gallery lesson of fifteen minutes' duration, to be fol-lowed by the criticism of his fellow-students, whilst the other half would be teaching in the classrooms under the super-vision of the rector.

Another feature of the course was the delivery of a Bible lesson by one of the students to a class made up of his fellows. The latter were informed as to the age and capacity of the children they were to represent, and were not allowed to answer questions out of the prescribed range of thought thus indicated. At these lessons a running criticism was kept up by the rector both upon the conduct of the lesson by the teacher and upon the answers of the class.

From time to time a "public criticism lesson" was held, and this was a solemn and momentous occasion, to which the terrors of the ordinary criticism lesson were as nothing. The selected student had to teach a class before an audience con-sisting of all the other students, reinforced by the rector, the secretary (Stow), and sometimes the heads of the various model schools. On these occasions the students did not criti-cise, that function being appropriated to the rector and his officers. So great was the strain of such a proceeding that we are told that "the female students take no active share in this exercise; they sit attentive and interested auditors".[1]

The criticisms of the inspector on the work of the seminary are illuminating. Of the institution which had originally set out to give no academic instruction at all, he found it neces-sary to say, a few years after its inception, that the course of instruction was too ambitious, and should be restricted to the minimum essentials, considering the brevity of the course. He regarded as essentials Biblical knowledge, reading,

[1] Committee of Council on Education, Minutes, 1840–1, p. 416.

geography, English grammar, arithmetic and book-keeping.[1]
He thought that the gallery lesson was stressed at the expense
of the ordinary class lesson, the students doing well in the
former type and badly in the latter. There was considerable
criticism, also, of the abuse of the elliptical question and
simultaneous answering, but these objections applied to
Stow's system of education as a whole rather than to his
methods of training

It was this tendency to overdo the instructional side of the
work of the seminary that led to Stow's severing his connection with it when, having accepted Government grant, its
work had to conform with the demands of the Education
Committee. Stow consistently maintained that the purpose
of the training college was purely professional, and that the
academic instruction of intending teachers should be carried
out in separate academies or preparatory colleges.

Upon general principles Stow was undoubtedly right, and
it is to be regretted that greater efforts were not made to keep
the seminary a centre for exclusively professional training.
Such an ideal would have been impossible in England, where
there was an almost complete lack of facilities for secondary
education for the type of student who would be willing to
take up teaching as an occupation, but in Scotland, with its
system of parochial schools and "academies", and its democratic university system, there were the possibilities of the
experiment being carried further. In England it was almost
inevitable that the training college should take upon itself
the functions of a secondary school when it became generally
recognised that a certain degree of culture was necessary in
the primary teachers. The real key to any effective teachers'
training is to be found in the existence of an efficient secondary school system, and it was the late organisation of secondary education in England that made the training of the
teachers such "a thing of shreds and patches". The best

[1] Committee of Council on Education, Minutes, 1840–1, pp. 417–18.

thought and the most strenuous effort put into the working of the pupil teacher system and the training college were not directed to real professional training at all, but were rather devoted to the "schooling" of the student. If the Glasgow Normal Seminary had only remained true to the intention of its founder, it would have been, in effect, a day training college of a type that was not to be heard of for another fifty years, but as things actually came to pass, it in time became assimilated to the standard type of training college in England, and ceased to be of particular interest in itself.

The fame and influence of the Glasgow Normal Seminary were very widespread. In Scotland there was none to challenge its supremacy, the only other training centre of any importance being the normal school at Edinburgh run by the Education Committee of the Church of Scotland. This institution was similar in type to Borough Road or Westminster (the home at this time of the National Society's Central School). From 1825 teachers had been sent to Wood's Sessional School in Tron Parish, Edinburgh, to learn the "system". The length of training rarely exceeded six months, and was frequently much less; the students were of poor quality, and the training they received was meagre.[1] In England no normal school could seriously challenge the superiority of Glasgow. Dr Kay (later Sir James Kay-Shuttleworth), giving evidence before the Select Committee of 1838, stated that "teachers from Scotland appear to me to be preferable to any others that I have yet seen",[2] and that the Glasgow Normal Seminary was "the most perfect school of this description".[3] Writing in 1843 an observer remarked that Glasgow, as compared with the other chief normal schools, was pre-eminent for mental and moral training, and

[1] Committee of Council on Education, Minutes, 1841–2, pp. 40–46.
[2] Select Committee on the Education of the Poorer Classes, 1838, *Report*, § 46.
[3] *Ibid.* § 265.

especially commended the training that the students received in the development of questioning on an inductive basis, and in the "simultaneous system" generally.[1] In a letter to Sir J. Graham in 1841 Stow made sweeping claims on behalf of his seminary: "We have had several deputations from the Church of England in consequence of which the diocesan training schools were established; the improvements in the Church of England Model School were copied from this institution; all the late improvements in the Borough Road school, gallery, etc., were professedly taken from us: the gallery system at Norwood and Battersea and throughout England was taken from this institution.... The Wesleyans throughout England are getting their teachers trained by us".[2] In all 442 Wesleyan students were trained, and when the Wesleyan Training College was established at Westminster, the influence of Glasgow was strongly marked, Sugden, the head of the practising schools, having been trained there.[3] Indeed it will be found that many of the pioneers in training during the next twenty years had had some connection with the seminary. The Glasgow-trained teacher could command the posts carrying the highest salaries. Stow himself wrote, "We preferred the true mercantile principle, to provide a superior article and then claim a higher price".[4] And most important of all, the "simultaneous system" popularised by the efforts of Stow, brought about the decline of the monitorial systems, and created a demand for cultured and trained teachers, with skill to manage children in the mass without resort to the mechanical devices of Lancaster and Bell.

The Glasgow Seminary is noteworthy as the first of the training colleges to attempt to devise a technique of training.

[1] A. R. Craig, *The Philosophy of Training*, 1843, p. 20.
[2] Committee of Council on Education, Minutes, 1841–2, p. 31.
[3] D. Stow, *The Training System and Normal Seminary*, 1859, p. 540.
[4] *Ibid.* pp. 527–8.

Elsewhere it was considered enough to pitch the student into the welter of the life of a school, giving him occasional instruction on the working of the "system". The work at Glasgow was carefully designed as a whole, and with reference to the best models. The monitorial student was never taught to deliver a lesson in the commonly accepted sense of the term to-day; what he did learn was to manipulate the machinery of instruction in vogue in the school. The "simultaneous" lesson at Glasgow was the forerunner of the "chalk and talk" lesson, and obviously preparation for this type of lesson was bound to be a more ambitious affair. So a detailed system of practice and criticism lessons was developed. Such lessons soon became standard in all the training colleges, with individual variations, and the criticism lesson is still with us. There was a certain formality about the method of teaching that Stow favoured, and no doubt the mechanical aspect was not altogether lacking. The elliptical lesson and "picturing out" only too often became fetishes, but on the whole the technique of instruction inculcated was sound enough. Stow's own directions were that question and ellipsis were to be combined in every lesson. "The question pumps the water from the well; the ellipsis directs its course. The master is the filterer who sends it back, as it were, in one pure stream to all."[1]

The second training college founded in the period 1830–40 was that of the Home and Colonial Infant School Society in the Gray's Inn Road. This was a college destined to play an individual part in the development of the training college system, and was noteworthy as the first institution to devote itself primarily to the training of teachers for infant schools (although the teaching of infants played an important part at Glasgow). The society was formed in 1836 with the special purpose of encouraging infant school work upon the prin-

[1] D. Stow, *Practical Hints on the Training System for Glasgow Normal Seminary Students*, 1838, p. 8.

ciples of Pestalozzi, and the preparing of teachers for this work. The college was opened on June 1st of the same year. A number of young women were received for training, together with acting teachers from the schools who came for short courses. The college adhered to Church of England principles, but candidates from any denomination were received if they held "the fundamental truths of the Bible". During the first year there was no practising school on the premises, but in 1837 a model school was established, together with two houses as students' hostels, one for mistresses and the other for married couples, with accommodation for twenty-one of the former and five of the latter. The course lasted twelve weeks, the cost to the student being eight shillings a week, but in 1838 the course was extended to fifteen weeks. The curriculum included both academic and professional instruction. Students were instructed in religious knowledge, natural history (with special reference to the adaptation of the several organs of each familiar animal to its peculiar habits), the first rules of arithmetic, elementary geography, singing, and the drawing of simple geometrical forms. On the professional side an explanation was given of the principles upon which the education of small children should be based, and an exposition of Pestalozzian methods of teaching.

A special feature of the college was the training of nursery governesses, and at a later date preparation was afforded for mistresses of middle-class schools.

The way in which the methods inculcated differed from those at Glasgow was explained in the Society's Report for 1839:

"In the Model School it is the practice to give less actual information; the children are rather called on by questions to exercise their own faculties, with a view to strengthen them. The plan pursued at Glasgow (the elliptical plan) is not used, except at the summing up or close of a lesson to aid in impressing the whole consecutively on the memory".[1]

Apart from the foundation of these two training colleges, the history of the decade 1830–40 is mainly concerned with criticism, discussion, and tentative experiment. With the first grant of 1833 the Government came into the arena, but it was not until after 1839 that it became of supreme importance in the matter of training.

Perhaps the most useful evidence upon the general state of teachers' training, and upon the general lines of contemporary criticism, is to be found in the reports of the evidence of witnesses to the Select Committees on Education which were published in 1834 and 1839.

Evidence was given by various representatives of the National and British and Foreign Societies concerning the training work done under their auspices. By 1834 the central school of the former society had trained 2039 teachers,[2] and the average period of training had been increased to as many as five months.[2] But in addition to the work of the central school (which had been moved from Baldwin's Gardens to Westminster in 1832), training was being carried on at thirty-five provincial centres.[2] No students were received under the age of twenty-one years,[3] and the superintendent of the central school, in reply to a question, said that he did not favour the idea of taking boys from the school and continuing their education until they were old enough to be trained as teachers, not so much upon general principles, as because of the very low class of boy attending the school and the immaturity of their characters when the normal age for leaving arrived.[4] On the other hand, he did not favour the setting up of institutions for training middle-class boys for

---

[1] See G. C. T. Bartley, *The Schools for the People*, 1871, pp. 481–3.
[2] Select Committee on Education, 1834, Minutes of Evidence, 79. (The references are to paragraphs.)
[3] *Ibid.* 102.   [4] *Ibid.* 117.

the profession.[1] The average age for admission for training at the central school was 25–30 years, and students were expected to maintain themselves, although those "especially distinguished in application and intelligence" might be advanced to the pay list, receiving a weekly allowance of a sum varying from a half to one guinea.[2] There was no library for the students other than that used by the children.[3] Practically no change had taken place in the method of training since the early days at Baldwin's Gardens. Certificates were not issued to the masters and mistresses trained, but after examination by the "clerical superintendent" a report was sent to the committee.[4] A proposal, however, was under consideration, to issue graded certificates, the class of certificate to determine the type of school in which the teacher might find employment, with the possibility of the teacher improving the grade of his certificate during the course of his teaching career.[5]

At the Borough Road students were usually somewhat younger, the age most favoured ranging between nineteen and twenty-four.[6] The best of the students were those who had been educated at the Borough school itself, and the worst were the private teachers who came to be trained.[7] The minimum length of training was officially three months, but it was difficult to keep masters even as long as this, so great was the demand.[8] There were three types of student: externals, who were merely connected with the institution for training; students who lived out, but had their dinners at the school; and foundation students who lived in entirely.[9] Here again there was little change in the mode of training. As the master of the school put it, it was his business to teach "the British system of teaching, irrespective of a young man's

---

[1] Select Committee on Education, 1834, Minutes of Evidence, 118.
[2] *Ibid.* 126.　　[3] *Ibid.* 130.　　[4] *Ibid.* 1838, 841.
[5] *Ibid.* 861.　　[6] *Ibid.* 1834, 227.　　[7] *Ibid.* 228.
[8] *Ibid.* 229.　　[9] *Ibid.* 993.

other attainments".[1] Compared with the students at the National Society's institution, "The masters at the Borough have evening training, and there is great attention paid to the improvement of their own minds, and they have the means of education through the medium of books at the British and Foreign School Society, more than is given to the masters of the National Society".[2]

In spite of all the efforts expended in providing training, the proportion of trained teachers in the schools was still lamentably low. In his evidence to the Select Committee of 1838, Dr Kay gave a number of figures showing the proportion of teachers with any training at all in the combined schools of all types in Manchester, Salford, Liverpool, Bury and York. The highest proportion of trained teachers was to be found in the "superior private schools", where 126 out of 324 teachers were trained, and in the endowed and charity schools, with forty-six out of 119. Then in order of merit came the infant schools, evening schools, common boys' and girls' schools, and last the dame schools with only fourteen trained teachers out of a total of 606.[3]

Trained or untrained, the masters were mostly of a poor quality. This was not merely due to the unattractiveness of the prospects of the profession, which was the reason most commonly given. So far as trained masters were concerned, great difficulty was caused by the gap that was bound to exist between the boy's leaving school and his entering a training institution. Generally the ablest and better-class boys became apprenticed to a trade on leaving school, and it was only the failures who turned to teaching at the age of about twenty-one. The best masters were those who had never lost touch with educational institutions of some kind or other. A good instance of this type was Crossley, the master of the

[1] Select Committee on Education, 1834, Minutes of Evidence, 1046.
[2] *Ibid.* 1664.   [3] *Ibid.* 1838, 261.

model schools at the Borough Road. He had been a pupil in Lancaster's school from 1805 until 1813, and, when the schism came, he went away with Lancaster for a year, returning as a resident student to be trained at the Borough Road after having received some instruction in Latin and other subjects from a benevolent clergyman. When his training was finished, he spent some time as an organiser of new rural schools, and then was appointed to the model schools in 1819.[1]

The difficulties arising from this gap were commented upon by several of the witnesses, and the secretary of the Harp Alley School expressed himself very clearly on the matter:

"We much regret that the boys generally leave us at the age of eleven and twelve, or even sooner, and that boys are perpetually leaving us who would make excellent schoolmasters, but we do not know what to do with them. We are obliged to let them go off to anything that their parents may find for them to do; when, if we had the opportunity, we should be glad to place them in some institution where they would be carrying on their education to a higher point, and preparing themselves to take charge of schools".[2]

It was left to Kay-Shuttleworth to bridge this gap by means of the pupil teacher system which came into being in 1846. The only solution that occurred at the time was that boys should be taken on at about fourteen in the training centres, and this the officials of those institutions looked upon with disfavour.[3] No suggestions were made as to a system of pupil teachers, but it must be remembered that such a system demands teachers qualified to instruct their pupil teachers, and that there were hardly any such at the time.

Criticism was levelled against the shortness of the training

[1] Select Committee on Education, 1834, Minutes of Evidence, 1094–6.
[2] *Ibid.* 2154.   [3] *Ibid.* 117, 230.

period, although the superintendent of the central model schools at Westminster professed himself quite satisfied. Asked the question, "If a man were sufficiently well skilled in writing, reading and arithmetic, he could learn in five months the difficult art of teaching?" he replied, "Yes, decidedly; and it may be learnt in three months, if he has tact".[1] Such was the estimation of the teacher's craft held by the officer responsible for the training of teachers for the largest educational society in England. On the other hand, the secretary of the British and Foreign Society expressed himself profoundly dissatisfied with the short time available for training. He would have liked a three-years' course, during which the student should actually teach in the first and last three months, whilst the science of teaching should be studied during the last year, the rest of the time being given up to general education.[2]

The nature of the training given came under the adverse criticism of the Rev. R. J. Bryce, principal of the Belfast Academy, who appears to have been one of the most enlightened of the witnesses. He complained that the training was concerned with methods, instead of with principles. "It appears to me", he asserted, "that the education of these schoolmasters is a thing of the same kind as if medical students, instead of studying general scientific principles to guide their medical practice, were simply to follow a physician or surgeon through the wards of an hospital and look at him while he felt the pulse and examined the symptoms of the patient, and then take notice what sort of prescription he afterwards wrote."[3]

His account of the elements involved in teaching skill is worth quoting verbatim.

"I think that skill in the art of teaching requires, in the first

[1] Select Committee on Education, 1834, Minutes of Evidence, 122.

[2] *Ibid.* 229, 240.   [3] *Ibid.* 1835, 1036.

place, a good general education, such as serves to enlarge and invigorate the mind, and make it capable of receiving and applying philosophical principles. In the second place it requires a knowledge of the laws of the human mind; I do not mean a familiarity with metaphysical controversies, but a sound acquaintance with all the ascertained and undoubted parts of mental philosophy, which are neither few nor unimportant, and most of which are capable of being practically applied to the business of education. Finally there ought to be constructed a science of education founded upon the ascertained facts and laws of the human mind, bearing the same relation to mental philosophy which the science of medicine bears to anatomy and physiology; and this is the third thing which I think every teacher ought to study."[1]

This is an ideal not yet attained, but Bryce's words might be taken to-day, with slight modification, to indicate the scope of a modern institution for the training of teachers. As practical guidance at that time it was not particularly helpful. The second and third qualifications are dependent upon the first, and until it was possible to give the prospective teacher a really thorough general education, it was hopeless to foist upon him the abstractions of a scientific theory of education. Moreover, the mental philosophy of the day had little to tell the teacher that would be of real significance and assistance to him. Until psychology came down to earth it could be of small use in the humdrum work of training teachers. A science of education cannot be built up on merely philosophical and theoretical considerations, but grows from experiments in the field of education itself, and even to-day the outlines of such a science are only slowly taking shape. Yet it is interesting to find a man at that date with so clear a conception of the rationale of training, at a time when empiricism reigned supreme.

[1] Select Committee on Education, 1835, Minutes of Evidence, 1034.

There were a number of suggestions as to ways in which the quality of the teachers might be improved. For example, considerable emphasis was laid upon the importance of having a standard certificate for teachers, and references were made to the practice of other countries, particularly to the "brevet de capacité" in France. In this connection the analogy between the medical and teaching professions was again stressed.

Three methods of training the teacher found supporters. Some witnesses considered that the best thing was to improve the normal schools in their existing form, but definitely to make all training centre about the work of model schools like Borough Road and Westminster. Others advocated the establishment of seminaries after the Continental model, mainly places of higher learning where prospective teachers were segregated. Others again would have liked to see the work of training taken up by the universities.

It was maintained that the model school was sufficient to prepare a teacher for elementary teaching, if the length of training was extended and the quality of the candidates improved. Good model schools should be set up in the great centres of population. One witness suggested that normal schools should be established in the great towns, "and those schools at first should be devoted to the training of normal teachers who are themselves to be distributed over the country, not perhaps immediately to teach pupils but again to teach teachers, so that an army of teachers should be prepared in the first instance".[1] The idea of basing the art of teaching upon a norm or standard that might be exemplified in an actual model school was one that died hard, and there were few to conceive of education as an art which depended for its success upon the spontaneity of the teacher. The difficulty was that what progress had been made in education was the

[1] Select Committee on Education, 1835, Minutes of Evidence, 472.

result of quasi-mechanical systems, and the quality of the teacher of the day did not encourage trust in his spontaneity.

The Continental seminary appealed more to the onlooker than to the man actually engaged in teaching or in the training of teachers. The amateur educational enthusiast was apt to be carried away with admiration for the range of studies followed in those colleges as compared with the meagre attainments of the English teacher. The schools attached to the seminaries were not "normal" or "model" schools, but merely practising schools, a very different thing. The three years' course in the normal seminaries of Germany made the English five months look very poor. However, there were objections to be raised to the seminary as the instrument for teachers' education and training. The Prussian seminaries were approved by Bryce because they gave due recognition to general principles, although too often these were merely general rules of method, but he doubted whether segregation was a good thing for the prospective teacher.[1]

It was to avoid this segregation that the utilisation of the university was suggested. Bryce's ideal of a training establishment was a university of the Scottish or German type, with a chair of education and a model school. In this way it would be possible for the general and professional education of teachers to go on simultaneously, and the teachers in training would have the opportunity of mixing with other classes of students. Candidates should enter between the ages of fifteen and twenty-five, having received a sound elementary school education.[2]

Another witness, whilst approving of the institution of university chairs of education, would have the normal schools as separate institutions, and it should be the duty of the masters of those schools (which were to be model schools,

---

[1] Select Committee on Education, 1835, Minutes of Evidence, 1038.
[2] *Ibid.* 1040 et seq.

not training colleges) to "instruct didactically" the "semi-nants". After passing through the normal school, some teachers in training would go on to the university. In the interests of uniformity a great central normal school should be established in London, "perfectly and philosophically organised", for the purpose of training masters for the provincial normal schools. The methods of this central school were to be universally adopted. At the same time a faculty of didactics should find a place in the universities. The main body of teachers should enter the profession through the normal schools, which would be the most satisfactory instruments for equipping teachers for the practical work of running a school, "and although perhaps a higher kind of accomplishment might be reaped by attendance in the university, he would not have the same confidence that the qualification of practically teaching an elementary school would be there attained".[1]

All this sounds surprisingly modern. The University Training Department has come to stay, but there are still those who claim that increase of knowledge has been purchased at the expense of teaching technique. In 1834, in England at any rate, there was not much chance of the co-operation of the universities. Oxford and Cambridge were not enthusiastically interested in popular education. Durham and London had been established only a very few years, and beyond these there were no universities in existence to do the work. In Scotland it was more possible, where the educational system had been always democratic, and, moreover, where the universities had been accustomed to devoting much of their time to what we now consider education of a merely secondary standard.

From the evidence given before the Select Committees it is clear that men of all types were becoming interested in the

[1] Select Committee on Education, 1835, Minutes of Evidence, pp. 154, 155, 180, 181, 182, 183.

problems of national elementary education. Ideas were incubating that were to bear fruit in later years. With the exception of the pupil teacher system, there is hardly a development of teachers' training which is not foreshadowed in some measure. The time was ripe for advance, and a man was raised up to lead the van.

The decade under consideration in this chapter saw the first timid interference by the State in elementary education, commencing with the first grant for the erection of schools made in 1833. That enlightened public opinion recognised the quality of the teacher to be the real crux of the education question was shown by the speeches of the educational pioneers in Parliament. When Roebuck introduced his Bill immediately before the first grant was made, normal schools were to play a considerable part in the educational system which he proposed. The first step actually taken by the State in connection with training was the result of a speech by Lord Brougham in the House of Lords in 1835, in which he upheld the voluntary system, but declared that it needed to be supplemented. The great need was for "seminaries where good schoolmasters might be trained and taught the duties of their profession", such as were already flourishing on the Continent. Following this speech, Parliament voted a grant of £10,000 "towards the erection of normal or model schools", but, because of sectarian jealousy, the grant was not finally made until after the failure of the scheme for a State normal school brought forward as the first act of the newly created Committee of Council on Education in 1839.

The "Committee of the Privy Council on Education" was set up by Melbourne's Government in April, 1839, "to superintend the application of any sums voted by Parliament for the purpose of promoting public education", and its first secretary, Dr James Phillips Kay, later Sir James Kay-Shuttleworth, was the man to whom the training of teachers owes a greater debt than to any other. Three days after it came into being, the committee celebrated its creation by plunging England into a first-rate educational controversy by its minute proposing the institution of a National Training College. This was a daring attempt to override the religious prejudices of the day in the true interests of education. The need for training was obvious, even to the most bigoted sectarian, and it was undeniable that the denominations, whatever might be their achievement in the erection of schools, showed no signs of grappling adequately with the problem of supplying teachers qualified for the staffing of the schools that were set up. If the committee were to do anything to improve matters, there were two alternatives before it. It could give substantial grants to the denominations for the specific purpose of establishing training colleges, or it could set up a State institution which should be open to all denominations. If the former alternative were chosen, there were four distinct groups interested in education, each of which would have a claim on the bounty of the committee: the Church of England, the Wesleyans, the Congregationalists and Friends, and the Roman Catholics.[1] The committee chose the latter alternative.

A model school[2] was to be set up, with a residential establishment for normal students attached. In the school the ages of the children were to range between three and fourteen years. Attention was to be paid both to industrial and moral training, and in addition to general religious training the children were to receive instruction according to the tenets of their several sects by authorised teachers. The proposed organisation of the school is significant as showing how the tide of public opinion was veering away from the monitorial system to the "simultaneous" method championed by David

[1] J. Kay-Shuttleworth, *Four Periods of Public Education*, 1862, p. 279.
[2] For details of scheme see *ibid.* "Explanation of the Measures of 1839", Chap. IV and pp. 179–81.

Stow. Every class was to consist of fifty scholars, but the classrooms were to be supplemented by "galleries", which were to be used for object lessons and others where it was desirable to have a large number of children attending to a subject at once.

No details were given as to the method of training to be followed, nor was it made clear to what extent students were to receive instruction as distinct from training. The institution was to be under the charge of a rector, who was to lecture on "method and matter of instruction and on the whole art of training children of the poor".[1] As far as can be gathered it was to be an institution not differing widely from the training establishments already in existence so far as methods of training were concerned, for the whole work was to centre on the "model school".

It is unnecessary to dwell on the outburst of sectarian protest which followed the proposal, or to discuss to what extent that outburst was justified. In these days it is difficult to understand the degree of indignation that was aroused, but it was patently evident that the proposal was in advance of public opinion, and the Government was forced to relinquish the project. By a minute of June 3rd, 1839, the £10,000 that had been voted in 1835 was divided between the National and British and Foreign Societies, with the significant recommendation that no further grant should be made unless the right of Government inspection were conceded.[2]

It is interesting to speculate what would have been the future of the training college movement had the State normal seminary been successfully established. Certainly at the outset it would have stimulated the voluntary societies to great efforts in the training of teachers, just as the institution of the School Boards in 1870 led to effort in the provision of education generally. But, as in the latter case, the competition would have been unequal, and probably the State would have

[1] J. Kay-Shuttleworth, *op. cit.* p. 181.   [2] *Ibid.* pp. 182, 183.

soon found itself with a monopoly of teachers' training. Whether the State would have wanted it is quite another question. We have recently seen the Board of Education delegate the conduct of the certificate examination for teachers in elementary schools, and it is not unlikely that something similar would have taken place sooner or later in respect of a State monopoly of training. A system of State training colleges would have been undoubtedly in the immediate interests of efficiency, and to-day we should have seen a better organised scheme for the training of teachers of various grades, but it is proverbial that the Englishman is suspicious of standardisation and centralisation, and in the present variegated system there is certainly to be found that "unity in diversity" which we are told is the characteristic of the living organism.

BIBLIOGRAPHY

Report from Select Committee on the State of Education, with Minutes of Evidence, 1834.

Report from Select Committee on Education in England and Wales, together with Minutes of Evidence, 1835.

Report from Select Committee on Education of the Poorer Classes in England and Wales, together with Minutes of Evidence, 1838.

COMMITTEE OF COUNCIL ON EDUCATION. Minutes, 1840–1.

J. KAY-SHUTTLEWORTH. *Four Periods of Public Education,* London, 1862.

BROUGHAM. *The Speech of Henry Lord Brougham in the House of Lords on Thursday May 21st, 1835, on the Education of the People,* London, 1835.

ROEBUCK. *The Speech of Mr Roebuck on National Education,* London, 1833.

J. KAY. *The Education of the Poor in England and Europe,* London, 1846.

F. SMITH. *Life of Sir James Kay-Shuttleworth,* London, 1923.

NATIONAL SCHOOL SOCIETY. *Annual Reports.*

BRITISH AND FOREIGN SCHOOL SOCIETY. *Annual Reports.*

H. BARNARD. *Normal Schools*, Hartford, U.S.A., 1851.

G. C. T. BARTLEY. *The Schools for the People*, London, 1871.

A. R. CRAIG. *The Philosophy of Training*, London, 1843 (much enlarged in later editions).

Edinburgh Review. Nos. 61 and 64 (articles on Fellenberg at Hofwyl).

—— No. 116 (article on Cousin's Report on German Education).

—— No. 117, "National Education in England and France", J. Pillans.

—— No. 120, "Seminaries for Teachers", J. Pillans.

V. COUSIN. *Rapport sur l'État de l'Instruction Publique dans quelques Pays de l'Allemagne et particulièrement en Prusse*, Paris, 1833.

—— *Report on the State of Public Instruction in Prussia*, translated by Sarah Austin, London, 1834.

—— *De l'Instruction Publique en Hollande*, Paris, 1837.

R. R. RUSK. *The Training of Teachers in Scotland*, Edinburgh, 1928.

GLASGOW EDUCATION SOCIETY. *Third Report*, Glasgow, 1839.

D. STOW. *The Training System and Normal Seminary*, 1st ed., 1836; nine subsequent editions, last 1853, Glasgow.

—— *Practical Hints on the Training System for the Use of Glasgow Normal Seminary Students*, 1838.

—— *Granny and Leezy*, London, 1860, 6th ed. (A popular exposition of the Glasgow system in dialogue form.)

W. FRASER. *Memoir of David Stow*, London, 1868.

J. WOOD. *Account of the Edinburgh Sessional School*, Edinburgh, 1829.

CHAPTER III

THE BATTERSEA EXPERIMENT

"THE indomitable man, who was founding our public education, determined to start a Normal School himself and to show how such an institution worked." The words are Matthew Arnold's,[1] the "indomitable man" is Kay-Shuttleworth, and the reference is to the founding of the Battersea Normal School. The secretary of the Committee of Council on Education had tried the temper of the country in respect of the establishment of a training college maintained by the State, and the country had responded with a decided and undeniable negative. We have his own word as witness that he had never really expected that the project for "training colleges purely civil" could be carried through. Many years afterwards, in a speech to the Battersea Club, composed of old students of the Battersea Training College, he said: "A scheme was devised and put before the public, with a conviction on my part that it would fail....I prepared the minute and presented it to the Government; I attended the Cabinet Council and it passed, and when they asked my opinion I said it would ignominiously fail".[2] Feeling strongly as he did that one of the crying necessities in English education was a central training college on an improved model, he realised at the same time that such a college would stand a far greater chance of success if run as a national affair than under the auspices of some private body. But when the country intimated that it would have none of such a scheme, Kay-Shuttleworth resolved to embark upon an adventure in

[1] T. Adkins, *History of St John's College, Battersea*, London, 1906, p. 32.
[2] *Ibid.* pp. 27, 28.

teachers' training on his own initiative, and largely at his own expense.

We have seen that he was profoundly impressed by what he had seen going on in the normal seminaries on the Continent, and particularly in Switzerland. There he had seen something which differed radically from anything known in England. It is true that some of the training institutions already in existence at home were residential, but the residence of the students was chiefly a matter of convenience, and the students remained for too short a time for corporate life to have much effect upon their character and outlook. His imagination was aroused by what he saw at Kreuzlingen, where Vehrli was exploiting the common life of a seminary in the interests primarily of character formation, but character formation with a vocational bias, and he was resolved to establish an institution in England after the Swiss model, so that all interested in education might see what could be accomplished by a method of training differing fundamentally from those hitherto adopted in this country.

Originally his project for a training college arose out of his work in connection with the administration of the Poor Law. He came to realise that some supply of teachers for Poor Law schools was needed other than that from the existing model schools. These Poor Law schools presented certain peculiar difficulties. Unlike the ordinary primary schools, they were residential, and the teachers who came to the work through the ordinary avenues of training or experience proved anything but satisfactory under conditions of living that were strange to them. The prospects of the Poor Law teacher were poor, even poorer than those of the ordinary elementary teacher. The life was in many ways sordid, and inevitably circumscribed, and Kay-Shuttleworth realised that the only motive that could carry a man on in the work efficiently and in the right spirit was a feeling of service and self-sacrifice combined with a happy acceptance of the limitations of the work. As it was, entrants to the work were commonly the dregs of the profession, whose one desire was to get out as soon as possible, and who were actuated by no sense of vocation. The shortness of their training was a disadvantage, and the fact that most of them were dependent upon patronage whilst at the normal school tended to produce an unfortunate attitude towards their work.

The founder of the Battersea Training College eloquently expressed the purpose of the experiment thus:

"We hoped to inspire them (i.e. the students) with a large sympathy for their own class. To implant in their minds the thought that their chief honour would be to aid in rescuing that class from the misery of ignorance and its attendant vices. To wean them from the influence of that personal competition in a commercial society which leads to sordid aims. To place before them the unsatisfied want of the uneasy and distressed multitude, and to breathe into them the charity which seeks to heal its mental and moral diseases".[1]

This being the aim, what method could be more attractive than that adopted for the preparation of schoolmasters for the popular schools of Switzerland, with its emphasis on community life, hard and incessant labour, both manual and intellectual, and strong religious tone? The life of the Swiss peasant schoolmaster was hard, but the life of the student preparing for that vocation was still harder. As one English observer remarked, "When they leave the Normal Schools they find that they have changed from a situation of humble toil to one of comparative ease".[2] By following similar lines Kay-Shuttleworth hoped to be able to raise up a race of Poor Law schoolmasters inured through several years of training to the simplest of living and the most strenuous of labour.

Before passing on to describe the foundation of the training

[1] J. Kay-Shuttleworth, *Four Periods of Public Education*, 1862, p. 309.
[2] J. Kay, *Education of the Poor in England and Europe*, 1846, p. 11.

institution at Battersea, we must turn our attention to certain experiments in the Poor Law schools a few years earlier, as it was from the product of these experiments, the earliest "pupil teachers" so-called, that the new college was to be recruited. The work of the Poor Law schools had been improved by the introduction of trained teachers from the Glasgow Normal Seminary and Wood's Sessional School in Edinburgh, and when Kay-Shuttleworth was responsible for the East Anglian district, he appointed Horne, from Wood's Sessional School, as an organising master.[1]

Kay-Shuttleworth tells us that his mind was first turned towards the possibility of some system of pupil teachers by the exploit of a certain William Rush in an East Anglian workhouse school.[2] In an emergency caused by the illness of the schoolmaster at the workhouse of Gressenhall, the work was successfully carried on by William Rush, who had reached the mature age of thirteen years. This occurrence suggested a solution to the problem of recruiting workhouse schoolmasters. Why should not this class be drawn from the abler members of the workhouse schools themselves? The success of this solution depended upon the possibility of providing the right sort of training. Writing many years afterwards, Kay-Shuttleworth described how the situation appealed to him:

"But could this youth, however gifted, complete his education so as to take charge of an independent school, without some other training which should transform his manners, habits and modes of thought, and give him some experience of the life of the world outside the workhouse walls? Was it expedient to launch this youth on a career which apparently must be abortive, because his preparation would necessarily be so limited and his experiences so incomplete?"[3]

[1] J. Kay-Shuttleworth, *op. cit.* p. 287.   [2] *Ibid.* p. 288.
[3] MS. 1877. See F. Smith, *Life of Sir J. Kay-Shuttleworth*, 1923, p. 51.

In 1838 Kay-Shuttleworth published a pamphlet *On the Training of Pauper Children, and on District Schools*, and soon afterwards resolved to experiment in training teachers at the Poor Law schools at Norwood, which were placed under the direction of McLeod, a trained teacher from Scotland, who was destined to play no mean part in the early history of the training institution at Battersea. In the matter of organisation his arrangements were not unlike those of Lancaster in his early experiments in training at the Borough Road. A number of the older and more promising pupils were raised to the rank of "probationers", and received special instruction in the evenings. If they made satisfactory progress, they were invested with a special distinguishing uniform and were known as "pupil teachers". The tangible rewards of their promotion were the allocation of separate rooms and the provision of better food than that supplied to the common herd of pupils. The pupil teachers were not all drawn from within the walls of Norwood. Kay-Shuttleworth conceived of Norwood's developing into a central place of training, and the most promising boys from pauper schools in various parts of the country were received, and were apprenticed for a period of five years. Private pupils also might be taken in, and a number were sent by patrons to receive training identical with that given to the pauper pupil teachers. A similar apprenticeship of five years was enforced in respect of these private students, and in addition their patrons were called upon to supply their uniform and pay a fee of five shillings a week. In the main this private class of students was drawn from the sons of schoolmasters, although there were others, including two from as far distant as Malta.[1]

There was an elaborate organisation of classes and teachers, just as in the monitorial training centres, and the work of the pupil teachers was carefully supervised. The school was di-

[1] F. Smith, *op. cit.* pp. 57–60, and J. Kay-Shuttleworth, *op. cit.* pp. 289–92.

vided up into classes of fifty, and to each class were appointed a pupil teacher and a monitor. For every two classes there were allocated a "teacher" and a "candidate teacher", these being the ranks next above that of "pupil teacher". Examinations were held every six months, and success in these led to promotion to higher ranks and more responsibility.

Kay-Shuttleworth realised that this pupil teacher organisation was only the first step in grappling with the problem of training, and that the pupil teacher period should be followed by a period of further education in an institution definitely designed for the purpose of training teachers. This conviction was strengthened by what he experienced on his extensive tour of the Continent with Tufnell, when, as has already been noted, he was vastly impressed by the work of the Swiss normal schools. He learnt much also in other countries. In Holland he found a pupil teacher system fully developed and working, the pupil teachers spending their days in gaining experience of teaching in the schools, and their evenings in improving their own knowledge in central classes. In Paris he was greatly interested in the work of the Christian Brethren, and his partiality for the segregated life of the seminary as an important element in the training of teachers of the poor was strengthened by the semi-monastic life led by the Brothers. He had his Norwood pupil teachers in mind when the project for the State normal school was mooted.[1] Such an institution might well have supplied the further education that they needed, whilst they in their turn would have formed a useful nucleus of students, pending the opening up of other sources of supply. The project, as we have seen, failed, the State normal college was sacrificed upon the altar of sectarianism, and Kay-Shuttleworth was forced to make his own arrangements for the carrying on of the adventure which he had embarked upon at Norwood.

He was satisfied that his pupil teacher system was a step

[1] See F. Smith, *op. cit.* p. 83.

in the right direction, and, with his quick eye for educational expedients, he foresaw that it was a system that was capable of expansion to meet national needs for better prepared teachers. Writing in 1877 he said:

"I conceived, therefore, that further experience would prove that for many years the pupil teachers would have to be chiefly selected from the most promising scholars of the elementary schools. There would even be difficulty in securing their services unless they were apprenticed at the age beyond which the most advanced scholars seldom remained at the schools.... My conception was that the form and limits of this system must be determined by the circumstances among which it came into existence. I saw in it the means of development of a class of certificated adult and assistant teachers: and when the popular appreciation of the value of elementary education should become more enlightened, this first step might, by improvement, be adapted to the wants of the schools rising to higher conditions of efficiency.

"If, as a first step, the schools of each denomination reared their own pupil teachers, the Government might secure the efficiency of their instruction by examinations, provided they granted aid to meet the expense. On similar conditions it might promote the building of Training Colleges in which the pupil teachers might complete their education".[1]

This extension of the system to meet national needs was brought about by the famous Minutes of the Committee of Council of 1846, and the scheme was to remain the central feature of our training system for sixty years and more.

Battersea was chosen as the site of the training college which Kay-Shuttleworth resolved to establish as a private undertaking. At that date it was a suburban village with much of its rural nature surviving, and there was a suitably large house and grounds available. The local clergyman, the

[1] F. Smith, *op. cit.* p. 91.

Rev. Robert Eden, was deeply interested in the project, and was willing to place the village school at the disposal of the college for practising and demonstration purposes. He also offered to supervise the students of the college in religious matters.

The college was opened in February, 1840, and the first batch of students consisted of eight pupil teachers from Norwood, all aged about thirteen years. These were indentured as apprentices for seven years, or until they reached the age of twenty-one. They were to receive at least three years' instruction in the training school, and for two years they were to act as pupil teachers in the village school for three hours a day. At the end of their apprenticeship they were to be subjected to examination, and if satisfactory were to receive certificates and be given employment as teachers in schools of industry for pauper children. During the period of apprenticeship they were to receive remuneration with annual increments.[1]

In addition to these young students who were receiving schooling themselves as well as professional training, a number of young men, with ages ranging between twenty and thirty years, were to be admitted for short courses of one year. In the year 1841 there were nine of these older students in the institution.[2] The situation was much like that which obtained in Lancaster's day at the Borough Road, when he mingled outside students with his own "family", and Kay-Shuttleworth was to find himself later faced by the same problems in this connection as faced the earlier educational pioneer.

Kay-Shuttleworth was himself the superintendent of the institution, and he installed his East Anglian organising master, Horne, as a tutor. A second tutor was appointed, Thomas Tate,[3] whose name was destined to appear subse-

[1] J. Kay-Shuttleworth, *op. cit.* p. 310 and F. Smith, *op. cit.* p. 106.
[2] J. Kay-Shuttleworth, *op. cit.* p. 311.   [3] *Ibid.* p. 312.

quently on a large number of works of an educational nature, whilst the village school was placed in the charge of McLeod,[1] whom he brought with him from Norwood. In the early days of the college the personal influence and supervision of Kay-Shuttleworth were of tremendous value, and such success as was met by the new institution was in the nature of a personal triumph. The difficulties to be faced were very great. At first the project was financed out of the superintendent's own purse, and even when the State came forward to assist the new venture, there was continual need for Kay-Shuttleworth to put his hand in his pocket. The "students" were anything but promising material, and to bring them to a suitable standard of culture for the work for which they were destined was a serious task. Oral teaching was bound to be the staple mode of instruction, since the students had little idea of the right use of books, and, indeed, a sad scarcity of books was characteristic of the institution. The superintendent tackled all difficulties with great enthusiasm, and managed to imbue both his assistants and his pupils with his keenness and vigour. Morning by morning he was at his post to receive the reports of the student "superintendents" or prefects, and he watched with an ever-vigilant eye the moral and intellectual progress of every individual.[2] Morning by morning he addressed all the students on the general principles determining the work of the institution, and explained the relationship between the discipline of the training school and the work that would lie before them when they passed from its walls.[3] Frequently he would accompany his flock on walking expeditions to places of interest, with the idea of getting them occasionally out of the seclusion of the school and into touch with nature and humanity, and making them acquainted with the real life of the countryman and with the extra occupations which they might be called upon

[1] J. Kay-Shuttleworth, *op. cit.* p. 360.   [2] *Ibid.* p. 332.
[3] *Ibid.* p. 332.

to follow as teachers of the poor, thus putting into practice in England a lesson learnt from the practice of the normal schools in Switzerland.[1] Often he was to be seen toiling in the garden with his students, accompanied by his two tutors, and sometimes by his friend Tufnell.[2] He realised to the full how much all depended upon his personal influence and control, and in his account of the early years of the training school he inserted the significant remark, "The Principal should be *wise as a serpent*".[3]

Speaking of the Battersea Training School and its significance in the development of the English training college system, Tufnell, Kay-Shuttleworth's staunch supporter, remarked in 1875, "We were pooh-poohed, then abused, then imitated; and now I have the satisfaction of seeing the establishment of forty training colleges all founded upon the principles first exemplified at Battersea".[4] That statement is substantially true. The form that Battersea took under Kay-Shuttleworth's guidance was to leave its mark upon the character of every training college established during the subsequent three decades. For good or ill Battersea was destined to be the model, and this being so, a clear understanding is necessary of its founder's conception of the aims and methods of such an institution. So far as what may be called educational politics were concerned, we have Kay-Shuttleworth's own word for it that his purpose was two-fold. He deliberately set out to establish a training college which should be an example and type to guide future efforts, and to show that masters trained in the spirit of Christian charity could conduct schools in which the children of all denominations were educated together.[5] But what is of more interest

---

[1] J. Kay-Shuttleworth, *op. cit.* pp. 319–23.
[2] T. Adkins, *op. cit.* p. 55.
[3] J. Kay-Shuttleworth, *op. cit.* p. 405.
[4] T. Adkins, *op. cit.* p. 106.
[5] J. Kay-Shuttleworth, *op. cit.* p. 426.

is his conception of the true work of a college for the training of teachers for the lower classes, and the means he considered necessary for carrying out that work and attaining
the end he had in mind.

Above all he maintained that the training college was concerned with education as well as professional training, and
with education in the moral sense rather than the intellectual,
although he always recognised the importance of practice in
teaching, and instruction in the methods and principles of
the art. This point of view he put forward explicitly in the
Second Report (1843) on Battersea: "The main object of a
Normal School is the *formation of the character of the schoolmaster*".[1] He was convinced that the drudgery of teaching
the lower classes could be successfully and conscientiously
carried out only by persons motivated by a real feeling of
vocation, and he felt it the duty of the training institution
to foster and develop such a feeling of vocation among the
students. If that were lacking, all intellectual advance was
of little avail. His great fear was that the little learning acquired during training might foster an empty intellectual
pride, which was the worst spirit in which to enter upon the
work of a schoolmaster. That this was no vain fear was shown
by the attitude of many of the schoolmasters who had received training at the Borough Road and similar training
schools. Of the older methods of training Kay-Shuttleworth
wrote:

"To select from the common drudgery of a handicraft, or
from the humble, if not mean pursuits of a petty trade, a
young man barely (if indeed at all) instructed in the humblest
elements of reading, writing and arithmetic, and to conceive
that a few months' attendance on a Model School can make
him acquainted with the theory of its organisation, convert
him into an adept in its methods, or even rivet upon his
stubborn memory any significant part of the technical know-

[1] J. Kay-Shuttleworth, *op, cit.* p. 399.

ledge of which he has immediate need, is a mistake too shameful to be permitted to survive its universal failure".[1]

Whilst realising the need for a broader intellectual training, he feared lest this danger of conceit might be enhanced, and the seeds of discontent sown, unless it were accompanied by the sternest of moral training. "He (the trained teacher) might become, not the gentle and pious guide of the children of the poor, but a hireling into whose mind had sunk the doubts of the sceptic; in whose heart was the worm of social discontent; and who had changed the docility of ignorance and dulness for the restless impatience of a vulgar and conceited sciolist." [2]

The remedy for this evil was to be found in religious training, and an introduction during training to a Spartan standard of living coupled with very hard work, both intellectual and manual. "The path of the teacher is strewn with disappointments if he commence with a mercenary spirit. It is full of encouragement if he be inspired with the spirit of Christian charity." [3]

In the deliberately fostered spirit of service which Kay-Shuttleworth met in education abroad he saw something that was conspicuously lacking at home. In Paris, for example, he was profoundly impressed by what he saw in connection with the "Mother Schools" of the Brothers of the Christian Doctrine, where a boy entered the service of education as if entering a monastery, starting his career at the age of twelve or fourteen. After a period of instruction and training he devoted his life to the education of the poor of Paris, working in the city schools during the day, but always residing in the Mother School. In spite of his religious prejudices, Kay-Shuttleworth was strongly attracted by this semi-monastic system.[4] He is reported by his friend Hullah to have exclaimed on a visit to one of the schools of the Brothers,

---

[1] J. Kay-Shuttleworth, *op. cit.* p. 410.   [2] *Ibid.* pp. 401–2.
[3] *Ibid.* p. 358.   [4] *Ibid.* pp. 388–93.

"Would to God we had anything like these men (he would have said 'Papists' an hour before) in our schools!"[1] and the work of the Christian Brothers was second as an inspiration only to what he saw done in the normal schools of Switzerland. Writing in his "First Report on Battersea" (1841) he said: "In the Orphan Schools which have emanated from Pestalozzi and De Fellenberg we found the type which has assisted us in our subsequent labours",[2] and the severe life of Battersea was modelled upon what he saw at Vehrli's Normal School at Kreuzlingen, where the pupils had a day of constant work commencing at four or five in the morning and lasting until nine at night with only three meals, and the normal school at Berne, where the students worked in the fields for eight hours a day in addition to their intellectual labour, wore the coarsest of peasant clothes, with wooden shoes and no stockings, and yet attained to a comparatively high academic standard.[3]

Constant activity was the keynote of life at Battersea. This in itself was no innovation in a training institution, but it was the inclusion of much manual work that was peculiar. For example, at the Borough Road the students were kept hard at work from five in the morning until nine or ten at night, but these long hours were looked upon rather as a regrettable necessity than a means of character training. Giving evidence before the Select Committee of 1834, Henry Dunn, the secretary of the British and Foreign School Society, said: "Our object is to keep them incessantly employed from five in the morning until nine or ten at night. We have rather exceeded, in the time devoted to study, the limit we would choose, on account of the very short period we are able to keep them, and we have found in some instances that their health has suffered on account of their having been previously

---

[1] T. Adkins, *op. cit.* p. 77.
[2] J. Kay-Shuttleworth, *op. cit.* p. 303.
[3] J. Kay-Shuttleworth, *op. cit.* pp. 303–8.

quite unaccustomed to mental occupation".[1] At Battersea there was not the necessity for the same pressure, as it was hoped that students would remain, many of them, for several years, but Kay-Shuttleworth was resolved to inure his prospective teachers from the outset to long hours of unremitting toil, whilst avoiding the danger of over-pressure by mingling work of hand with work of brain throughout the day. Holidays were unknown, and as a deliberate policy no leisure time was left for the students to dispose of as they pleased, for fear of "associations formed among the students inconsistent with discipline",[2] and the suspicion that free time "might be spent in listless sauntering or in violent exertion".[3] It was felt that constant supervision was the only safeguard both in intellectual and moral matters. "In so brief a training it is necessary that the entire conduct of the student should be guided by a superior mind."[4] Accordingly the students were never away from the watchful eyes of the superintendent or his assistants, whether they were at work in the classrooms or in the garden, and this supervision was augmented by a system of student "superintendents" or prefects, whose duty it was to report misdemeanours promptly to the authorities.

From the beginning it was intended that the school should be as self-supporting as possible, and the grounds be brought under cultivation to supply vegetables. Gradually livestock was introduced, first a cow, then three pigs, then three goats (the head of one of which was long preserved stuffed and mounted in the college),[5] and subsequently poultry and another cow.[6] As part of the day's routine, three (originally four) hours were devoted to gardening or looking after the livestock, milking, and so forth. All students had to take

[1] Select Committee on Education, 1834, Minutes of Evidence, 232.
[2] J. Kay-Shuttleworth, *op. cit.* p. 403.   [3] *Ibid.*   [4] *Ibid.*
[5] T. Adkins, *op. cit.* p. 53.
[6] J. Kay-Shuttleworth, *op. cit.* p. 313.

part, and their tutors laboured with them. In the early days the students appeared to find this a severe physical strain, but as time progressed it proved to be a very salutary form of outdoor exercise.[1] In addition, the students had a number of domestic tasks to perform. Only one servant was kept, to do the cooking, and all the work of cleaning dormitories and making beds fell on the students themselves.

The day's work began at 5.30 a.m., and after domestic duties had been performed everyone turned out to milk the cows or work in the garden. At 7.30 there was a short religious service, and afterwards the superintendent received the reports of the prefects, and frequently gave a short address. Breakfast was at 8.30, consisting of porridge and milk, and at this, as at every other meal, the tutors had the same fare as the students. Half an hour was more than sufficient for this frugal meal, fortified by which the students passed on to three hours' work in classes till noon, the first half-hour being devoted to religious instruction. An appetite for dinner was stimulated by an hour's work in the garden. Dinner was the main meal of the day, and was a substantial, if plain, repast. From 2 till 5 p.m. was spent in class again, with another hour of outdoor activity to follow. At 6.15 supper was taken, consisting of bread and milk, and at 7 the students turned out for drill. The rest of the evening was spent in miscellaneous but useful activities like copying music, making notes on geography or mechanics, or practising singing. The day came to a close with evening prayers at 9, and all were in bed by 9.20.[2] The proverbial Satan was not given much scope in the Battersea Normal School. "By this laborious and frugal life, economy of management is reconciled with efficiency both of the moral and intellectual training of the School, and the master goes forth into the world humble, industrious and instructed."[3]

[1] J. Kay-Shuttleworth, *op. cit.* pp. 314, 315.
[2] *Ibid.* pp. 328-9.   [3] *Ibid.* pp. 404-5.

There was no attempt at maintaining a monastic seclusion from the world, however. Kay-Shuttleworth was particularly anxious that his students should be kept in touch with everyday things. He organised what would now be called "school journeys", when he would lead his little company to visit places of historic, scientific or educational interest. Sometimes they were merely long country walks, when the purpose was to bring the students into contact with real peasant life.[1] Later the superintendent introduced definite instruction in the "collateral duties of a country schoolmaster", such as the management of a garden, the pruning and grafting of trees, the "domestic economy of the poor", the "means of preserving health", and the relations of capital and labour (!).[2] On Sundays all attended the services at the village church, the pupil teachers attired in their uniform "rifle-green" suits and peaked caps which earned them the nickname of the "Green Birds", the rest of the day being spent in studies of an appropriately religious nature which included the writing of "copious extracts" of the sermon to be read and publicly commented upon in the evening.[3]

In his organisation of the academic side of the life at Battersea, Kay-Shuttleworth was influenced by what he knew of the work of the schools for the training of teachers in Germany. The problem was complicated by the presence of pupils of varying ages. So far as the youngest students were concerned, the first years of the course were to be devoted mainly to general education, the normal school doing the work carried out in Germany by the "preparatory training schools".[4] Certificates were to be awarded to the pupil teachers at various stages of their course; a "Candidate's" certificate at the end of the first year, a "Scholar's" at the

[1] J. Kay-Shuttleworth, *op. cit.* pp. 319–23.
[2] *Ibid.* pp. 365–6.
[3] *Ibid.* p. 325 and T. Adkins, *op. cit.* p. 62.
[4] J. Kay-Shuttleworth, *op. cit.* p. 326.

end of the second, and a "Master's" at the end of the third.[1] A careful check was kept on progress by means of weekly examinations, and a complicated system of marking was adopted, which took into account punctuality, subordination, industry, cleanliness and order, the whole being combined in a kind of "moral coefficient".[2]

The curriculum was a wide one, and in each subject an attempt was made to teach according to the most approved "modern" methods of the day, so that these methods might be applied by the students in their own teaching. Thus in reading, the German "phonic" method was adopted.[3] In English the methods worked out at Wood's Sessional School, Edinburgh, were followed.[4] Grammar and etymology were studied, and literature was accorded an important place as the prime cultural instrument in popular education. "A thorough acquaintance with the English language can alone make the labouring classes accessible to the best influences of English civilisation."[5] The "Mulhauser" method was used in writing, and in arithmetic the "synthetic" methods of Pestalozzi, as modified by the Kildare Place Society, were adopted.[6] Additional subjects were the elements of mechanics, regarded as important because of the increasing prominence of machinery in the national life, geography, particularly physical geography, drawing, and vocal music after the method of Wilhem.[7] In the latter subject the school was especially fortunate to have the services of Hullah, who was doing fine work in popularising music throughout the country, and who later on was to be helped in his lectures by illustrations given by his "Battersea Boys".[8]

When it was considered that the preparatory course was sufficiently advanced, a series of lectures was commenced on

[1] J. Kay-Shuttleworth, *op. cit.* p. 327.   [2] *Ibid.* pp. 330-2.
[3] *Ibid.* p. 338.   [4] *Ibid.* p. 338.   [5] *Ibid.* p. 339.
[6] *Ibid.* pp. 340-2.   [7] *Ibid.* pp. 344-54.
[8] T. Adkins, *op. cit.* Chap. VI.

the instruction and organisation of elementary schools, based on the model of the German lectures on "Pädagogik" customary in the normal schools. The chief topics dealt with were the general objects of education, the structure and arrangement of schools, methods of discipline, main methods of communicating knowledge, and the teaching of special subjects.[1]

Practical experience in teaching was gained in the village school. At first this was not very definitely organised, owing to the difficulty already mentioned of the wide age range of the students and the need for completing the preparatory stage of the course. After 1843, however, when it had been decided to take no more students under the age of 18, a definite routine of practice was arranged. Students in the "first class", i.e. those whose preliminary education was considered to be sufficiently advanced, were divided into two groups, one group attending the village school in the morning, the other in the afternoon. Thus, in a training period of eighteen months, it was usual to have three hours' daily practice for six or eight months.[2]

At the school the students observed the methods employed, which were those they had been brought up on in the normal school, and had the opportunity of doing some teaching themselves, under the supervision of McLeod, who also lectured to them on the special methods of the different subjects, the art of managing and instructing a class, the art of giving gallery lessons, and the discipline and organisation of schools.[3]

Kay-Shuttleworth had no particular desire to keep the Battersea Normal School independent of Government supervision or of Government assistance. From the first, the newly-created inspectors were invited to visit the institution, and their co-operation was sought in connection with the awarding of the various certificates. As the financial burden

[1] J. Kay-Shuttleworth, *op. cit.* pp. 356–8.   [2] *Ibid.* p. 421.
[3] *Ibid.* p. 420.

was very heavy, and fell upon a few individuals, it was hoped that the Government might be prepared to give some help by way of grant, and if that were to come about, Kay-Shuttleworth considered that the Government should have the right to veto any appointments that might be made, and that any of the staff might be dismissed on the report of an inspector.[1] This hope of assistance was realised in 1842, when a grant of £1000 was made, followed in the next year by a further grant of £2200 for the carrying out of certain improvements.[2]

By this time Kay-Shuttleworth was not altogether satisfied with the working of his experiment. He realised that the normal school was preparing teachers for a very definite type of work, that of the rural teacher or the teacher in a Poor Law school, and that the training given was not well fitted for teachers who were going to work in towns or manufacturing districts. He would have liked to institute a "Town Normal School", complementary to Battersea, after the model of the central schools for "pupil teachers" which he had seen in Holland. In such a normal school the students would reside and carry out their studies under the supervision of a principal, whilst they would go out day by day into the schools of the town for practice in teaching. Such a project, however, was out of the question at the time, since all resources were strained to the uttermost to keep Battersea going.[3]

Moreover, certain important modifications of procedure had been rendered necessary at Battersea itself. The original plan had been that the body of students should include both boys and persons of more mature years, but it was found in practice very difficult to carry on work satisfactorily with both these classes in the same institution. Methods suitable with boys were inapplicable to adults, and difficulties were likely to arise when boys who had been a year or two in the

---

[1] J. Kay-Shuttleworth, *op. cit.* pp. 369–71.   [2] *Ibid.* p. 387.
[3] *Ibid.* pp. 391–4.

college were far ahead in class of students much older and more experienced than themselves. Combined with this was the difficulty of keeping students for a long course. Accordingly the age of admission was fixed at eighteen years as a minimum, although twenty was looked upon as the best age for entering, and two years was about the longest course that could be hoped for.[1] So Kay-Shuttleworth's more ambitious hopes were overcome by the same difficulties that had been met with by Lancaster in his dealings with his "family", and the attempt to bridge the gap between the age for leaving the elementary school and the age for starting serious teaching had once again failed.

There was considerable variation in the conditions under which students were admitted. Students who could pay all their own expenses or who had patrons to pay them might settle in what schools they liked after their course of training. Students who could find £30, and who gave security for the payment of a further £25 within one year of leaving, were similarly free. Students who could only manage to pay the £30 and made no promise of future payment bound themselves to serve in Government-aided schools for five years after leaving the normal school. Students might be helped financially by an entrance exhibition of £25, or by a leaving exhibition of £25 which was awarded once every quarter.[2]

The students admitted were generally recruited from the lower or lower-middle classes, mostly "sons of small tradesmen, of bailiffs, of servants or of superior mechanics".[3] Their attainments were generally meagre in the extreme. Few, if any, had had any schooling beyond that afforded by the ordinary parochial school. Their skill both in reading and writing was imperfect. Few could compose a decent letter, and a student was rare who could display skill in applying the four simple rules of arithmetic. In spite of the supposed

[1] J. Kay-Shuttleworth, *op. cit.* pp. 397–8.
[2] *Ibid.* pp. 424–5 footnote.   [3] *Ibid.* p. 400.

religious character of the education they had received in the elementary school, their Biblical knowledge was meagre and inaccurate. They were quite unfitted for the severely regular work of the normal school, and took fully three months to settle down to the new mode of life.[1] It was accordingly necessary to confine instruction almost exclusively to oral teaching. Books were scarce, and the students had no idea of the right use of books even when available. Such text-books as there were were used chiefly for recapitulation.[2]

The Government grant had been made on condition that the institution should be made permanent, and the only feasible way of providing for this seemed to be to place the college under the control of one of the existing organisations interested in education, and especially in the training of teachers. Kay-Shuttleworth was a staunch believer in the religious principle, and a firm supporter of the Church of England, so it was natural that he should turn to the National Society, particularly as that organisation had shown great activity in recent years in providing facilities for the training of teachers. Negotiations for the transfer were commenced, and eventually the Battersea Normal School was handed over to the society,[3] and the period of the "Battersea Experiment" may be said to end with that transfer in 1843, followed by the appointment of the Rev. Thomas Jackson as principal in 1844. Henceforward there is little to distinguish it in type from the other training colleges of the Church of England.

Kay-Shuttleworth's experiment at Battersea is the most significant event in the history of the development of the English training college, for it was the type to which all subsequently founded training colleges conformed until the advent of the Day Training College. For good or for ill it established the residential college as the type. To a certain

[1] J. Kay-Shuttleworth, *op. cit.* p. 401.
[2] Committee of Council on Education, Minutes, 1842–3, p. 65.
[3] J. Kay-Shuttleworth, *op. cit.* pp. 429–30.

extent previously founded training institutions in England had been residential, but the residence had been for convenience sake merely. At Battersea life in college was regarded as a definite educational instrument. For many years corporate life of this kind was looked upon as of the highest value in the education and training of the teacher, and the English training college has developed a type of "corporate consciousness" all its own. The founder of Battersea conceived the training college essentially as a seminary in which candidates for a vocation were to be segregated from the world, but evidence is not lacking that he realised the dangers of such segregation, and took steps to prevent its becoming absolute. Under the direction of men less wise, these safeguards were often omitted, and a dangerous narrowness came to mark the life and work of the training colleges. With the advent of the Government certificate, and the partial dependence of college finances upon success in Government examinations, preparation for those examinations came to dominate the work of the colleges, and out-of-door activities, such as found a prominent place at Battersea, tended to disappear, it being felt that time spent in such a way was largely wasted. This being the case, residential life in a training college became commonly narrow and comparatively unrelated to the life of the outside world.

The Battersea Normal School, like the institutions of the two great educational societies, and unlike Stow's Glasgow Normal Seminary in its early days, set out to teach the subjects of school instruction as well as to give training in the technique of teaching method, and that dual function has characterised the residential training college until the present day. Much criticism has been directed against the work of the training colleges of recent years on this account, and there is no doubt that the future will see a steady movement towards clearly differentiating between academic work and professional training, the organisation of each being kept separate, even though both types of work be carried on in one institution. Possibly training college tradition has proved a hindrance to such development, but it has to be admitted that the dual-function institution was the only solution in the middle of the nineteenth century of the problem of providing teachers for the elementary schools reasonably acquainted with the subjects they were to teach, and in some degree trained in the technique of the teacher's craft.

On the academic side the problem of the training of the teacher was in effect simply one aspect of the far wider problem of national secondary education. Many of the developments in the training of teachers during the second half of the nineteenth century were concerned with the devising of makeshifts to provide for intending teachers that education which should properly be given in post-primary institutions unconnected with the specific business of preparing teachers for their work. We have seen that Kay-Shuttleworth realised the importance of bridging the gap between the time of leaving the elementary school and entering the training college. His first attempt at solution failed, as it was bound to do. His second attempt, by the establishment of the pupil teacher system, was more successful.

With the great development of secondary education during the present century, and with the spread of university education, the problem of the training of the teacher has taken on quite a fresh aspect. In the last century the training college was bound to attempt academic as well as professional training, much as such a combination may be deplored on general grounds. It is very easy to criticise with supercilious condescension the academic work of the early training colleges, but it must be realised that they were embarking upon something quite new in English education, something that was not to be found in any other type of educational institution. They were trying to do the work of the secondary school before such a school was contemplated, and working out a curriculum quite unlike that of any school or university of the time.

In the matter of professional training, Battersea set the example for subsequent training schools. The "model school" and the "master of method" are two characteristic features of the Victorian training college, and the latter officer was in nearly every case the master of the model school. McLeod combined the duties of teaching the Battersea village school (which, unlike many later model schools, was not built for that express purpose) and instructing the students in the technique of their future calling. He appears to have been the first man in England to whom the title of "master of method" was applied,[1] and masters of method conformed commonly to his type throughout the century.

It is doubtful whether the master of method and the model school were altogether desirable adjuncts to the training college, and without doubt they were responsible for much of the narrowness and stereotyped quality of the professional training that was given. The alternative title for the master of method is "normal master", and the use of the term "normal" in connection with teachers' training is significant of an "idol" of the training college—the idea that there exists some norm or type in teaching, and the nearer the teacher comes to that norm the better will his teaching be. It is this conception that explains the popularity of the model school, which was looked upon as the concrete embodiment of the norm so far as the school as an institution was concerned, whilst the teaching of the master of method was to be regarded as the norm in the technique of class teaching. There is something to be said for the idea, given requisite excellence in both model school and normal master, but in hard fact that excellence was rarely attained. Moreover, the normal master was nearly always a man whose experience was limited to the training college and elementary school,

[1] Committee of Council on Education, Minutes, 1842–3, p. 69.

and his methods, good enough in their way, did not merit exaltation as models of general and exclusive imitation.

But here again it is essential to remember the state of education as a whole at the time. With better educated students, and with a profusion of passably good schools, it is possible to-day for those responsible for training teachers to send out their apprentices to take part in the life of ordinary schools at their daily work, and to apply the principles of spontaneity and self-development in professional training as much as in education generally, trusting that students in training will arrive at their own methods with judicious guidance, without the imposition of a pattern or model of method from above. But the situation was vastly different when the training college movement began in earnest. The quality of the students was such that the trainer of teachers was bound to play for safety by imposing a method which was at least sound, even at the expense of a sad loss of originality. The general average of efficiency of elementary schools was lamentably low, and this same playing for safety on the part of training college authorities showed itself in a reluctance to pitch students into the rough and tumble of ordinary school life, and a preference for bringing them up in the artificial atmosphere of the model school.

BIBLIOGRAPHY

J. KAY-SHUTTLEWORTH. *Four Periods of Public Education*, London, 1862.

T. ADKINS. *History of St John's College, Battersea*, London, 1906.

F. SMITH. *Life of Sir J. Kay-Shuttleworth*, London, 1923.

COMMITTEE OF COUNCIL ON EDUCATION. Minutes, 1842–3. (Report on Battersea Training School by Rev. John Allen.)

J. KAY. *The Education of the Poor in England and Europe*, London, 1846.

H. MANN. *Report of an Educational Tour*, ed. W. B. Hodgson, London, 1847.

CHAPTER IV

THE DEVELOPMENT OF THE TRAINING
COLLEGE SYSTEM, 1839–1846

THE period 1839–46 was one of great activity in the foundation of training institutions, apart from the establishment of the normal school at Battersea. In the Minutes of the Committee of Council for 1845 is included a list of Church of England training colleges, the number of students in each, and the length of the course pursued in each. From this list a vivid conception may be gained of the progress that had been made in the seven years mentioned, and of the great variety that was to be found among the colleges at the end of that period. The table (slightly abbreviated) is as follows:

College	Number in training	Length of course
St Mark's (men)	53	3 years
Battersea (men)	71	1½ years minimum
Whitelands (women)	54	2 years minimum
Westminster (men)	40	6–12 months
„ (women)	51	6–12 months
Canterbury (men)	5	6 months desirable
„ (women)	4	6 months desirable
York and Ripon (men)	36	1–3 years
„ (women)	8	1–3 years
Durham (men)	13	6 months average
Winchester (men)	19	6 months minimum
Chichester (men)	10	2 years
Brighton (women)	11	1 year
Exeter (men)	19	3 years maximum
Bristol (men)	6	3 years
Lichfield (men)	26	2 years
Lincoln (training department attached to middle class school)	—	2 years maximum, mostly less

College	Number in training	Length of course
Llandaff (non-residential)		
(men)	2	3–12 months
(women)	2	3–12 months
Norwich (men)	3	3 months
„ (women)	7	3 months
Oxford (men)	14	1 year minimum
Kidlington (women)	6	6 months minimum
Salisbury (men)	26	6 months–3 years
Chester (men)	41	1 year minimum
Warrington (women)	20	1–5 years[1]

To make the tale of training colleges of all kinds complete, the Home and Colonial and the Borough Road Colleges must be added.

In 1839 the only training colleges in existence in England were the Borough Road, the Central Schools of the National Society at Westminster, and the Home and Colonial Training College. How then did all these fresh institutions come into being? Battersea we have already dealt with in some detail. St Mark's and Whitelands were established by the National Society in 1840 and 1841 respectively. The rest were the outcome of diocesan enterprise, which had been vastly stimulated by the assistance which could be obtained from the Government for the erection of buildings. There had previously existed in many of the dioceses "central schools" where a certain amount of training work was carried out, along much the same lines as at Westminster, but they had not been in any sense organised colleges. The average stay of a student was brief, and he gained little more than an insight into the workings of the monitorial system, and the opportunity of "brushing up" his probably scanty acquaintance with the subjects of the elementary school curriculum. The opportunity of Government assistance was now seized in order to develop a more definite organisation for these

[1] Committee of Council on Education, Minutes, 1845, pp. 333, 334.

provincial centres, and most of the diocesan colleges mentioned in this list took distinct form between 1839 and 1841.

Chester and York may be taken as interesting examples of the development of diocesan training colleges. The college at Chester started in two houses in January, 1840, and a proper college building was opened in 1843. This housed seventy students in training and a boarding school of fifty middle-class boys whose fees were to help towards the upkeep of the training college. Students entering the college had to sign an agreement with the Diocesan Board to take up teaching under the Board, when required by the principal, within a year of leaving the college, and they bound themselves to continue teaching under the Board for at least four years after leaving. The penalty from an ex-student who refused to honour this contract was a sum equal to twice the money that had been spent on his training. The minimum age of entry was fifteen years, and no student could be recognised as a qualified teacher before reaching the age of eighteen years. In addition to regular students, however, practising schoolmasters might enter for periods varying between three and eight months, being aided by exhibitions given by the National Society for that purpose.[1]

The academic work of the college was not ambitious, and was largely limited to subjects of direct usefulness in elementary school teaching.[2] A large proportion of time was devoted to scriptural knowledge, English, arithmetic, drawing and music. A great feature of the college was the attention paid to practical activity of all kinds, as distinct from the exclusively agricultural and domestic activities which found a place in other institutions. Most of the students had been brought up to some trade, and they were encouraged to keep up their skill in those occupations, and to spend some of their time in teaching them to others. Common activities were

[1] Committee of Council on Education, Minutes, 1844, pp. 630–4.
[2] See Appendix A at end of this chapter.

carpentry, cabinet-making, brasswork, bookbinding, paint-
ing and graining, stone-cutting and lithographing. The
manual skill of the students was put to practical use as far as
possible. The college chapel, for example, was very largely
erected by the students themselves. Moseley, reporting on
the work of the college, thought that possibly these manual
occupations flourished at the expense of outdoor exercise
and literary culture, and pointed out that of forty students
eighteen spelled incorrectly, twelve read and eight wrote
incorrectly, and ten might be characterised as illiterate.[1]

On the professional side, a good deal of time was devoted
to lectures and reading with reference to National School
teaching, and about six weeks in the year were devoted to
teaching practice.

The Chester students seem to have been a hardy and stout
lot of men, comparing well with students in the metropolitan
colleges. One of the reports by an inspector on the college
declares "They are generally robust and athletic men, four
of whom would, I should think, weigh as much as five at
Battersea and six at St Mark's".[2] On official occasions they
appeared in all the glory of cap and gown.

The training college for men at York was opened in 1841
under the auspices of the York Diocesan Board, but in 1843
it became the college for the Ripon diocese as well. It re-
sembled Chester in being connected with a boys' boarding
school, and at neither college was the arrangement a success.
At York the arrangement was made without the consent of
the Committee of Council. Teaching practice was carried out
in this middle-class school, and was a poor form of preparation for teaching in elementary schools for the working

[1] Committee of Council on Education, Minutes, 1844, pp. 628–9,
639. See also article in *English Journal of Education*, 1851, p. 103,
and H. Barnard, *Normal Schools*.
[2] Committee of Council on Education, Minutes, 1847–8, vol. II,
p. 477.

classes. There was very little supervision of practice, and the teaching was almost exclusively catechetical.[1] The women's college at York was founded in 1846 when the men moved into new premises, and the old premises were taken over by the women.

It will be seen by reference to the list at the beginning of this chapter that many of the diocesan "colleges" contained very few students, and that some gave only a very short course. There was no uniformity, and there is no doubt that the figures in the column "Length of course" represent in many cases pious hopes rather than hard facts. Many of the smaller diocesan institutions were doing work not very much in advance of that of the provincial training centres out of which they so often grew. It was the Minutes of 1846 that imposed a certain uniformity upon all the colleges, and some of the smaller places of training were unable to keep up to the mark, and disappeared.

It is interesting to notice the varying fates that have attended the training colleges in existence in 1846. Of the non-diocesan colleges Borough Road and Whitelands still exist, St John's Battersea and St Mark's Chelsea have been amalgamated (the lion has lain down with the lamb), the National Society's Westminster Training Schools have passed out of existence, and the Home and Colonial Training College has recently brought to a close its long and distinguished career. Of the diocesan colleges, Canterbury, Lichfield, Llandaff, Kidlington, and Oxford have disappeared, although Culham is descended from the Oxford institution. The rest have survived, although sometimes with a change with regard to the sex of the students.

The foundation of St Mark's Training College, Chelsea, by the National Society, is a noteworthy date in the history of English training colleges, because it marks the inception

[1] Committee of Council on Education, Minutes, 1847–8, vol. II, pp. 525–40.

of yet another experiment, another feeling out after the right form for a training college.

During 1838 and 1839 the National Society had been negotiating with the Committee of Council for a grant towards the cost of erection of a new training college to supplement the training schools at Westminster. The committee had insisted upon inspection as a condition of such a grant, and ultimately the society declined to accept a grant on such a condition, and set to work independently.

The motive behind the project was not purely enthusiasm for the training of teachers for elementary schools. There was a section of the Anglican party which saw in the training colleges an instrument of propaganda, and an opportunity for the education of the lower-middle class which was nowhere else obtainable. One of the leaders of this section was G. F. Mathison, who published in 1844 a pamphlet entitled *"How Can the Church Educate the People?* by a Member of the National Society". In this pamphlet he refers regretfully to the failure of a scheme for the establishment of training colleges in cathedral centres where the principalship might carry with it a stall, and suggests that national boarding schools admitting day scholars should be set up in connection with the training colleges to be both practising schools and recruiting grounds for the colleges. From such schools and the training colleges themselves a steady supply of recruits to the lower ranks of the clergy might be forthcoming. In the British Museum copy of the pamphlet is an autographed letter from the author to the Hon. Thomas Grenville, which expresses an attitude shared by a number of the Church party: "I confess that elementary day schools for little children who go to plough at 8, and always earn their bread in some way at 12, have never appeared to me as great a panacea as to many others, for national wants....I cannot help thinking, however, that Colleges, where select youths may be trained and loyalised, are now a real desideratum".

The scope of the new college was thus expressed in a letter addressed to the Committee of Council on July 30th, 1839:

"The primary object of the Institution which the Society has in view is to prepare young persons to become teachers in Parochial and National Schools, by giving them a sound general education and training them up as attached and intelligent members of the Church. For this purpose they will be admitted at the age of 15 and upwards, and will remain two or three years; but in order to meet the urgent and immediate demand for competent instructors, accommodation will also be provided for older persons who, having in some degree received a general education elsewhere, require a more systematic course of discipline and instruction".[1]

The house and grounds of Stanley Grove in Chelsea were chosen as the site of the new venture, although the original intention had been to erect the new college near the already existing institution at Westminster. In the early part of 1841 the college opened with ten students under the Rev. Derwent Coleridge, a man of strong personality and very definite views upon the things necessary in the training of the teacher, who was destined to make for St Mark's a unique position among the early training colleges.

Students were admitted commonly about the age of fifteen, and if accepted, they were clothed, educated and maintained until the age of twenty-one. The course at the college was normally one of three years' duration, and the rest of the apprenticeship was carried out in teaching under the direction of the National Society.[2] Care was taken to make quite clear to candidates the nature of the life they were embarking upon, and the following questions were put to each entrant:

"Are you sincerely desirous of becoming a schoolmaster, and do you seek admission into the National Society's Train-

[1] G. W. Gent, *Memorials of St Mark's College*, p. 3.
[2] Derwent Coleridge, *Letter on Training College*, Chelsea, 1842, pp. 39–40.

ing College expressly to be fitted for that difficult and responsible office?

"Are you prepared to lead in the College a simple and laborious life; working with your hands as well as acquiring book-knowledge, and rendering an exact obedience to the discipline of the place?

"Are you aware that your path of duty on leaving the College will be principally, if not entirely, among the poor?

"Are you willing to apprentice yourself to the Society on that understanding?"[1]

The students who applied for entrance were mostly poorly qualified on the academic side. Many of them were sent up to St Mark's by Diocesan Boards, and early in its career the college was augmented by the wholesale addition of the training school at Wells.[2]

Derwent Coleridge shared with Kay-Shuttleworth the idea that the great and primary function of the training college was the giving of a culture to its students which included both religious and intellectual elements, but his conception differed on one very important point. At Battersea little or no appeal was made to the students' desire for self-advancement in the worldly sense, and we have seen that the whole of the life of the normal school was organised so as to reconcile them to a life of hard work and comparative penury. Coleridge did not belittle the importance of the "missionary spirit" as a motive, but he thought that it was well also to appeal to "that keen sense and appreciation of social respectability, together with that energetic desire of social advancement, which unite to form at once the moving spring, the self-acting safety valve and self-adjusting regulator, of that great machine which we call the British community".[3] "The better the schoolmaster is bred, the more highly he is trained,

[1] H. Barnard, *op. cit.* p. 350.
[2] Derwent Coleridge, *Second Letter on St Mark's*, 1844, p. 4.
[3] Derwent Coleridge, *The Teachers of the People*, 1862, p. 30.

and the more he is socially respected, the more ready will he
be to combat the difficulties, to submit to the monotony, and
to move with quiet dignity in the humbleness of his vocation."[1]

Hence he considered that it was part of the work of the
training college deliberately to raise the students above their
stations. "All the arrangements of the Training College, even
its nomenclature, were conformed, as far as possible, to these
views. They must not be wholly new nor obtrusively distinctive. The new was untried, and carried with it no charm
to those who were to be drawn within its walls. The College
must be an adapted copy, *mutatis mutandis*, of the elder
educational institutions of the country, originally intended,
even those of the higher class, with their noble courts, solemn
chapels, and serious cloisters, for clerks to the full as humble
as those whom I had to train. My judgment consorted as
little as my taste with the bald utilities and whitewashed
parallelograms which have sometimes been set forth as a
model. I looked, not in foreign lands, but at home for my
exemplar, not of course to be followed blindly: it must be
modified, lowered, yet remain the same in kind: the same
theme transmodulated. It must awaken the same or similar
associations. It must create the same *esprit du corps* among
its alumni. As time went on it must be consecrated with the
same *religio loci*. In a word, it must be rendered attractive
both to the student and to his friends. It must first attract,
then elevate, refine, ennoble."[2]

He realised the lurking meanness behind the Battersea conception of teachers' training. Writing over twenty years later
he said: "Once more recurring to a time when the system of
training had yet to be formed, and the position of the popular
schoolmaster was far other than that which it has since become, How, I asked, were candidates to be found, and how

[1] Derwent Coleridge, *The Teachers of the People*, 1862, p. 37.
[2] *Ibid.* pp. 33-4.

were they to be prepared for such a career? Such was the problem which lay before me, and other most zealous and efficient labourers in the same field. Humbling and laborious discipline; a rigid simplicity in dress, diet and external accommodation; sound elementary instruction; above all the substitution of religious principle for worldly motive; all this looked well upon paper, and recommended itself strongly to the religious mind of the country;—recommended itself also to many not specially religious persons, who thought that such discipline was very proper for the national schoolmaster, though it had nothing to do with them or with theirs. In itself it was a noble scheme; there was a meaning in it with which I fully agreed, a feeling in it with which I deeply sympathised. It must never be lost sight of. But for myself I felt persuaded, that taken alone it would not work. Not to mention that this ascetic discipline, religiously considered, seemed proper rather to bring down the lofty looks of the proud, than to raise the low estate of the humble, and that those with whom we had to deal appeared to require a different, and in some respects an opposite treatment,—there lay in the scheme itself, as in many similar projects for improving the manners and condition of inferior people, a latent injustice unperceived, and unintended by its authors and abettors, but sure to be keenly felt by those to whom it was addressed. It seemed to say, 'We are about to bestow upon you a privilege of a high and spiritual nature, but we do not intend that you shall reap the worldly advantages with which it is ordinarily accompanied. Your hearts must be fixed on nobler objects. Education is a great boon; you will receive it freely at our hands; but you must not look for its temporal rewards, nor follow it out to its natural results in you own persons. In outward circumstances you must remain as you are. You must remember the rock from which you are hewn. *We* are differently placed. Our rights and duties are different. No such restriction lies on us. We may rise in the world, according to our talents and opportunities. It is the order of Providence'".[1]

In accordance with these views, Coleridge emphasised the academic side of the work at Chelsea, and adopted a more ambitious programme than had hitherto been attempted in a training college. The first two years of the course were to be devoted entirely to the culture of the students, and the curriculum they followed was to be in the main literary. Coleridge had been brought up in the classical tradition and shared the unbounded faith, common in his age, in the efficacy of Latin grammar as an educational instrument. Accordingly a study of Latin was given a prominent place in the curriculum, and was regarded as a panacea for the backwardness of his students when they entered the college. "Where this fails", he said, "I have found nothing else to answer."[2]

The religious element in the collegiate life was emphasised by a development of chapel services unheard of at Battersea. The chapel was to be "the keystone of the arch".[3] Much contemporary controversy, which it is out of our province to discuss, was aroused by the religious life of St Mark's. The exaltation of the chapel service to supreme importance, and the introduction of sung services and what was then an advanced ritual caused the cry of "Popery!" to be raised. An hour's service took place every morning, the students all joining in the rendering of the music, helped out by boy choristers. On festival days and on Sundays the services were longer and more elaborate.[4]

As was common, the student's day in college was long and laborious. He rose at 5.30 a.m., and at 6 he applied himself to household tasks which had to be finished by 6.45, when

[1] Derwent Coleridge, *The Teachers of the People*, 1862, pp. 29–30.
[2] Derwent Coleridge, *Second Letter on St Mark's*, 1844, p. 21.
[3] Derwent Coleridge, *Letter on Training College, Chelsea*, p. 31.
[4] See *Record*, 1845.

he embarked upon 1½ hours of study, the period opening with prayer. Breakfast was at 8.15. At 8.40 he prepared for chapel, and the morning service lasted from 9 till 10. Then followed two hours of study and fifty minutes of "industrial occupations". Dinner was at 1 p.m., and study recommenced at 2 o'clock, lasting until 4, and followed by further "industrial occupations" until 5.30. Then came more than an hour of music, and tea took place at 7. After tea the student turned to his books again at 7.30 and worked until 9, when there were evening prayers followed by a short lecture. At 9.35 he retired to bed, and lights had to be out by 10. On Wednesdays after 4 an hour and a half was devoted to recreation, and the student was free at the same time of the day on Saturdays after the necessary domestic duties had been performed. This routine held good throughout the year, except that it was modified in the case of senior students who were doing teaching practice. On festivals there was practically no study, these days being filled with religious exercises of one kind or another.[1]

The students were divided into three classes corresponding to the three "years", and each class was divided into two sections. The senior class was Class 1, and of that class each section practised on alternate weeks during the year. The college was provided with a library of serious works, and a careful censorship was maintained over the private books and reading of each individual, the "frivolous" being rigidly excluded.[2]

The practising school was erected in the grounds of the college, and was a peculiar structure, octagonal in shape. The original building was an imitation of the form of an Italian baptistery, and it was so placed with relation to the chapel as to symbolise the school as the porch to the Church. The building contained three classrooms and a gallery, and each

[1] Derwent Coleridge, *Second Letter on St Mark's*, 1844, p. 15.
[2] *Ibid.* pp. 22–4.

classroom was divided into two by a curtain. Thus accommodation was afforded in the practising school for six classes, and in 1844 two rooms were taken over in a cottage near the porter's lodge to house the more advanced scholars. Three years after its establishment the school contained 152 children, who paid fourpence a week for their education. The scholars were expected to attend the college chapel every morning, although this arrangement was abandoned after a time owing to practical difficulties. The boy choristers of the chapel were scholars, and formed the first class. The first normal master was B. G. Johns, who had been an assistant master under Coleridge at Helston Grammar School, and his only assistants in the school were the drafts of students who came for practice. The hours of teaching were from 10 to 12 and from 2 to 5, Wednesdays and Saturdays being half-holidays.[1] Some use was made in addition of the Chelsea village school for the purpose of teaching practice.

The students were sent down in batches of eight, and each student was put in charge of a class. One of the students was nominated "Master in Charge", and his duty was to supervise the school in the absence of the normal master. A tabulated report of the work of each draft was submitted each week to the principal.[2] To judge from the reports of inspectors, after the college had agreed to receive them, as it was soon constrained to do for financial reasons, the training of the students in the art of teaching was not very successful. The questions set to the third class by Moseley in 1844[3] illustrate well the scope of the instruction given. It was concerned almost exclusively with "method". Considerable attention was paid to the organisation of schools, this being particularly important because nearly all the students would

[1] Derwent Coleridge, *Second Letter on St Mark's,* 1844, pp. 31–4.
[2] See Appendix B at end of this chapter.
[3] See Appendix D at end of this chapter.

go straight from college to assume the responsibility for the complete running of a school. (Later, when assistant teachers became more common in schools, and the student usually left college for such a post, the problem of training changed its aspect considerably.) Some attention was devoted to various "systems", including the best known of those in vogue abroad, and a good deal of time was given to what is to-day called "special method".

The weakness in the actual professional training at St Mark's may be ascribed to the fact that this side of the college's work was looked upon as of secondary importance, and as having no integral connection with the academic work. Moseley, ever a wise and discerning critic, realised this when he wrote the following comments:

"I am not urging the claims of any of the particular schemes or methods of instruction, which may at any time have been compounded, although I believe that the students at such an institution should be conversant with all of them: I am simply insisting on the necessity of making teaching *as an art* the subject of study in a training college, in respect to *each subject* taught; of viewing each such subject under a double aspect, as that which is to become an element of the student's own knowledge, and as that which he is to be made capable of presenting under so simple a form, that it may become an element of the knowledge of a child.... It is not the fact that the teacher knows too much, which makes him unintelligible to the child, but that he knows nothing which the child can comprehend or that he has never studied what he has to teach in the light in which a child can be made to comprehend it".[1]

There we have one of the main problems of teachers' training in a nutshell. It is a problem which we are far from solving to-day, and, indeed, the growing separation between

[1] Committee of Council on Education, Minutes, 1847–8, vol. II, p. 440.

academic and professional training is making the problem more difficult of solution. In the old training college, the good master of method, who also taught academic subjects in the college, could achieve what Moseley suggested, but most commonly the gap between the subject as learnt and the subject as taught remained unbridged.

As might be expected, much adverse criticism was aroused by Coleridge's avowed intent of educating his students "above their station". It was thought that the establishment of St Mark's was in accordance with the scheme, already mentioned, of utilising "training colleges" for middle-class education rather than for producing effective teachers of elementary schools. It was contended that the course followed was too elaborate, and was likely to unsettle the students and make them averse to the simple duties of teachers of the poor. To such critics, and those who maintained that practical and scientific pursuits should find a more prominent place, Coleridge made a spirited reply in his *Second Letter on St Mark's* College. He argued that morality was the central point in the education of the teacher, and that the great instrument of morality was to be found in culture. When it was said that highly educated schoolmasters would desert the profession of elementary teaching, he replied: "Such men may have been taught a great deal, but they have not been *educated* enough; they have something else to learn of more value than all that they have hitherto acquired. To qualify by a *suitable* education, which will be both general and specific, a number of young men for the work above described, who shall be induced by the necessity of their position, as well as disposed from a sense of duty, to enter upon this field of labour—this is the matter in hand".[1] "There are some", he said, "who seem to look upon the weak and the uneducated as in a sort of privileged state, over which it becomes their pastoral guides to watch with

[1] Derwent Coleridge, *Second Letter on St Mark's*, p. 18.

reverential care, lest it should be disturbed with an intrusive enlightenment."[1]

Events proved that these suspicions were by no means groundless. During the whole of Coleridge's principalship St Mark's was notorious for the number of its students who took up educational work in schools of a higher grade than elementary, or entered the Church, or took up work of no educational character. When Coleridge retired in 1864, little more than half of the men trained at Chelsea were engaged in inspected schools.[2] This was the cause of continual friction between the authorities of the college and the Committee of Council when the latter began making annual contributions to college expenses in the form of Queen's Scholarships (in 1846). The official attitude was clearly expressed by an inspector on the occasion of the retirement:

"Now Mr Coleridge has always maintained that his object was to raise the education of the middle grade as well as the lower grade; and hence he endeavoured to leaven the body of teachers of middle class schools with the better article which he manufactured at St Mark's. He has done this with considerable success; and the friends of education may well be pleased with that success. But this work should be done and paid for by those *who wish to do it*".[3] . . ."The aim Mr Coleridge has had in view is not exactly that which the Parliamentary votes contemplate, and this wider range over which Mr Coleridge has extended his influence is one which the friends of Church education may be glad to cover, but which the public money is not intended to reach."[4]

Modern sympathies will probably be on Coleridge's side in this controversy. It has come to be recognised that it is inexpedient and short-sighted to regard educational grants in the light purely of a business proposition, even those

---

[1] Derwent Coleridge, *Second Letter on St Mark's*, p. 19.
[2] Committee of Council on Education, Minutes, 1864–5, p. 334.
[3] *Ibid.*   [4] *Ibid.* p. 333.

which are made for the training of teachers. The attempt to restrict the recipients of training grants to any one type of educational service at the completion of their training has been abandoned, and the suggestion has been brought forward and widely discussed that specific training grants to university students should be abolished, the money being devoted to exhibitions of a general kind. This raises important administrative questions which lie beyond the scope of the present essay. Certainly Coleridge made a great contribution to the development of the English training system in standing up for the best culture possible for prospective teachers. It was a hard fight that he waged, and the coming of the Revised Code seemed to mark the victory of the opposite party, but the principles he laid down have triumphed in the end. Before teachers are trained the most must be made of them as human beings.[1]

The Borough Road College presented a striking contrast to St Mark's at this time, and this chapter may profitably conclude with an account of the methods in vogue and the developments that took place at that institution during the years 1839–46.

When grants became available for training colleges as a result of the failure of the State normal school scheme, the British and Foreign School Society were much troubled in mind over the question of accepting grants, and with it the principle of Government inspection. Considerable correspondence took place between the society and the Committee of Council, which makes clear the main grounds of distrust. The element of denominational suspicion was present, and was particularly aroused by the power of veto that had been accorded to the archbishops on the appointment of inspectors of National Schools. There was, moreover, a fear that inspectors' reports on the Borough Road institution might have an adverse effect on the efforts of the society in

[1] See Appendix C at end of this chapter.

general. The secretary of the society, Henry Dunn, referred to the reports made public on the Glasgow and Edinburgh training institutions, in which there had been much criticism of their methods, the lack of real educational training and the type of student that was attracted. Then, to bring the matter nearer home, the inspector's report on the British Schools in London had been adverse, and this was attributed to his dislike of the monitorial system, which was still the British and Foreign Society's darling. If a similar report was to be made on the Borough, it was contended, it would mean a serious loss of confidence on the part of voluntary supporters, upon whose interest the work for the most part depended. "It seems difficult to imagine", wrote Dunn, "that any number of gentlemen would long continue to sacrifice their time and money in the gratuitous management of any institution subject to control of this character, nor would it be found practicable to retain the services of teachers whose prospects for life might be ruined by the authoritative publication year by year of their supposed deficiencies." Fear also was entertained that inspection might be adverse to the Borough tradition of taking persons of mature years, and would encourage mere intellectual power at the expense of professional skill, since older students could not be expected to shine in an examination.[1] However, scruples were overcome and fears laid to rest, grant was accepted, and new buildings were opened in 1843, a speech at the opening ceremony being delivered by Lord John Russell.[2]

The British and Foreign School Society had been carrying on training work along the old lines with few changes of policy or improvements in procedure. The students came only for short periods, and the main emphasis in the training course was upon the practical business of teaching. The institution had grown greatly in numbers. In 1818 forty-four teachers

[1] Committee of Council, Minutes, 1842–3, pp. 401–538.
[2] British and Foreign School Society, *Annual Report*, 1843, pp. 3–7.

had been trained, as compared with 207 in the year 1840–1.[1]
Most of the students were of mature years, and little attempt
was made to improve their general education. The monitorial
system was still expounded at the Borough, and in 1838
Dunn's *Normal School Manual*, which was the authorised
exposition of that system, had been presented to every teacher
in a British School.[2] But even at the Borough some recognition had been given to the claims of the "simultaneous
method". In 1839, on the recommendation of Crossley, the
head of the model school, the committee passed a resolution
that in order to afford greater facilities for the instruction of
the students in the "art of communicating", one or more
additional classrooms should be erected, and equipped with
galleries for teaching on the "collective or simultaneous
system".[3]

The very practical nature of the work at the Borough
shows itself in the personnel of the staff, all the members of
which were teachers who had been through the Borough
"mill" themselves. Cornwell, the principal, had been trained
there, and had subsequently continued his education at University College, London. Crossley, the head of the model
school, had been one of Lancaster's monitors, whilst Saunders,
the vice-principal, had been the headmaster of a large British
school in Plymouth.[4]

The students were described by Her Majesty's Inspector
Fletcher in his report of 1847 thus:

"They are healthy in appearance, of fair muscular development, open in countenance and unaffected in their manners,
of which the predominant characteristic is *earnestness*. Indeed, the few months' course of exertion in which they find
themselves here involved is one which no infirmity of purpose or of health could safely encounter, and the positively

[1] British and Foreign School Society, *Annual Report*, 1843, p. 6.
[2] *Ibid.* 1838, p. 8.   [3] *Ibid.* 1839, p. 3.
[4] Committee of Council, Minutes, 1846, vol. II, p. 345.

weakly are advised at once to seek some other career".[1] They were gluttons for work. "The morning bell rings at six o'clock; but many are up at four, and two-thirds at five, for the sake of gaining more time for their preparation of lessons to which the first $1\frac{1}{2}$ hour of the ordinary working day is devoted."[2]

This earnestness was deliberately fostered, and each student was presented with a paper of "hints", the main headings being:

"(1) Let your mind frequently and seriously revert to the *objects* which are to be obtained by your residence in the Society's House.

(2) Redeem your Time.

(3) Cultivate Habits of Order.

(4) Cherish a kind and friendly disposition towards your Associates.

(5) Exercise a constant spirit of 'Watchfulness unto Prayer'".[3]

In spite of repeated efforts over a number of years, little success had attended the attempts of the committee of the society to prolong the period of training. In the year 1846–7 only four men, and no women, stayed longer than six months.[4] Three months was about the average, and the "method unit" for instruction in the college was the quarter. The student on entering the institution was placed in the "Junior Class", and at the end of the quarter was promoted to the "Upper Class", but it was quite common for students to leave before they passed out of the lower group. This meant that the numbers "trained" seemed immense, but the fact of the case was that the student body was in a state of constant flux. So in the year 1844–5, the junior class started with ten students, 165 were admitted in the course of the year, and at the end of the year there remained eleven in the

[1] Committee of Council, Minutes, 1846, vol. II, p. 346.
[2] *Ibid.* p. 349.   [3] *Ibid.* pp. 421–2.   [4] *Ibid.* p. 297.

class, the rest having passed out to schools or to the upper class.[1] Those who attended for less than three months were those sent up by patrons for a short period of training.

A great part of the work of both senior and junior classes consisted of teaching in the great Borough Model Schools; academic instruction was a secondary matter, and was related as far as possible to the practice of teaching.[2] Thus the junior class started the work of the week with a grammar lesson at 6 on Monday morning, which was a kind of criticism lesson at the same time. The substance of the lesson had been previously prepared, and one student was appointed to examine the rest, questions being addressed to individuals. If no satisfactory answer was forthcoming the examiner had to explain the matter to the class. Then the students were called upon to criticise the way in which the questions had been put, faults of pronunciation, and similar defects. In other lessons, geography for instance, members of the class were grouped on a gallery and one student instructed whilst another interrogated afterwards. Another variation was that a tutor gave a lesson, and then a student had to come out and explain the matter of the lesson in more detail to the class.[3] The subjects studied were those taught in the schools, and nothing much was attempted beyond the school standard of attainment.

Practice in teaching was the main business of the place, and every day the students of both classes spent $4\frac{1}{2}$ or 5 hours in the model schools. The tutor was always present to supervise. The student started in the lowest class, and worked his way right through the school, following the traditional method of the monitorial training centres. Mistakes in method might be corrected in private discussion between tutor

[1] British and Foreign School Society, *Annual Report*, 1845, p. 47. See Appendix E.
[2] See Appendix A at end of this chapter.
[3] British and Foreign School Society, *Annual Report*, 1845, pp. 49–52.

and student, or, if they were of a general nature, they were publicly talked over in the lecture theatre. The criticism lesson was a regular event. All the students gathered in one of the gallery classrooms and one victim gave a collective lesson to 100 boys, the students the while making notes as to "grammar, manner, knowledge, government, etc." After the lesson they all repaired to the theatre, and each student in turn was called upon to give an opinion on the lesson. Then followed observations by the tutor, first on the criticisms, then on the lesson itself. In connection with these lessons the inevitable happened, and we are told: "On the entrance of some students, the observations have been rather intended to show the acuteness of the speaker than to benefit the teacher who has given the lesson".[1] But it appears that the criticisms were kindly and useful as a rule.

It is interesting to note that Fletcher reports that the technique of collective teaching was not really appreciated at the Borough, and the practice gained in the model schools was mainly in the working of the monitorial plan.[2]

A series of lectures was delivered lasting over three months, and repeated with each new batch of students, on the "impartation of knowledge", one lecture being given every day. This course included a number of lectures on "Mental Philosophy", an attempt to raise the training above the merely empirical level. Students were expected to make abstracts of these lectures, and we are informed that "Through these lectures the science of education is understood".[3]

A consideration of the work at the Borough shows clearly the great significance of the experiments at Battersea and Chelsea, where the attempt was made to make the training

[1] British and Foreign School Society, *Annual Report*, 1845, pp. 45, 46.
[2] Committee of Council, Minutes, 1846, vol. II, pp. 377–8.
[3] British and Foreign School Society, *Annual Report*, 1845, p. 45. See Appendix E.

college a place of education as well as of mere training, possibly to some extent at the expense of mere training. From the standpoint of immediate efficiency in the school the Borough students were probably much superior. That result was almost bound to follow from the general and wide nature of the aims of Battersea and Chelsea as compared with the definite and narrow aims of the Borough Road College. The Borough wagon was hitched to no very lofty star. "And if we have to regret that some when they leave us, are far from finished scholars, yet none go without a good deal of information of the kind most immediately wanted by them; all have practically learnt the value of time, and been engaged in the systematic study of those subjects which are to them the most important; have been supplied with a list of the most useful books, and thus are enabled to turn their time to the best account in their own attempts at self-improvement. They have learnt, too, experimentally, what is meant by *hard work*."[1] Perhaps as much as possible was accomplished in the short time available, but the development of the work at the Borough was hindered by the traditional adherence of the society to the monitorial methods derived from its founder Lancaster, when the times were crying out for a change to the "simultaneous" method. But whilst a student could be fairly drilled in the monitorial method in a few months, the collective method demanded a training very different in scope and duration. The future lay with colleges of the Battersea and Chelsea type, and to that type the Borough Road College gradually came to conform under the influence of Government grants and examinations.

[1] British and Foreign School Society, *Annual Report*, 1845, pp. 46–7.

BIBLIOGRAPHY

COMMITTEE OF COUNCIL ON EDUCATION. Minutes and Inspectors' Reports.

NATIONAL SCHOOL SOCIETY. *Annual Reports.*

BRITISH AND FOREIGN SCHOOL SOCIETY. *Annual Reports.*

H. BARNARD. *Normal Schools,* Hartford, U.S.A., 1851.

DERWENT COLERIDGE. *A Letter on the National Society's Training College for Schoolmasters, Stanley Grove, Chelsea,* London, 1842.

—— *A Second Letter on the National Society's Training Institution for Schoolmasters, St Mark's College, Chelsea,* London, 1844.

—— *The Teachers of the People,* London, 1862.

ST MARK'S COLLEGE, CHELSEA. *Occasional Report, December,* 1864, *with a list of the students trained showing their present employments.*

G. F. MATHISON. *How Can the Church Educate the People?* (by a Member of the National Society), London, 1844.

G. W. GENT. *Memorials of St Mark's College,* London, 1899.

The Record, 1845. "Popish Character of the Religious Instruction provided for the pupils and children of the Training Institutions at Westminster and St Mark's College."

EXETER DIOCESAN BOARD OF EDUCATION. *A Plea for the Training College,* presented by J. T. Toye, M.A., Exeter, 1849.

G. MARTIN. *A Sermon Preached...on the Occasion of Laying the Foundation Stone of the Exeter Training School,* Exeter and London, 1853 (containing a claim of priority of foundation of Exeter over Battersea).

APPENDIX A

Subjects studied, and Distribution of Time, at Battersea,
St Mark's, Chester, and Borough Road

1. BATTERSEA (Minutes of Committee of Council, 1842–3, p. 115):

	Hours of work (per week)	
Subject	1st class hr.	2nd class hr.
Religious instruction	6	6
Geography	3	3
Reading, etymology and grammar	5	8
English composition	2	2
English history	2	2
Arithmetic	2	2
Pure mathematics and mensuration	4	2
Mechanics and natural philosophy	6	5
Pestalozzi	1	2
Music	6	6
(Teaching in village school)	15	15
(Preparation for teaching)	5	5
(Garden work)	16	16

2. ST MARK'S (H. Barnard, *op. cit.* p. 352):

	Hours of work (per week)			
	Top class		Bottom class	
Subject	hr.	min.	hr.	min.
(Chapel)	6	0	6	0
(Evening worship)	3	30	3	30
Scripture and Christian doctrine	2	5	3	40
Church history and Bible literature	2	20	2	40
Latin	6	15	6	0
English grammar, literature, and history	7	10	3	50
Geography	2	30	5	20
Writing		30	4	0
Arithmetic		20	3	30

Subject	Hours of work (per week)			
	Top class hr. min.		Bottom class hr. min.	
Geometry	2	50	—	
Algebra and trigonometry	2	20	—	
Mechanics and natural philosophy	2	0	—	
Music	7	10	7	10
Drawing	4	0	4	0
Normal lessons	3	0	—	
Private reading	1	30	—	
Preparing lessons[1]	—		9	0
(Meals)	8	45	8	45
(Leisure)	6	0	6	0
Practising chapel music	6	0	6	0

[1] This does not mean preparation of lessons to be taught.

3. CHESTER (H. Barnard, *op. cit.* p. 400):

Subject	Hours per week hr. min.	
Scriptural knowledge	8	0
Evidences of Christianity	1	0
Church history	1	20
English grammar	3	30
English history	1	0
English literature (including themes and writing from memory)	2	40
Education (lectures, reading and essays)	12	0
Arithmetic	5	10
Algebra	1	0
Euclid	1	0
Mensuration	1	0
Natural and experimental philosophy		40
Lecture (subject not specified)	1	0
Writing	1	40
Geography	2	0
Vocal music	3	0
Linear drawing	2	0
Preparation for lessons	4	30
(Leisure)	15	0

4. BOROUGH ROAD (summarised from Tutor's Report on the
   Upper and Junior Classes, British and Foreign School
   Society, *Annual Report,* 1845, pp. 41–50):

Upper Class: Syllabus of Subjects.

English: (1) Grammar, (2) Formation and derivation of
words, (3) Composition. No systematic course on
Literature.

Geography: Inductive study as far as possible. Etymology
of geographical names.

History: Salient events in various countries, chiefly England.

Mathematics: Full and systematic study of principles of arithmetic. "Demonstrative geometry" (individual study).

Natural philosophy: Popular treatment, reference to common
instances.

Natural history: Only zoology, including visits to the Zoo-
logical Gardens and Museums.

These subjects were studied for 2½ hours on three evenings a
week, the method adopted being conversational lectures based on
the society's lesson books. Each morning from 6 to 8.30 was
spent in private study, and there was an hour's lecture on pedagogy each day. Two evenings were devoted to instruction in
singing.

Junior Class:

English grammar	3 hours and weekly examination (1 hour).		
Geography and history	2 hours	,,	,,
Arithmetic	2 hours	,,	,,
Geometry	1 hour		
Physics	1½ hours		
Reading	1 hour		
Elocution	1 hour		
Copybooks	½ hour		
Drawing	½ hour		

Students wrote one dictation a week (marked by two students
under supervision of tutor) and wrote weekly letter to tutor.
Regular Bible study took place, and there was a weekly examination in "Sacred history and Geography".

APPENDIX B

St Mark's—Specimen of weekly report on teaching

For the week ending October —, 1844.

Master	Class	No. in class	Attendance	Temper	As a teacher
A	1	11	Good	Tolerable	Good
B	2	19	Good	Good	Improving. Good disciplinarian
C	3	10	Good	Tolerable	Indifferent
D	4	20	Good	Good	Good: but wants decision
E	5	22	Good	Tolerable	Improving: but still rather noisy
F	6	22	Good	Good	Good
G	7	19	Good	Improving	Diligent
H	8	21	Good	Good	Good, especially in lower class

Master in charge: D. Will do well when he has had more experience; as yet rather nervous.

(Derwent Coleridge: *Second Letter on St Mark's*, p. 39.)

APPENDIX C

Careers of St Mark's Students

1. From Gent, *Memorials of St Mark's College.*

Of the original ten students when the college opened, four were subsequently ordained. Of these, one became Principal of Peterborough Training College in later years, two became masters of secondary schools, and one rector of a parish. Of the rest, one became eventually clerk to a School Board, one an accountant in the London City Mission Office, one a master at the Greenwich Naval School. All these were living in 1891. The other three were dead, and it was not known what their occupations had been (presumably elementary schoolmasters!). Of seven more students who entered in October, 1841, one did not complete his training, one was retained on the college staff as a tutor, and subsequently became principal of Warrington Training College, one became vicar of a parish and another a minor canon of Salisbury Cathedral, one the proprietor of a private school.

2. From Committee of Council, Minutes 1864–5 (H.M.I. Cowie's *Annual Report on St Mark's*) and the *Occasional Report* presented by Derwent Coleridge on his retirement in 1864.

In his *Annual Report,* Cowie pointed out that the Government's contribution to the building expenses at St Mark's had been comparatively small, £8192. 15s. 5d. as against £34,554. 17s. 0d. total expenditure. On his retirement Coleridge had printed an address giving careers of St Mark's students of great interest to all concerned in Church education. The following are the statistics given in that address (published as *Occasional Report*).

Between April 1841 and the end of 1864, 708 students completed a course of training or were still in the college. Their occupations could be thus classified:

"Now employed in National Schools	329
Now employed in Schools for the Poor other than National	48
Students beginning work in 1865	49
Employed in Training Schools or other work connected with Normal Training and School Organisation ..	14
	440
Employed in Grammar, Middle-class and Private Schools, or private tutors	99
In Holy Orders and engaged in work not directly connected with elementary education	13
Laymen not engaged in education	35
Unemployed, chiefly from ill-health	9
Employment unknown	29
In Colonies (Educational or Missionary Work).. ..	43
In Colonies (not known to be engaged in educational work)	8
	676
Deceased	32
	708"

(p. 15).

Cowie, by referring to the records of the Education Department, was able to criticise the accuracy of these figures, maintaining that actually less than half the number trained at Chelsea were engaged in inspected schools (Minutes, 1864–5, p. 334). The inspector considered that the case of St Mark's was an eminent justification for the new methods of administering grant to training colleges under the Revised Code (*vide infra*, p. 184). "There cannot be a more evident proof of the necessity of recent measures in order to secure the application of Parliamentary funds to their intended object than is shown by the tabulated results of the 25 years' work at St Mark's....As Government aid to training schools is now directly proportional to the number of teachers who work in inspected schools for the poor, this system of training young men for the higher branch of the teacher's profession must either be abandoned or the funds must be provided by the National Society, or from some other source. If neither of these conclusions is accepted, I do not believe that St Mark's College can stand" (pp. 334, 335).

In his *Occasional Report* Derwent Coleridge did not deny that the education given at St Mark's, especially in the early days, fitted students in many cases for educational posts more highly paid and estimated than that of master of a National School (p. 9). In all forty-six men had been ordained, thirty-four before the coming of the first group of Queen's Scholars (i.e. those paid for by the State) to the college. "If these promotions," said Coleridge, "the result and the reward of faithful and efficient services, are to be considered as in any degree detracting from the usefulness of the Institution, or as interfering with its proper object—the loss, if loss it be, must be regarded as the accompaniment of a great effort, made for the general improvement of elementary education among the poor, and as the price which has been paid for it. It is believed, however, that the gain, estimated exclusively with reference to the children of the labouring class, has greatly, very greatly, preponderated" (p. 9).

3. From *The Teachers of the People*, Derwent Coleridge, 1862. (A parable on the Training of Teachers.)

"A certain man was employed to manage a cider-orchard. The cider had been execrably bad, and ruinous to the constitution: nothing but pale faces and dragging limbs wherever it was drunk. So he sent for new plants, manured freely, and employed better methods of cultivation. Well, the cider was quite another thing and gave general satisfaction; but alas, though the general produce was nothing better or worse than good cider-apples, with quite sufficient harshness, some of the grafts got to bear golden pippins and nonpareils. It is true that these improved the general quality of the beverage, so most people thought; but then they came to be considered too good for the cider-press: so some of them were sold for table-fruit at double and treble the profit.

"By and by this came to the ears of the owner, who took it much amiss, and having sent for the manager, he said to him, Sir, I employed you to make cider for the country people, whence come these golden pippins and nonpareils? I shall take care to check your charge for manure, and do you keep clear of those superior grafts.

"So the manure was stinted, and by a careful selection of inferior trees they soon got back to the old crabs" (pp. 17, 18).

APPENDIX D

Questions set by H.M. Inspector Moseley to the Third Class at St Mark's on Teaching 1844 (Committee of Council Minutes, 1844, vol. II, p. 615)

"1. By whom, and for what purpose, was the monitorial system introduced into elementary instruction? What are the evils essential to it, and the abuses to which it is liable; and what are the systems which have been proposed to replace it in part or altogether?

"2. State generally what would be the subjects of instruction, and what the classification you would adopt, in a school of 60 children, assembled under the ordinary circumstances, in an agricultural district?

"3. State the same in respect to a school of 150 children, in a manufacturing district, and give a time table for each school, specifying thereon the portions of the course of instruction which you would reserve to yourself, and the periods you would allot to them.

"4. Mention some of the passages of Scripture which appear to you best suited to form the subjects of Scriptural instruction addressed to children.

"5. Give a practical exposition of a passage of Scripture in the words in which you would address it to a class in your school.

"6. Give some particulars of the methods of elementary instruction adopted in Prussia and in Holland.

"7. Explain what is meant by the simultaneous method of instruction, and what the elliptical and interrogative methods, and point out the advantages and evils attendant upon them."

APPENDIX E

Table illustrating fluctuating numbers in the Junior Class at the Borough Road Training College (Tutor's Report on the Junior Class, B. and F.S. Soc. Annual Report, 1845, *p.* 47)

	No. of students	No. left				Passed to upper class
		1st month	2nd month	3rd month	Withdrew	
1st quarter	38	2	4	4	2	26
2nd „	57	3	6	4	6	38
3rd „	38	1	3	4	10	20
4th „	53	1	2	5	8	37

APPENDIX F

List of "Conversational Lectures" at the Borough Road Training College (*H. Barnard*, Normal Schools, *p.* 319)

Delivered daily, these covered a quarter. The first thirty-six were given by the principal, the remaining twenty-four by the vice-principal.

1. On the objects which a teacher should have in view in adopting his profession.
2. On the circumstances which make a teacher happy in a school.
3. On some of the essential moral qualifications of a teacher.
4. On the essential intellectual qualifications of a teacher.
5. On the establishment of authority.
6. On gaining ascendancy over the minds of children.
7. On combination and arrangement.
8. On routines of instruction and formation of plans.
9. On the monitorial system: its use and abuse.
10. On the selection of monitors.
11. On the training of monitors.
12. On the collective or simultaneous system.
13. On the art of teaching the elements of reading to very young children.
14. Illustrations of the mode of using the First Lesson Book.
15. On various methods of teaching spelling.
16. On the mode of using the Second Lesson Book.
17. On object lessons for young children.
18. On the interrogative system, with illustrations.
19. On analytical teaching generally, with illustrations from the Third Lesson Book.
20. On synthetical teaching; illustrations from the Third Lesson Book.
21. On the art of reading with animation and expression.
22. On scripture questioning generally; on scripture geography and methods of teaching it.

23. On teaching writing.
24. On the use and nature of numbers.
25. On teaching arithmetic.
26. On the mode of using the Fourth Lesson Book.
27. On teaching geography.
28. On teaching grammar.
29. On teaching drawing.
30. On teaching vocal music.
31. On the philosophy of the human mind as applicable to education.
32. On attention and memory.
33. On association.
34. On conception.
35. On imagination.
36. On the principal writers on education.
37. On rewards and punishments.
38. On emulation.
39. On common errors relating to punishments, and on corporeal punishments.
40. On moral and religious influence generally.
41. On the promotion of a love of truth, honesty and benevolence and other virtues among children.
42. On cleanliness and neatness, kindness to animals and gentleness.
43. On promoting obedience to parents, respectful demeanour to elders, and general submission to authority.
44. On the private studies of a teacher.
45. On the course to be pursued in organising a new school.
46. On keeping the various registers of attendance and progress.
47. On the ventilation of schoolrooms and dwellings.
48. On school furniture generally.
49. On some of the circumstances which affect the condition of the labouring classes.
50. On the elements of political economy.
51. On machinery and its results.
52. On cottage economy and savings' banks.

53. On the duties of the teacher to the parents of the children and to the Committee.
54. On the formation of museums and collection of apparatus, and the management of school libraries.
55. On keeping up a connection with old scholars.
56. On the *order* in which a teacher should attempt to accomplish the various objects he has in view.
57. On school examinations generally.
58. On raising and filling a school and on the circumstances which make a school popular.
59. On the various ways in which a teacher may co-operate with other benevolent efforts, such as temperance societies and Sabbath schools.
60. Brief summary of the teacher's duties *in* school, *out of* school, and in relation to the children, their parents, the committee, and to society at large.

CHAPTER V

THE PERIOD OF STABILISATION, 1846–1860

(a) ADMINISTRATIVE ACTIVITY OF THE COMMITTEE OF COUNCIL; THE PUPIL-TEACHER SYSTEM

THE year 1846 is one of the most important dates in the story of the training of teachers in England. The highly important Minutes of the Committee of Council in that year put a new complexion on the whole question of national education, and the period between that date and the Newcastle Commission was one of great progress under the liberal and encouraging direction of the committee, whose attitude was largely determined by the views of its secretary, Kay-Shuttleworth. The period saw the establishment of a State-financed pupil-teacher system, and the application of the principle of Government assistance in the maintenance of the training colleges. It saw also the establishment of certificates for teachers, issued by the Government and carrying with them emoluments guaranteed from State funds. Government interference and control of this kind meant the stabilisation of the training system, and they were bound to result in the emergence of a uniformity lacking in previous years. Hence it follows that the story to be told is one of steady development, and is much concerned with questions of administration and finance. It is not a period of striking experiments and outstanding personalities, and the hero is to be found, not in any one man (unless it be Kay-Shuttleworth), but in the Education Committee itself. This being the case, it will be convenient to deal first with the various Minutes of the Committee which bear upon the question of training, and then to discuss the general life and activities of the training colleges under this *régime* of central direction.

By the year 1846, as has been seen, much had been done in grappling with the problem of the provision of better equipped teachers for the primary schools of the country. Since 1836 a large number of institutions had been established, the majority with Government assistance, for the purpose of continuing the education of prospective teachers and giving them a modicum of professional training. It is, however, one thing to erect colleges, and another to fill them and keep them filled with satisfactory students. It was this question of supply that was now the outstanding problem, and it was one to which Kay-Shuttleworth had been acutely alive for years past, and one with which he had already made private attempts to deal.

There were three main elements in the problem. In the first place, and this is unfortunately nothing unique in English educational history, it was a question of hard cash. The training colleges, being private institutions and almost altogether unblessed with endowments, were dependent for their existence upon private liberality. A few received annual grants from "My Lords", but in most cases the grants given were akin to those made to schools, i.e. they were grants for building and not for maintenance. Private liberality might take the form of direct subscription, or the payment of students' fees by benevolent patrons. Only a very small proportion of the students could be expected to be in a position to pay the fees themselves. This financial precariousness reacted in a number of undesirable ways. The state of popular education precluded the hope of getting really decently educated students, and among possible candidates selection depended rather upon chance patronage than merit. The colleges could afford to turn away none who came backed by some charitable person or organisation prepared to foot the colleges' bill. The financial difficulty meant also that the establishment of a good standard of academic achievement or of professional training was out of the question. It was impossible to insist upon anything like an adequate period of residence in college, and the heterogeneous nature of the student body made sound teaching an extremely difficult matter.

In the second place the problem was an integral part of the whole question of the existing facilities for popular education. Even had the prospective students been possessed of a reasonable financial competence, where were the schools to be found in which they might receive their education preparatory to entering upon a training college course? The public schools catered for a quite different class, and, even had it not been so, their curriculum would have been a poor preparation for the work of the training college. The grammar schools of the country were in a chaotic state, the best being wedded to an exclusively classical tradition, and the worst being little better, if at all, than the ordinary elementary schools. Here and there a private school was doing good work, but the majority approximated more to Dotheboys Hall than Bruce Castle. It was inevitable that the training colleges should be recruited from the elementary schools, where it was extremely rare for even the best scholars to remain after the age of thirteen. How was the gap between leaving the elementary school and entering the training college to be bridged? The attempt to include the schooling of boys as part of the work of the training college had proved a failure. Until the secondary education of the country had been put in order, the break had to be accepted as inevitable, or some scheme must be devised to keep prospective teachers in the elementary schools until they were old enough to go to college.

The position was clearly put by Kay-Shuttleworth himself:

"It is of the utmost importance to the future prosperity of

the Normal Schools, that the elementary schools should be rendered the means of educating a class of candidates for admission, who in their earliest youth should have been selected on account of their proficiency and skill and whose progress in the several grades of monitor, pupil teacher and assistant teacher, should not only have been the object of systematic care and continual vigilance, but whose ultimate selection should be made by the Inspector on the ground of their superiority, as proved by the experience of years, in all the qualifications required for success in the vocation of a schoolmaster".[1]

The third element in the problem was connected with the lack of attractiveness in the teaching profession as a whole. The financial prospects of the elementary teacher were extremely poor, and there was no compensating social respectability, for the primary schoolmaster was still commonly despised. Until better recruits were obtained for the profession it was likely to remain despicable, and until the profession was made more reputable there was little hope of obtaining better recruits. A country which is too poor to provide a decent remuneration for its teachers is too poor to educate itself.

The Minutes of 1846 showed that the committee had grasped the essentials of the problem, which was attacked along each of the three lines indicated. It was clearly realised that if English elementary education was to be improved, the improvement must start with the teachers themselves. "The Normal School is the most important institution in a system of elementary education."[2] The institution of certificates issued by the Committee of Council, one of the measures of 1846, aimed at improving the qualifications of the teachers, and the grants that these certificates carried both for the augmenting of the teacher's salary and the maintenance of the college training him rendered the profession more

[1] J. Kay-Shuttleworth, *Four Periods of Public Education*, pp. 480–1.
[2] *Ibid.* p. 487.

attractive financially and did much to ease the financial strain felt by the colleges. The inauguration of a pensions scheme added still more to the attractions of the profession. The pupil-teacher system was designed to bridge the gap between leaving school and entering college by subsidising promising pupils for a period of years which were to be devoted to gaining practice in teaching and to carrying on the study at the same time of those subjects essential to the primary teacher. Thus was provision made for a steady supply of better qualified students for the colleges.

The new epoch in the history of English education was inaugurated by the Committee's Minutes of December 21st, 1846, following after preliminary resolutions of August 25th in the same year.[1] A scheme was propounded which provided that selected scholars in the elementary schools might remain in the schools for a period of five years, during which time they were to be apprenticed to the school managers. They were to serve as teachers during the school day and receive instruction from the master of the school after school hours. For their services as teachers they were to receive some payment, and their progress was to be checked by yearly examinations carried out by Her Majesty's inspectors.

If the managers of a school applied to have pupil teachers, the appropriate inspector had to report upon the suitability of the school for the purpose. He had to be sure that the master or mistress of the school was qualified to carry out the further education of the pupil teacher. The school must be well equipped with books and apparatus. It should be organised in classes, and the standard of teaching should be good. The discipline was to be "mild and conducive to order". Moreover it was essential that there should be good prospects that the expenses of the school as a whole, and of the pupil teacher's salary, would be satisfactorily met during the five years of the apprenticeship.

[1] Committee of Council, Minutes, 1846, vol. I, pp. 1–9.

Candidates for the post of pupil teacher were to be of not less than thirteen years of age, and attention was directed to home conditions. If these were unsatisfactory, provision was to be made for "boarding out". Candidates would be required:

"1. To read with fluency, ease and expression.

"2. To write in a neat hand, with correct spelling and punctuation, a simple prose narrative slowly read to them.

"3. To write from dictation sums in the first four rules of arithmetic, simple and compound; to work them correctly, and to know the tables of weights and measures.

"4. To point out the parts of speech in a simple sentence.

"5. To have an elementary knowledge of geography.

"6. In schools connected with the Church of England, to repeat the Catechism, and to show that they understand its meaning, and are acquainted with the outline of Scripture history. The parochial clergyman will assist in this part of the examination.

"In other schools the state of the religious knowledge will be certified by the managers.

"7. To teach a junior class to the satisfaction of the Inspector.

"8. Girls should also be able to sew neatly and to knit".[1]

These qualifications throw an interesting light on the state of the schools. The pupil teachers were to be drawn from the cream of the scholars, so that the attainments here enumerated denote the high-watermark of scholastic achievement. So qualified, the pupil teacher was to enter upon full-time teaching, and upon a course of further instruction from the master or mistress. This instruction was to last for $1\frac{1}{2}$ hours for five days in the week, and was to be given either before or after school hours.[2] A syllabus was laid down for each year, and upon this syllabus the inspector would inspect

[1] Committee of Council, Minutes, 1846, vol. I, pp. 3–4.
[2] *Ibid.* p. 9.

the pupil teachers under his supervision. The progress that was to be made during the five years' apprenticeship is indicated by the scope of the examination that was to mark the end of service as a pupil teacher.

"1. In the composition of an essay on some subject connected with the art of teaching.

"2. In the rudiments of algebra, or the practice of land surveying and levelling.

"3. In syntax, etymology, and prosody.

"4. In the use of the globes, or in the geography of the British Empire and Europe, as connected with the outlines of English history.

"In this year girls may be examined in the historical geography of Great Britain.

"5. More completely in the Holy Scriptures, Liturgy, and Catechism in Church of England schools, the parochial clergyman assisting in the examination.

"6. In their ability to give a gallery lesson, and to conduct the instruction of the first class in any subject selected by the Inspector."[1]

The syllabus was considerably modified in the case of girl pupil teachers. These were not necessarily examined in algebra, or surveying, or levelling, or the globes, or the geography of the British Empire and Europe, but as a compensation they were expected to show a special proficiency in sewing.

A school might have one pupil teacher for every twenty-five scholars, and the master was to receive payment for his services in instructing apprentices at the rate of £5 for one, £9 for two, £12 for three, and £3 for each one above three. In addition the teacher was to receive a gratuity if boy pupil teachers were instructed in gardening or in some craft-work suitable for schools of industry, or girls in sewing, cooking, baking, and washing. The pupil teachers themselves were to

[1] Committee of Council, Minutes, 1846, vol. 1, pp. 5, 6.

be paid, irrespective of other emoluments, upon a scale which started at £10 in the first year, and rose by increments of £2. 10s. 0d. to £20 in the last.[1]

In schools where the teacher was not qualified to undertake the instruction and training of pupil teachers, the teaching staff might be augmented by the appointment of "stipendiary monitors", who were to remain in the school without apprenticeship to assist in the teaching. They were not to be retained after the age of seventeen, and their payment was on a scale ranging from £5 to £12. 10s. 0d. They were to receive daily instruction from the master or mistress of the school, who in turn was to be paid for instructing them on a scale lower than that for pupil teachers. This provision did something towards the solution of the immediate staffing problem, but had little bearing on the general question of teachers' training.[2]

When the pupil teacher had completed his apprenticeship, there were various courses open to him, and he was not necessarily considered as bound to follow the teaching profession at all, since the money he had received was not an "intending teacher's grant", but was payment for services rendered. It was quite legitimate to look upon the apprenticeship merely as a means to further education (though a somewhat heroic one), and the certificate that was granted at its completion might be regarded as a general educational qualification, much as we regard the School Certificate today. But candidates were encouraged to continue their education and training at a training college by the institution of "Queen's Scholarships", which were to be awarded upon the results of an annual examination, and which were to carry with them a maintenance grant of £20 or £25 annually. Candidates unsuccessful in obtaining scholarships might be admitted into the lower branches of the Civil Service.[3] On

[1] Committee of Council, Minutes, 1846, vol. I, pp. 8, 9.
[2] *Ibid.* pp. 6–9.   [3] *Ibid.* p. 10.

the other hand pupil teachers completing their apprenticeship might immediately take posts as schoolmasters or school-mistresses.

This scheme afforded some solution to the problem of providing and financing out of State funds a supply of better qualified candidates for the training colleges. In Kay-Shuttleworth's own words: "The Queen's Scholars will have passed through an elementary course of instruction in religion, in English Grammar, and Composition, in the history of their country, in arithmetic, algebra, mensuration, the rudiments of mechanics, in the art of land-surveying and levelling, in geography, and such elements of nautical astronomy as are comprised in the use of the globes. Their skill in conducting a class will have been developed by five years' experience as assistants in a common school. To these attainments will in many cases be added a knowledge of the theory and skill in the art of vocal music, and also, in some cases, of drawing from models, or linear drawing".[1] The grants given to the Queen's Scholars, however, were insufficient to meet the whole of the expenses of the training colleges incurred on their behalf, and the problem of professional prospects was still left untouched.

These aspects of the general problem were dealt with by the institution of annual training college examinations, success at which carried with it a grant to the college and an augmentation of the student's salary when he commenced teaching. At the same time the profession was made still more attractive by the inauguration of a pensions scheme.[2]

There were to be annually three examinations for training college students, according as the candidates had been at college one, two or three years. Upon the results of these examinations leaving certificates were to be awarded, a First Class Certificate for those successfully completing the first

[1] J. Kay-Shuttleworth, *Four Periods of Public Education*, p. 488.
[2] Committee of Council, Minutes, 1846, vol. I, pp. 10–12.

year of training, a Second Class Certificate for the second year examination, and so on. These certificate examinations were to be open to teachers who had not been trained in college, and, if successful, such were to receive the same augmentations of salary. These augmentations were dependent upon the managers of the school to which the teacher was appointed providing a house rent free, and an equal sum by way of salary. The scale of augmentations was as follows:

For men: First Class Certificate: £15 or £20.
                  Second Class Certificate: £20 or £25.
                  Third Class Certificate: £25 or £30.

For women: Two-thirds of these amounts.[1]

Thus a man with three years' successful training might look forward to a salary of £60 with a house. It is noteworthy that this scheme of augmentations to teachers' salaries was the first grant made for teaching as distinct from the erection of schools, and the first institution of national certification for teachers.

For every successful student, Queen's Scholar or otherwise, the training college received £20 for a first-year candidate, £25 for a second-year candidate, and £30 for a third-year candidate. The examinations were not to be uniform throughout the country, but the inspector was to fit his examination to the training college he was examining.[2]

Nothing could better illustrate the benevolence of the Committee of Council than the solicitude they manifested to popularise the new schemes among schoolmasters and managers. The first certificate examination took place in 1848, and instructions were given to the inspectors to be as pleasant as possible with candidates, and to encourage them to sit for the

---

[1] Committee of Council, Minutes, 1846, vol. 1, p. 11, and J. Kay-Shuttleworth, *op. cit.* p. 484.

[2] Committee of Council, Minutes, 1846, vol. 1, p. 11.

examination again if they were unsuccessful. In a letter to their inspectors "My Lords" said:

"The fact that the candidates are called upon in the first instance to prove their qualifications might be interpreted as a sign of rigour, instead of that sympathy for the position of the teacher, and that desire to raise him to credit or distinction, of which this examination is a necessary preliminary. You would obviously increase the chances of such misinterpretation, if your demeanour during the examination were either stern or reserved or if you were betrayed into impatience by fatigue or even by misconduct of the candidates. On the contrary, by cheerfulness, affability, anxiety to consult the convenience of all, and such sympathy with their success as is consistent with the impartial discharge of your duties, it is hoped that you will not only leave on their minds the most grateful personal impressions, but that you will inspire them with a just confidence that the Government is anxious to recognise every legitimate claim on the public resources, for their proper remuneration, and to give the sanction of public authority to every well-qualified schoolmaster".[1]

Thus the inspectors of "My Lords" were, by their "nods and becks and wreathed smiles", to dissipate the suspicions of the teaching world, and by their winning ways entice the reluctant pedagogue into the examination room. But the harmlessness of the dove was not unmixed with the wisdom of the serpent. Kay-Shuttleworth knew that inspection was one of the great factors in educational improvement, and many schools still fought shy of it. Accordingly it was laid down that untrained schoolmasters sitting for the examination must come from inspected schools, and a broad hint was dropped in a circular sent round to non-Church of England schools that schoolmasters might do well to use their powers of persuasion on their managers to accept inspec-

[1] Committee of Council, Minutes, 1847–8, vol. I, p. cviii.

tion, so that they, the schoolmasters, might be eligible for certification.[1]

Everything possible was done to popularise the pupil-teacher system. Realising that the majority of school teachers there and then would be unqualified to conduct the whole of the five years' instruction of the pupil teacher, the committee laid down that a teacher would be considered as qualified to instruct pupil teachers if at the end of any one year he could prove himself qualified for the work of the next year. Here again the benevolent cunning of the committee is evident. In order to be qualified to receive the benefits associated with the presence of apprentices in the school, the teacher had to be polishing up his own knowledge, and increasing it year by year, so that by the time he had piloted a pupil teacher to the end of the apprenticeship, he would be well on the way to an adequate knowledge for sitting for a certificate.[2] To make the certificate and pupil teacher schemes plain, "broad-sheets" were issued which showed in a tabulated form all the conditions connected with pupil teachers and certificates of merit.

Even the cold wind of failure in the examination was tempered as far as possible to the scholastic lambs. Who would not feel that even failure has its compensations on receiving a communication from the nabobs of Whitehall such as this?

"COMMITTEE OF COUNCIL ON EDUCATION,
PRIVY COUNCIL OFFICES,
WHITEHALL.

SIR,

I am directed by the Lord President of the Council to inform you that, although their Lordships have been unable to grant you a certificate on this examination, they hope that your present failure will only stimulate you to increased dili-

[1] Committee of Council, Minutes, 1847–8, vol. I, p. cxxvii.
[2] *Ibid.* p. cxxviii.

gence, both in your own studies and in the improvement of your school, so that on another trial their Lordships may have the pleasure of rewarding your perseverance.

I am etc.

(signed)   R. W. LINGEN.

To............

Master of the .... School.[1]

The examination all took place on one day, in three sections, the first from 8 to 11, the second from 1 to 4, and the last from 6 to 8, a pretty heavy day's work for candidates who had, most of them, never sat for a serious examination in their lives before. Questions were to be answered on four or five of the following sections: religious knowledge (in Church of England schools and colleges), English grammar and paraphrase of passages from English authors, English history, general geography, especially the British Empire and Palestine, geometry (Euclid, Books 1 and 2), algebra up to simple equations, mensuration of plane figures, elements of mechanics, popular astronomy, in addition to the composition of notes for a lesson, or observations on the practical duties of the teacher, and teaching a class before the inspector. Alternative subjects which might be substituted for any of the above academic subjects were vocal music, drawing from models, history and etymology of the English language, modern history, modern languages, ancient history, physical science, higher mathematics, Latin and Greek. Success in sufficient of the latter group of subjects, in addition to those necessary for the lowest certificate in the first group, entitled the candidate to a higher certificate.[2]

These Minutes of 1846 determined the lines along which training was to proceed until the revolution wrought by the

[1] Committee of Council, Minutes, 1851–2, vol. I, p. 121.
[2] *Ibid.* 1847–8, vol. I, p. cx.

Revised Code. During the period 1846–60 a number of modifications of the original scheme were effected by Minutes, and it will be convenient to consider these together before passing on to a discussion of the scheme as a whole.

In 1849, following upon a report by H.M.I. Moseley[1] on the southern district, in which he gave it as his opinion that certificates were granted too much on mere attainment and too little on professional efficiency, it was decided to withhold certificates obtained by training college students until they had been in charge of a school and had been reported upon favourably by the inspector.[2]

In 1850 certain additional rules were laid down in respect of Queen's Scholarships. Pupil teachers completing their apprenticeship, and such would then be appearing for the first time, were to decide for themselves which of the training colleges they desired to enter, and they were to sit for the ordinary Christmas examination in the college of their choice. They were not to attempt all subjects, but must satisfy the examiner in scripture (if Church of England), English history, geography, arithmetic, grammar and composition, and lesson notes. For qualifications in an extra subject ("My Lords" preferring Euclid), there would be an increase of £5 in the value of the scholarship. Every candidate was to teach before the inspector, read intelligently, write a fair hand and spell correctly. The number of scholarships to be awarded at any college was limited to 25 per cent. of the students resident there at the time of the examination who were of one year's standing or more.[3] A Queen's Scholarship was awarded for one year, but was to be renewable for another year at the training college.[4]

Additional financial assistance was given to the training colleges by a Minute of 1851 which made certificated teachers

[1] Committee of Council, Minutes, 1848–49–50, vol. I, pp. 26, 27.
[2] *Ibid.* pp. xxxiv–xxxv.   [3] *Ibid.* 1850–1, pp. xvii–xix.
[4] *Ibid.* pp. xx, xxi.

in normal schools eligible for the ordinary augmentations received by their fellows in ordinary elementary schools.[1] By the same set of minutes, grants of ten shillings per student for books were to be paid to any training college, provided that the college supplied £1 per head for the same purpose.[2] These provisions were part of the committee's policy of fostering the academic side of the colleges, which were suffering from the difficulty of maintaining adequate staffs because they were unable to pay their tutors salaries that made it worth their while to do training college work instead of going into the elementary schools where their certificates carried augmentations of salary.

This policy was continued by one clause in a very important set of Minutes in 1853, whereby it was provided that an augmentation of £100 should be made to the salary of qualified lecturers in certain subjects, provided that they received from the college authorities £150, or £100 and their board and lodging. In order to be eligible for this augmentation, lecturers had to pass an examination in one or two of the following subjects: history, English literature, geography, physical science, or applied mathematics.[3]

By various short Minutes in 1851 and 1852 certain regulations were laid down for the certification of pupil teachers who had finished their apprenticeship. These could only sit for the certificate examination if they had been for at least a year in a training college, or had served for three years as a principal or assistant teacher in an inspected elementary school.[4] The clause in the original scheme which had made an apprenticeship as a pupil teacher a qualification for minor posts in the Civil Service was rescinded.[5] Ex-pupil teachers might be appointed as assistants to certificated teachers at £25 a year (£20 for women), and such might sit for their

[1] Committee of Council, Minutes, 1851–2, vol. I, p. 24.
[2] *Ibid.* p. 31. [3] *Ibid.* 1853–4, vol. I, p. 24.
[4] *Ibid.* 1852–3, vol. I, p. 9. [5] *Ibid.* p. 9.

certificate after three years. One assistant was considered to be the equivalent of two pupil teachers on the staffing strength of the school.[1] This provision for adult assistant teachers in the schools was a significant thing. Previously the elementary school had been looked upon as essentially a one-man place, but as the monitorial system came more and more into disrepute, and the "simultaneous" method became more and more popular, the need for class teachers as distinct from head teachers was felt. As the assistant teacher became an established institution in the schools, it became increasingly common for students from training colleges to become assistant teachers before taking on the responsibility of a head teacher. This change of policy in the schools had an obvious bearing on the work of the training colleges, for an assistant teacher did not need the same knowledge of actual school organisation as the sole teacher of a school.

So far no provision had been made for the certification of teachers in infant schools, who were not expected to attain to the academic heights reached by their fully certificated colleagues. This omission was rectified in 1854, when training colleges were authorised to provide a one-year course for infant teachers, who were to sit for a special certificate examination. The certificates awarded were to be of two classes, carrying augmentation of salary and grant to the training college on analogy with the already established certificates. Teachers obtaining First Class Certificates were to be allowed to have pupil teachers. The certificate examinations were to be open to all teachers in infant schools.[2]

In 1853 the committee passed a number of important resolutions, and in a preamble the reasons for the changes thus effected were given. It was felt that the certificates were awarded too much on book learning, and that too little

[1] Committee of Council, Minutes, 1852–3, vol. I, p. 10.
[2] *Ibid.* 1853–4, vol. I, pp. 33–5.

recognition was afforded to excellence in teaching. Even with the existing supply of subsidised students and Government grants, the training colleges were finding it difficult to keep going, and none of them was full. Many pupil teachers finishing their apprenticeship never saw the inside of a training college at all. Nor was all well within the colleges. The standard of instruction was not good, and there was no encouragement for students to remain for more than a year of training.[1]

In order to fill the colleges, the existing limitation on the number of Queen's Scholars was abolished, and the scholarships made available for a second year on the scholar passing the first-year examination. Sufficient scholarships were to be awarded to fill the training colleges after all private students had been admitted. In order to facilitate the administration of admission to training colleges, all pupil teachers' indentures were to expire at Christmas. Candidates for Queen's Scholarships were to sit for the examination immediately after the students had been examined, and one list would be published of successful candidates, who would then be free to choose the colleges to which they would apply for admission.

The certificate examination was to be amended by the inclusion of drawing as a compulsory subject, and no certificates were to be awarded until a teacher had had two years of successful experience. In order to give some mark of recognition to efficient older teachers, who could not be expected to take the ordinary certificate examinations, a new class of "Registered Teachers" was instituted. Candidates had to be over thirty-five, and pass an examination composed of simple questions on scripture, English history, geography, arithmetic, English grammar and composition, and the theory and practice of teaching. "The object of the examination will be to ascertain sound, if humble, attainment", said "My

[1] Committee of Council, Minutes, 1853–4, vol. 1, pp. 23–7.

Lords". Every teacher with pupil teachers was to be either certificated or registered.

Following up the establishment of officially recognised assistant teachers, any such of three years' standing might obtain a Queen's Scholarship without examination.

Finally, an attempt was made to render a longer course of training common by an amendment of the method of payment of grant to training colleges. Grants were only to be paid in respect of students who resided for two years, with the exception that grants would be paid for one year's training in the case of students over twenty-four years of age, or over twenty-two years and placed in the Second Class of Merit in the examination, or ex-assistants. In order to encourage a third year of training, twice the ordinary grant would be paid in respect of students taking an approved course in a third year.[1] In spite of the fact that colleges could remain under the old Minutes should they elect to do so,[2] there was such an outcry on the part of the colleges against the new Minutes concerning the administration of grant, that it was necessary to fall back on a compromise, and by Minutes of June 28th, 1854, the new rules were modified to provide a scale of payments of grant for each year of training. This scale was replaced by a flat rate in 1855.[3]

So far there had been no standard syllabus for all the training colleges, and students had hitherto been examined without regard to their standing in the colleges. A number of heads of some of the larger colleges expressed a desire for an authorised syllabus to be published by the Committee of Council. The latter approved of the proposal and Moseley was set to draw up a scheme with a syllabus for each of three years. This scheme was circulated among the college authorities, amended freely in the light of their comments, and

[1] Committee of Council, Minutes, 1853–4, vol. 1, p. 29.
[2] *Ibid.* p. 29.
[3] *Ibid.* pp. 35, 36 and Minutes, 1855–6, p. 5.

published in 1855. The syllabus for the third year was designed for students of outstanding ability who would be likely to fill specially responsible posts in later life.

The principles underlying the syllabus were three. First, not to add to or take from the existing subjects of examination. Second, to give greatest weight to the subjects of elementary instruction. And third, to inculcate the principle of "not attempting more than can be done well", which "lies at the root of all truthfulness and reality in the teacher". The "subjects of elementary education" were taken to be religious knowledge, reading, penmanship, arithmetic, English grammar, geography, English history, physical science and vocal music (and in many schools mensuration, bookkeeping, geometry and algebra). Candidates were also to be examined in either classics or higher mathematics.[1]

The financing of the training colleges was made still easier by the institution in 1856 of the "Schedule". Previous to this, if a student failed in the examination at the end of the first year, the college received no grant for him, but by Minutes of June 2nd, 1856, students who did not fail hopelessly might be placed on the "Schedule". Such students had to take the examination again, but their scholarships were continued, and the colleges continued to receive grants for them.[2]

The way into the teaching profession through the training college was made still more open at the same time. In 1855 H.M.I. Cook had recommended that some Queen's Scholarships should be awarded in open competition, in the hope of attracting well-qualified candidates for the training colleges who had not been pupil teachers.[3] Accordingly in 1856 Queen's Scholarships were made available to all recommended by the colleges, pupil teachers and otherwise,

[1] Committee of Council, Minutes, 1854–5, pp. 14–17 (for Syllabus see p. 17).
[2] *Ibid.* 1856–7, pp. 2, 3.   [3] *Ibid.* 1855–6, pp. 760–1.

provided that they were over eighteen years of age. A list of those successful in obtaining scholarships was to be drawn up in order of merit, and from this the colleges were to make their selections. No more than 10 per cent. of the accommodation of a college might be taken up by non-pupil teachers.[1]

Similarly, in 1857, it was laid down that 10 per cent. of the scholarships for infant school training might be awarded to non-pupil-teacher candidates who were over eighteen years of age. Such candidates were expected to read an easy narrative, write simple sentences from dictation, and work easy sums in the first four rules, simple and compound. Students in training for infant school work were set a special certificate paper, were submitted to an oral examination as well, and must satisfy in music and drawing. When certificated, they were to serve only in schools where the pupils were under seven years old.[2]

The policy of opening up the way to the training college was carried a little farther in 1858, when permission was given for candidates over sixteen years to become pupil teachers of fourth-year standing provided they could pass the third-year examination for pupil teachers.[3]

Shades of the Revised Code appeared in 1860, when it was announced that no further grants were to be given for building or enlarging training colleges.[4] It was a sign of the close of the training college "boom".

The scheme of training devised by the Committee of Council stands as one of the ablest administrative contributions ever made to the development of English elementary education. It followed the traditional English method of utilising existing facilities rather than making a clean sweep and starting anew. Kay-Shuttleworth's scheme for a State normal school had been defeated by adverse public opinion,

[1] Committee of Council, Minutes, 1856–7, p. 3.
[2] *Ibid.* pp. 29, 30.   [3] *Ibid.* 1858–9, p. xii.
[4] *Ibid.* 1859–60, p. xxvi.

but much more than could have been achieved by such an institution was accomplished by the plan of encouraging and supporting denominational and privately owned training colleges, whilst directing their policy by the regulations determining the distribution of grant, and stimulating their efficiency by the establishment of nationally recognised tests for application to their products. The outlook of the Committee of Council during the period preceding the Newcastle Commission was one of great liberality, both financially and educationally, and, given a few more years of similar administration, a really sound system of teachers' training might have been evolved. It must be admitted that the scheme was more impressive in theory than in practice, but that is the way with schemes, and it must be remembered that the closure was put on the liberal policy by the Newcastle Commission before enough time had elapsed for a fair trial.

Probably the pupil-teacher system has been more discussed than any other aspect of the problem of teachers' training in England. Now that the system is almost entirely a thing of the past (though it dies hard), it is easy to see all its defects and the hardships it entailed, but the fact that a system has become obsolete with the changing years does not condemn it. In criticising the system we must think of the problem for the solution of which it was devised, the circumstances of education in general at the time of its inception, and the contribution it made to the solution of the problem. Criticisms which were fair in 1870 or 1901 would have been quite misplaced if directed against the pupil-teacher system at the outset. The problem was one more truly of secondary education than of teachers' training, and perhaps the most pertinent complaint that can be made of the scheme initiated by the Minutes of 1846 is that the pupil-teacher system was so good a stop-gap that it delayed the day when an adequate provision of popular secondary education should be made. It is an old story in English education. We are always ready to see the necessity of education for specific ends long before we realise it as desirable in a general way. The State needed teachers who had received something of a secondary education, so a makeshift secondary education for teachers was organised, and the only way for the elementary scholar who desired to prolong his studies was to become a teacher. We have the same thing, perhaps not quite to the same extent, to-day. The State decides that it is a very desirable thing that its teachers should have the benefit of a university training. Accordingly university education for prospective teachers is heavily subsidised. The result is that for many secondary school pupils the only hope of a university education is to promise to become teachers, whilst in many of the modern universities the arts sides are swamped by "intending teachers", and the finances of the university come largely to depend upon the business of educating them.

That the pupil-teacher-cum-training-college system was a fairly effective stop-gap is shown by the fact that reform in secondary education did not come for about a half-century after its inception. A distinct contribution was made to the formulation of content and technique of secondary education by good teachers of apprentices, by the pupil-teacher centres which were evolved later, and by the training colleges. Many a municipality and county found secondary schools ready to hand in the centres that had sprung up for the education of pupil teachers. Perhaps the time is not far distant when a similar thing may take place in regard to the training colleges, and these institutions will become agencies for some general educational purpose rather than remain dedicated to a narrow professional end.

There was nothing particularly original in the idea of using older girls and boys for teaching in the schools. In many ways it was the logical outcome of the monitorial system. Something similar had been attempted at the Borough, at Battersea, and at St Mark's, by the admission of juvenile students. A pupil-teacher system was in full swing in Holland, and Kay-Shuttleworth had been greatly attracted by it, and no doubt his scheme was partly influenced thereby. Moreover, a system very like that of the 1846 Minutes had been established earlier by the London Diocesan Board. Exhibitions of £10 a year or more were offered for competition among scholars fourteen years old, and the successful candidates acted as assistants in the larger schools and received instruction from the schoolmaster or the local clergyman. They served for three years, receiving annual increases of wages, and each year three boys and three girls of two years' standing were chosen to be sent on to a training college at no expense to themselves.[1] In a Memorial by the Diocesan Board to the Committee of Council in 1846 it was stated that there were thirty pupil teachers then at work, and the Memorial continued: "Their services are generally much valued, and their progress in preparing themselves for training institutions, as tested by periodical examinations, is most satisfactory".[2]

Thus the scheme in itself was no innovation. The genius of Kay-Shuttleworth lay in the manner in which he seized upon and improved such schemes as he knew, and modified them to meet a national need. Government support and interference were inevitable, sectarian suspicion was as strong as ever, and yet he succeeded virtually in nationalising the training of teachers without excessive wounding of religious susceptibilities. The rock upon which his ship eventually split was not that of religious controversy, but a mistaken conception of the meaning of "value for money spent" in education.

One of the strongest supporters of the pupil-teacher system was Matthew Arnold. In an article in Ward's *The Reign of Queen Victoria*, he described its inauguration as "the grand

[1] Committee of Council, Minutes, 1845, vol. I, pp. viii–xiii.
[2] *Ibid.* p. ix.

and chief merit of the Minutes of 1846".[1] He regarded the
system as particularly suited for English schools, where the
monitorial system had accustomed schoolmasters to sole control of their schools coupled with the provision of juvenile
assistance. "The English schoolmaster", said Arnold in
the same article, "has proved himself to have a remarkable
aptitude for managing boy helpers, and not by any means
an equal aptitude for managing adult helpers." This latter
argument in favour of the system shows clearly its danger as
a successful makeshift. If the Apostle of Sweetness and Light
had been honest with himself, he would have recognised that
a bad tradition was no excuse for an indifferent present organisation, and that the crying need of the country was an adequate supply of educated and trained adult teachers.

In a report on French education which he submitted to
the Newcastle Commissioners, Matthew Arnold rose to quite
lyrical heights in pleading the cause of the pupil teacher.

"Popular education in France will gain more by the introduction of pupil teachers into a single school than by libraries
of discussion upon the mutual and simultaneous systems.

"Pupil teachers—the sinews of English primary instruction; whose institution is the grand merit of our English
State-system, and its chief title to public respect;—this, and
I will boldly say, the honesty with which that system has
been administered. Pupil teachers—the conception, for
England, of the founder of English popular education, Sir
James Shuttleworth. In naming them, I pause to implore
you to use your powerful influence to preserve this institution to us unimpaired. Entreat ministerial economy to respect a pensioner who has repaid the outlay upon him a
thousand times; entreat Chancellors of the Exchequer to lay
their retrenching hands anywhere but here; entreat the Privy
Council Office to propose for sacrifice some less precious
victim. Forms less multiplied, examinations less elaborate,

[1] T. H. Ward, *The Reign of Queen Victoria*, 1887, vol. II, p. 256.

inspectors of a lower grade; let all these reductions be endured rather than that the number of pupil teachers should be lessened. If these are insufficient, a far graver retrenchment, the retrenchment of the grants paid to holders of our certificates of merit would be yet far less grave than considerable loss of pupil teachers. A certificate indeed is properly a guarantee of capacity, and not an order for money. There is no more reason that it should entitle its possessor to £20 than that it should entitle him to a box at the Opera. Private liberality can repair the salaries of the schoolmasters, but no private liberality can create a body like the pupil teachers. Neither can a few of them do the work of many. 'Classes of 25 and an efficient teacher to each class'—that school-system is the best which inscribes these words on its banners."[1]

This is enthusiastic, and, it must be confessed, somewhat incoherent praise, but there are soberer estimates to show that the pupil teachers were making a definite and valuable contribution to the education of the country. The Newcastle Commission subjected the whole educational system to a very thorough and stringent criticism, and on the whole the pupil teachers came well out of the ordeal. In the Report of that Commission we are informed that they were "persons of respectability in the best sense of the word",[2] and that their conduct was "extremely satisfactory and not surpassed by that of any other body of young people in any class of life".[3] Indeed, in 1854 only three out of 556 were dismissed for bad conduct.[4] The work of the schools had improved greatly as the result of the introduction of pupil teachers, although in some schools an unwise policy was followed of giving the youngest apprentices charge of the lowest classes. With regard to their usefulness in teaching, an inspector's report is quoted with approval, in which it was stated that

[1] *Newcastle Commission*, vol. IV, pp. 74, 75.
[2] *Ibid.* vol. I, p. 100.   [3] *Ibid.*   [4] *Ibid.*

they conducted lessons in reading, arithmetic and writing better than many adults. Many of them taught and examined in grammar, geography and English history, and the subject-matter of books of general information, with less waste of time and greater facility of illustration than the generality of untrained masters.[1]

The system was well described by one of the witnesses to the Commission: "It is, in military parlance, a tenable position which admits of being strengthened".[2] Considered from the absolute standpoint, the pupil teacher was bound to be a poor pupil and an indifferent teacher, but if the situation in the schools after the introduction of the pupil-teacher system be compared with that obtaining before, a favourable verdict must be given. The apprentices might teach badly, but they at least made possible a more adequate classification of scholars. They might learn badly, but when they reached the training colleges they were better candidates than those institutions had ever known before.

So far as the teaching of the apprentices was concerned, it was bound to be mechanical and arid, especially when, as was most often the case, the teaching of the schoolmaster was mechanical and arid also. Pedantry early began to set its mark on them. "They are apt to fall into the faults of meagreness, dryness and emptiness, or the opposite and not less mischievous evils of presumption and ostentation",[3] was the verdict of one inspector. There was a tendency for them to neglect their business as teachers for their other business as learners preparing for an examination.

The apprentices as pupils were equally open to criticism. At the commencement of the scheme, the fundamental defect in this connection was that there were no teachers who were really qualified to carry on the instruction of the apprentices to the standard laid down by "My Lords", and, since the

[1] *Newcastle Commission*, vol. I, p. 103.   [2] *Ibid.* vol. v, p. 58.
[3] Committee of Council, Minutes, 1853–4, vol. II, p. 18.

pupil-teacher gratuity was an attraction, large numbers of schoolmasters and schoolmistresses set to work to cram up subjects in order that they might cram the pupil teachers in their turn. It was hoped that this would gradually improve as the standard of the teachers improved generally, but until the coming of the municipal and county secondary schools there was never an adequate personnel to undertake the education of the pupil teachers. Under the circumstances the best had to be made of a bad job, and certainly the bait of the apprentice gratuity did impel many teachers to Herculean efforts to improve their own knowledge.

The knowledge gained by the pupil teacher was bound to be bookish and artificial, since he was being taught by a half-educated man during periods added on to hard days of teaching. It was inevitable that commonly the memory should be developed at the expense of the intelligence. An inspector reporting in 1856 said, "Those who are provided with good memories can retain an immense amount of crude, undigested facts, but very few gain from their apprenticeship what is tenfold more valuable, precision of ideas, the power of expressing themselves well in their own language, and the ability to give a sensible opinion on any common abstract question. They become overlaid with facts. Playing upon the surface of many objects, and mastering none, their memory is unwholesomely stimulated, their judgment stunted and baffled".[1]

Even with the safeguard of annual examinations, the standard of attainment of the apprentices when they came on to the training colleges was lamentably low, and, unfortunately, they commonly thought very well of themselves and of their knowledge. The complaint of a certain reverend gentleman to an inspector is typical. There was, in his opinion, a tendency for the pupil teachers to become "only eye-servants, inflated with self-importance, overbearing towards the younger chil-

[1] Committee of Council, Minutes, 1856–7, p. 451.

dren, contemptuous towards their social equals, high-minded towards their parents, brothers, sisters and other relatives, very dressy out of school, and forward and deficient in outward tokens of respect towards their betters".[1]

The strain upon the pupil teachers, the younger ones in particular, was heavy, and this was one of the darkest aspects of the system. In a time when it was customary for young people to work long hours in mine and factory, presumably the lot of the apprentice in the school was considered a light one, but there is no doubt that many teachers, especially women, paid a severe price in health for their apprenticeship, both at the time and in after-life. The following picture of the life of a girl apprentice was given by a witness to the Newcastle Commission.

"Ordinarily she is the daughter of a handicraftsman, or a labourer, or a domestic servant, or a farm servant. Her parents earn from 30 shillings down to 12 shillings, or it may be less, a week. She is not unfrequently one of several children, sometimes the only girl, or the only girl above infancy. It is a great wrong to her mother, father, brothers and sisters, if she be prevented from bearing her fair share of the usual household work of her home, and a greater injury to herself if she be excused from this. She ought to bear her part of the family house-cleaning, the family cooking, the family washing and the family clothes-making and clothes-mending. Otherwise, if she fail to obtain a Queen's Scholarship, or if she marry an elementary schoolmaster, or a small shopkeeper, or a small yeoman, she will be anything but a good housewife; or if she become a certified schoolmistress, she will not be the person whom sensible and thoughtful parents of humble life will care to intrust with the formation of the character of their girls.

"These home duties claim at least on an average an hour a day of her time.

[1] *Newcastle Commission*, vol. III, p. 85.

"Next, she is an apprentice teacher in an elementary school. She may have charge of a section of 40 children. She must be engaged in teaching daily for not less than 5½ hours; and in preparing the school for her class, and putting things away etc. for another half-hour daily.

"These school duties claim at least 6 hours a day, on an average of 5 days in the week.

"Again those school managers who have the interests of their female apprentices really at heart, and the interests of the children, who are already so much influenced by their example, or who will hereafter be under their care, require the female apprentices with the assistance of the elder girls and monitors, to do sometimes all the household work of the school premises, sometimes all this except scrubbing the larger and rougher floors. They also require them to visit, to inquire after absent children, dividing the duty between them and the principal teacher. These duties provide healthy bodily exercise.

"These duties, which are a most important detail in the training which is to fit them for their office, claim on an average another hour a day, or six hours a week.

"Already we have taken up *eight hours* a day on an average of 6 days in the week.

"But there is yet a claim on their time for one and a half hours daily. They have to spend an hour and a half a day for five days in the week in a class with the mistress; when she is to revise and correct the exercises they have prepared for her at home: to submit them to written examinations; to direct them as to what they are to study by themselves; to point out to them the difficulties they will meet, and when they have failed to overcome them without assistance to aid their own efforts to do so; to practise them in arithmetic and English grammar; to improve them in reading and penmanship; to exercise them in the fourth and fifth years in composition on some given subject; to instruct them in the art of teaching; to make up with their assistance the *voluminous school registers and school accounts*; and to give them such admonitions as occasion may require.

"This makes nine and a half hours a day for five days in the week, or nearly *eight hours* a day for *six days* in the week."[1]

Undoubtedly in the majority of cases the routine was not quite so rigorous as this would imply, but even so the pupil teacher's career had few attractions for those with a dislike of hard work. Not the least interesting part of this account of the pupil teacher's life is the catalogue of the duties which were to be carried out by the devoted teacher in return for his gratuity and the teaching assistance rendered by his apprentices. It would demand a scholastic Admirable Crichton to carry out the programme with success.

The institution of the pupil-teacher system was a great boon to the educational publishers. The market became flooded with books and periodicals designed to help the apprentice to get through his examinations, and the teacher to assist in that desirable object. As a supplement to the outline just given of the pupil teacher's week of work, here is the programme of work laid down in a Manual of Method of 1854 as a preparation for the annual examinations:

"Monday Evening: Sketch a map and learn by heart facts in Physical and Political Geography. Work examples in one of the Mathematical subjects.

"Tuesday Evening: Learn by heart a lesson in the Church Catechism, with Scripture texts. Work examples in one or more of the Mathematical subjects.

"Wednesday Evening: Write a short essay upon some subject previously given, or write an account of some reign in English History, or paraphrase a piece of Poetry. Learn a lesson in Grammar or Etymology and learn to Parse from the next day's reading lesson.

[1] *Newcastle Commission*, vol. III, p. 135.

"Thursday Evening: Prepare for repetition a lesson on the Liturgy. Work examples in one or more of the Mathematical subjects.

"Friday Evening and Saturday: Prepare a lesson on Scripture History, and sketch a Map to illustrate the places mentioned in it. Work examples in two or more of the Mathematical subjects".[1]

This programme was to be carried out in addition to teaching, and to the instruction received from the teacher. Nothing can better illustrate the aridity that characterised the "academic" training of the apprentices than the quality of the works produced for their assistance and edification.

There were certain defects in the scheme from the standpoint of administration. The payments to teachers in respect of pupil teachers were dependent on the success of the latter in the inspectors' annual examinations, and this success depended on a favourable report on the apprentice from the teacher. This put a premium on dishonesty, because, if a teacher was frank about an unsatisfactory apprentice, he lost his remuneration, and was thus penalised for doing his duty.[2] Pupil teachers, and ex-pupil teachers who did not proceed to college, tended to oust the trained teachers from the schools. For instance, schoolmasters were not inclined to have certificated assistants in their schools, since they took the place of pupil teachers, and so the pupil-teacher gratuities were lost.

[1] W. F. Richards, *Manual of Method*, 1854, p. 135.
[2] See Alfred Jones, "The Principles of Privy Council Legislation", a lecture delivered before the United Association of Schoolmasters of Great Britain, February 25th, 1859, pp. 26–34.

BIBLIOGRAPHY. See end of next chapter.

CHAPTER VI

THE PERIOD OF STABILISATION, 1846–1860

(b) THE WORK OF THE TRAINING COLLEGES

TURNING from the pupil teachers to the training colleges, we find that the Minutes of the Committee of Council had a most marked effect, and it was during the period 1846–60 that the training college system took upon itself a form which has survived, with modifications and additions, down to the present day. The principle of Government aid for privately owned colleges became established, and the project of a State training college did not again appear, so that the training colleges of the orthodox type had no competitors until the advent of the day training colleges, and later the training colleges set up by Local Education Authorities. The price of State aid was State supervision, and one by one the colleges either put up their shutters or came into line with the requirements of the Committee of Council on Education. Efficiency and uniformity increased side by side. The curricula of the colleges were determined by the certificate examinations, for on success in these their finances largely depended. The qualifications of the lecturers and tutors tended to become uniform, because their salaries to a large extent were dependent upon their passing the committee's examinations for lectureships. There was still considerable variation in the duration of courses, but the minimum of one year was firmly established, although the efforts of the Education Committee to enforce a longer period were in the main unavailing.

Colleges varied greatly in the rapidity with which they came into the committee's fold. In 1849, of the diocesan training colleges twelve were earning no grant; that is to say they were presenting no candidates for certificates.[1] At the Borough Road College no certificates were obtained by students in residence before 1851.[2] One by one, however, the colleges brought themselves up to the required standard, and year by year the grant increased by leaps and bounds. For Church of England colleges alone in the years 1854–9 the grant increased from £10,808 to £29,582.[3]

A number of new colleges were established by various bodies. Under the auspices of the Church of England, colleges for men were set up at Carnarvon, Carmarthen, Highbury (the Metropolitan Training College), Saltley, Culham (replacing the Oxford training centre) and Peterborough; for women at York, Truro, Derby, Bishop's Stortford, Bristol and Durham; for men and women at Cheltenham. Other denominations took the field for the first time. The Roman Catholics established colleges at Hammersmith (men), Liverpool (women) and St Leonards-on-Sea (women). The Wesleyans opened their Westminster Training College for both sexes, and the Congregationalists instituted the Homerton Training College, again both for men and women. With the help of the British and Foreign Society, although not under its control, a non-denominational college was established at Bangor.

The early history of Homerton College is of interest as the one attempt during this period to establish a college and carry it on independently of State assistance. In 1843 the Congregational Board of Education was formed, and in 1845 there came a definite breach with the British and Foreign Society on the question of accepting Government grant and interference. Other denominations shared the scruples of the Congregationalists, and in the same year a conference was held at Llandovery, at which Independents, Calvinistic

[1] Committee of Council, Minutes, 1850–51, p. 31.
[2] *Ibid.* 1851–52, p. 400.   [3] *Ibid.* 1859–60, p. 288.

Methodists, Wesleyans and Baptists were represented. As a result an independent training college was set up at Brecon. In the next year a training institution for women was established at Rotherhithe, a corresponding institution being opened for men in 1848, with the Rev. W. J. Unwin as principal, in Liverpool Street. In 1852 the two separate departments were united in the Homerton College, which started with eighteen students, but soon increased to forty-nine. The system favoured was a modified form of the "Glasgow Plan" devised by David Stow, and the period of training was one year. The students were to teach in Congregational schools, and independent examinations were conducted, and diplomas and certificates of merit awarded.

It was a gallant bid for freedom from the yoke of "My Lords", but a body neither very rich nor very powerful could not hope to succeed. It was gradually borne upon the Voluntarists that the fight was hopeless. Many of their fears were allayed by the scrupulous way in which the Education Department[1] administered the grant, without interference with religious teaching, and the struggle was given up after a Conference held at Manchester in 1867, when Edward Baines, the leader of the Voluntary movement, in his "Address" announced the reversal of his views. Overtures were made to the Education Department, Matthew Arnold was sent to inspect the college, found it efficient, and grant was offered and accepted. The work of the college was too similar to that of the grant-earning colleges to make it interesting educationally, and it is much to be regretted that there was no body in a position to experiment along lines distinct from those laid down by the Committee of Council.[2]

[1] Established in 1856 by amalgamation of the Committee of Council's Office and the Science and Art Department.

[2] Congregational Board of Education, *Tracts on Popular Education*, Tract 1, pp. 1–4, and Bartley, *The Schools for the People*, pp. 473–80.

The Wesleyan College at Westminster was well equipped, and provided with five practising schools. It was placed deliberately amid the slums of Westminster. The Wesleyan Education Committee "did not wish their students to be spoiled in training, and by a lengthened residence away from the dwellings of the poor and amongst the attractions of superior life, disinclined and rendered unfit to undertake the arduous and self-denying duties of school teachers. They hoped that, surrounded as their students were at Westminster, by the families of the poor, their want of education with its attendant degradation and misery would excite their best feeling".[1]

The work of the training colleges came to centre round the certificate examinations, which in effect largely determined their curricula and methods of instruction, although in the earlier days there was no general syllabus and examination for all colleges. At all times, and especially when the examination was a novelty, the coming of the examination day was a terrifying event. An entry in the accounts of the Battersea College tells its own tale: "Supplementary Account (Housekeeper)—£2. 10s. 0d. for wines and brandy given to students who were low and nervous at the time of the inspection", though at Battersea, after this, spirituous support was no longer provided out of college funds, for this expenditure was followed by a Minute of the College Committee recommending that "for the future the Supplementary Account be discontinued".[2]

In spite of all the efforts of the Committee of Council and its inspectors to avoid imposing their ideas too strongly upon the colleges, and to mitigate the terrors of the examination by winning manners, it was inevitable that the culmination of the activities of the colleges should be the obtaining of certificates. All efforts were directed to that end. The one

[1] Committee of Council, Minutes, 1853–4, p. 563.
[2] T. Adkins, *History of St John's College, Battersea*, 1906, p. 124.

criterion of method became its utility in preparing for the examination, and all college business which was unrelated to the demands of the inspectors tended to disappear. That is the unfortunate outcome of any examination system, particularly when the passing of an examination is an essential preliminary to a professional career, and also bears directly on the financial position of the institution that prepares candidates for the examination. The certificate examinations certainly did much to raise the standard of the qualifications of the school teachers, but that desirable end was attained at a great price. But here, as in the case of the pupil-teacher system, the circumstances must be borne in mind. By the recent action of the Board of Education, centralised dictation of the course which is to lead to certification of teachers has almost completely disappeared, and it is a thing to be welcomed. But this has only become possible by the advance which has been made in education generally. Possibly a similar leap in the dark would have been the best policy, even in the forties, but the Government was not concerned so much with the long run as with immediate demands for well-qualified teachers. Such teachers must be forthcoming, even at the cost of standardisation. Once again it was a case of making the best of a bad job, and, compared with the policy that came in with the Revised Code, the yoke of "My Lords" at this time was an easy one. Moreover, educational theory to-day is largely dominated by the ideas of "self-realisation" and the value of individuality, and at last we are prepared to apply these ideas even to the training of the teacher; but in the forties and fifties such ideas were not fashionable, and the well informed was too often looked upon as the well educated, irrespective of the way in which the information had been gained.

This confusion between information and education lay like a blight on the training college world. It was recognised readily enough that the demand was for teachers who were well informed, well trained for their profession, and of desirable character, but these things were catered for separately in the colleges. The giving of information, leading up to the obtaining of a certificate, had no connection with the training of character. There was much talk of morality in the colleges, often many religious exercises, always a multitude of rules to keep wandering feet in the paths of respectability, but all this was something quite distinct from the business of instruction. Much the same was true of the professional training, which again was often unrelated to the other business of the colleges, and, as will be seen, was often scamped because practical skill did not loom very large in the examination.

The demands made upon the candidates for certification were the result of conscientious thought on the part of the Education Department and its inspectors, but the resulting syllabus was on the whole imperfectly related both to the business of school teaching and the true education of the students. Nor was the central authority completely to blame. At first their demands were very largely conditioned by what the colleges were trying to do, and some of the inspectors raised their voices in protest against the over-ambitious schemes that were common in the colleges. For example, the following remarks were included in the report for 1847 by the Rev. Alex. Thurtell. After condemning the curricula of most of the colleges as too pretentious, he said:

"Why should we, in our training colleges, set at nought the principles on which the instruction in our best schools and our Universities is founded; viz. that of teaching well a limited number of subjects; and such subjects only as most call forth and exercise the intellectual powers with comparatively small regard to the mere acquisition of knowledge? Let us see that the trained master possesses the knowledge which he will be called upon to communicate; and more: let us lay in his mind a sound scientific foundation for every part of this knowledge to rest steadily upon: so that the structure may have connexion, unity and completeness as far as it extends".[1] That surely is sound doctrine in all education, not merely the preparation of the teacher for his task, and it was sound criticism of the training colleges. Unfortunately it is a doctrine which may easily be garbled into the educational heresy of the Revised Code, which, in fact, was to a considerable extent the outcome of much similarly sound criticism.

Criticism of a similar kind was voiced by the teachers themselves, particularly by those who had received no college training. There was much truth in the racy denunciation of "Government pretentiousness" given in evidence by a schoolmaster to the Newcastle Commissioners:

"The fact is, our theorists and amateur educationists have been rather *fast*. It is easy work to talk of the advantage of this science, or the paramount importance of the other, of the philosophy of common things (a hit at the Rev. Inspector Moseley, this!), and the modus operandi of uncommon things. Teachers have allowed themselves to be deluded by inexperienced persons, who, with confidence equal to their ignorance, insist upon the introduction of all the -ologies, and a boy educated according to their fancy would be well up in history, would comprehend the knotty points of political economy, would tell you all about the composition of air, fire, earth and water, and everything else, including a great deal of his own composition, inside and outside, from the hair of the head to the little toenail".[2]

Of course, the pretentiousness was in the syllabuses rather than in the attainments of the students. Like the grammarian, the training college, aiming at the million, succeeded often in missing the unit. As one critic somewhat cynically remarked, "It is a comfort to reflect that there is a mighty

[1] Committee of Council, Minutes, 1847–8, vol. II, p. 537.
[2] *Newcastle Commission*, evidence by J. Snell, vol. v, p. 391.

difference between the standard suggested by the answers and that suggested by the questions, otherwise we should be in danger of having a race of poor schoolmasters and mistresses too accomplished to form our houses of legislature, and so the anathema might ensue that the tail should govern the head".[1] The crude and undigested knowledge acquired during the pupil-teacher period was augmented by further crude and undigested knowledge imparted by diligent tutors in the training colleges, and in many cases the finished product was a pedant of the first water.

Some attempts were made by the Education Committee to remedy the trouble. As early as 1849, when the colleges were examined individually, Moseley, whose services to the cause of teachers' training can hardly be estimated too highly, in his report on the Southern District, expressed his opinion that certificates were granted too much on attainment, and that the teachers tended to get a smattering of all subjects for the certificate examination. As a reform he suggested that the subjects for the examination should be divided into divisions: (1) subjects proper to elementary instruction, (2) the exact sciences, (3) literature, (4) the experimental sciences, (5) the natural sciences, and that students should satisfy in the first group and one other.[2] Nothing, however, was done at the time. Then again in 1854 the same inspector brought forward the suggestion that in place of the very wide requirements then in force, designed so as to avoid interference with the curricula of the colleges, an official and definite syllabus should be drawn up for all the colleges.[3] This suggestion, as we have seen, was put into effect later, and the first detailed syllabus was printed in the 1854–5 Blue Book, but it meant little more than that the stereotyped nature of the colleges' work became more marked.

---

[1] *Newcastle Commission*, vol. v, p. 42.
[2] Committee of Council, Minutes, 1848–49–50, vol. I, pp. 26–9.
[3] *Ibid.* 1854–5, pp. 286, 287.

Moseley's idea that the students in the training colleges should be educated primarily through a thorough study of the subjects of elementary instruction was found to be impracticable, partly through the lack of appropriate books, and partly because the academic training of the principals of the colleges, who were commonly clergymen and graduates of Oxford or Cambridge, was such as to put them out of sympathy with any such project.[1] Accordingly more advanced subjects were included for "mental culture", and the old trouble remained. "The subjects relied upon for the general cultivation of the students' minds are, in the first year, the first four books of Euclid, algebra as far as quadratic equations, or instead, that part of the Latin grammar which relates to accidence, concords, genders of nouns, perfect tenses and supines of verbs"[2]—admirable fare for minds already made sterile by five years of pupil-teacher apprenticeship!

Thus, by the time of the Newcastle Commission, the syllabus had been made definite and universal, but retained most of the objectionable features which had characterised it from the commencement. The time was ripe for a simplification of the curriculum. Temple, one of the inspectors, was voicing the opinion of most thoughtful critics when he said: "I think that it would be far better if you could get schoolmasters with less knowledge and more education, which is what is commonly meant by people who ask for what they call a lower standard, but it really is a much higher standard".[3] Unfortunately this principle, as interpreted by Mr Lowe, when applied meant that the country got schoolmasters with less knowledge and with even less education.

The defects arising out of the pretentiousness of the examination system were enhanced by the nature of the training college staffs and the methods they adopted. It must be remembered that the colleges were breaking new ground and

[1] *Newcastle Commission*, General Report, vol. I, p. 118.
[2] *Ibid.* p. 119.   [3] *Ibid.* p. 132.

that they had no traditions to guide them. In such circumstances it was particularly regrettable that at so early a point in their career their activities should become orientated around an examination syllabus. With greater freedom in these early days it might well have been that the narrowness of outlook and method that settled on the whole training college system might have been avoided. As it was, the teaching personnel of the colleges was cramped from the outset. Principals and lecturers came into a branch of education which should still have been in the adventurous and experimental stage, but found the work already defined, and all too readily acquiesced in recognising "My Lords" as the supreme arbiters in training college work.

The principals were commonly drawn from two sources. In the Church of England colleges they were usually clergymen. In the larger colleges the appointment was commonly given to a man from Oxford or Cambridge, brought up in the old academic tradition. Amongst these there were many men of marked energy and ability, but too often they were out of touch with the work of the elementary schools, and tended to regard the professional work of their colleges as of secondary importance. With their academic outlook, they were too prone to regard instruction as their main business, coupled with efforts to provide for the moral training of their students. That subjects should be taught with a definitely vocational bias was a conception fundamentally opposed to the point of view at which they had arrived as a result of their previous education and experience.

But not all clerical principals came from the ancient universities. In the smaller provincial colleges the principal was frequently a man who had passed through a training college and had subsequently taken orders. St Mark's in particular supplied principals and other training college officers in this way. As early as 1852 this college had provided two principals of diocesan training colleges, three vice-principals, three normal masters, two tutors and two organising masters.[1] Some of such men had served for a time as elementary school-masters, but quite often they had passed directly to the staff of their own colleges as soon as their period of training was completed. Such men were likely to suffer from the narrow-ness of their upbringing. The greater part of their lives had been spent within the walls of their respective colleges, and their outlook tended to be bounded by those circumscribed limits. Compared with the Oxford and Cambridge men, they were likely to have greater sympathy with the pro-fessional end of training college work, but they lacked that breadth of vision which might characterise those who came new to the business.

The lecturers and tutors were usually trained teachers, although the post of vice-principal was occasionally filled by an outsider of some academic distinction. At first it was diffi-cult to obtain reasonably well-qualified certificated teachers on the staff, because by taking up work in a training college a man lost the Government augmentation due to him in respect of his certificate. A young student might remain for a year or two, but soon the superior pecuniary attraction of ordinary school work would entice him away. This state of affairs was remedied first by the Minute rendering certificated teachers in the training colleges eligible for the augmenta-tions, and later by the institution of the "lecturers' grants" to those passing a qualifying examination. But mere book knowledge is only a part of the training college tutor's equip-ment, and it was rare to find among the staffs of the colleges men endowed with breadth of vision and a philosophic out-look on educational matters. Too often the tutor was a mere instructor, whose life was made up of passing on in a more or less digestible form the stores of information that he had himself gained as a result of years of strenuous self-education.

[1] Committee of Council, Minutes, 1852–3, vol. I, p. 273.

The problem of staffing a training college or a university training department is not easy of solution. A knowledge of the philosophy and history of education, wide experience of teaching in various types of school coupled with a lively and critical interest in new methods, high academic attainment, the tact that is necessary in dealing with young adults, all these things are necessary, and it is unlikely that they will be found united in individuals. The last qualification should belong to every tutor, but in practice it is often absent, because it is something which cannot be tested in a candidate for appointment. For the rest, the ideal training college staff is recruited from various sources of supply. Here again the development of secondary education has done much to facilitate the solution of the problem. Generally the lecturers in academic subjects are experienced secondary school teachers. It is by no means usual for such to have taught in elementary schools, but it is very likely that many of them will have been pupils in elementary schools at the commencement of their educational careers, and, after all, experience of teaching in any type of school is very much better than none at all. Nor is it desirable that every training college tutor should have had elementary school experience. Such experience should be represented somewhere on the training college staff, and if it is lacking the college is greatly the loser.

To-day what is, perhaps, most conspicuously absent is the philosophic outlook on education. That in particular should be the mark of the principal, though it should characterise the work of every member of the staff. Unfortunately, in too many instances, the training college is too much like a superior secondary school, and fails in opening the minds of its students to the broad vistas of educational thought. In this respect the university department has the advantage, not merely because the philosophical attitude is expected of the university teacher, but because the whole situation is changed in an organisation that is concerned with the theory and practice of education solely, and is freed from responsibility in the matter of academic instruction.

Lecturing was the staple method of instruction, but there was much variation in the extent to which it was combined with study of books. In 1850 Moseley made a series of calculations based on examination results, to discover whether there was any correlation with the method of instruction adopted, and the result, in the light of modern contempt for "chalk and talk", is at first sight somewhat surprising.[1] The list was headed by Cheltenham and Battersea, and in each of these much the greater stress was laid upon oral instruction. This, of course, does not mean that an oral method is better than a "study" method from the absolute standpoint. The test was a rough one, and the criterion was a doubtfully conceived written examination. What it does mean is that the oral method proved to be the most satisfactory one for the business which the training colleges had come to regard as their reason for existence—the gaining of certificates. Hence the lecture occupied the central position in academic instruction. The students came up with no training in the use of books, and, if ex-pupil teachers, with minds that had lost all resilience as a result of the mechanical instruction they had received during apprenticeship and the meagre text-books they had been in the habit of using. The libraries of the colleges were very deficient, and the tutors were thrown back upon oral teaching. Nor was this of the most desirable kind. Very frequently the lecture consisted of little more than the dictation of notes, which were to serve the purpose of a text-book for the examination. Apart from the educational defects of such a method, notes of this kind were liable to be inaccurate, and constant revision was necessary. The minds of the students became loaded with facts, and the knowledge gained was often highly abstruse, since the tutors had not that deep knowledge of their subjects which renders

[1] Committee of Council, Minutes, 1850–51, pp. 43–6.

lively and effective presentation possible. Except in rare instances the whole business was a kind of specialised "window-dressing".

It is interesting to note that the training college was one of the first educational institutions to make a serious attempt at organised science teaching. Most of such teaching was extremely defective, science being treated entirely as an information subject, divorced from experimental work. Moseley, however, made a definite contribution to the development of science teaching by his plea for the "science of everyday things". In his Report for 1853 he outlined his conception of the place such work should take in the elementary school, and his views were far in advance of those in vogue at the time.

He first commented on the verbal nature of the instruction given in the training colleges in this connection, and urged the need for systematic study. He then went on to say:

"Having laid a sound foundation of knowledge in physical science, the next step is to apply it to the work of the elementary teacher. This application is obviously to the things which immediately surround the life of a poor child, and which stand in a close relationship to its material and its moral wellbeing: the things on which, under the providence of God, depend health or sickness, clothing or nakedness, want or abundance. The desire to know about such things is instinctive to the child, and from his earliest years the tendency is apparent to apply such knowledge. To *make*, with an adoption to some purpose and for some end, supposes a beginning of such knowledge, however imperfect. And the character of the *maker*, if it be not *innate*, manifests itself, at least, with the first steps the child takes out of infancy. It is for this end that God has associated thinking and acting in a pleasurable relation, so that what we do in the exercise of our judgment for some object, and with an adaptation to some end, we do with pleasure: whilst labour, without thought or contrivance, for no object to which our endeavours are directed, and which we adapt to no end, is irksome to us. To develop this character of the *maker* in the child, as contrasted with the *worker*, is the function of physical science in elementary education....This I hold to be industrial education in its only reasonable form".[1]

This is a principle still to be striven after in popular education, and we are still far from applying it universally. Those responsible for the organisation of the work of the "modern school" of the future would do well to ponder this wise counsel. The challenge thus thrown out to the training colleges was never taken up. Such progress as was made lay in the direction of the improvement of teaching science as an academic subject, and in this connection the contribution of the training colleges must not be overlooked.

The life of the training college was cloistral and full of hard work. As the policy of subsidising the student in training became established, it was noticed that there was not that seriousness and self-devotion that had characterised the older generation of training college students, but instead there was greater enthusiasm and emulation. Conceit and self-sufficiency were the commonest defects, and these were enhanced by the herding together of men and women who had all gone through the same previous training, and who were all preparing for the same walk in life. One of the more enlightened college principals expressed to the Newcastle Commission his doubts as to the value of the intense corporate life which marked the average training college. "Students in a training school are, considering their age and circumstances, too gregarious; they live too much in a mass. They study together, they take all their meals together, they occupy a common room in the intervals of recreation, they have no privacy, they are scarcely ever alone except when in bed. Hence there is little opportunity for self-recollection or private medita-

[1] Committee of Council, Minutes, 1853–4, pp. 442, 443.

tion, little opportunity for the practice of private religious exercises....It cannot be altogether good for young men to be made to pass through this phase of schoolboy life, but it cannot, I suppose, be helped."[1]

Discipline was strict, and great emphasis was laid upon morality. This was partly because of the religious motive which still predominated in the promotion of popular education, and partly because of the fear of loss of grant should there be any complaints on this score. At times it seemed as though the training college authorities conceived of moral training as their chief business, the sordid occupation of training people to teach being a secondary consideration. There was often considerable justification for the remarks of an inspector in 1849. "These ends (the teaching of the three R's), homely and simple as they are, will no more be attained (nor are they) by the unaided exhibition of those moral qualifications just adverted to, admirable and indispensable as they are, than mere good temper will enable a man who never learned watchmaking to repair a ruptured escapement, or than mere sobriety will qualify a person ignorant of engines to conduct the express train in safety from Warrington to London."[2]

One result that followed from this excessive gregariousness, with its concomitant emphasis upon moral training and the high calling of the elementary schoolmaster, was that the students tended to have too high an estimate of the place of the teacher in the order of things, and to exaggerate their own qualifications for such a vocation. "They gradually acquire a wrong belief that the work of a schoolmaster is the one great work of the day, and that they are the men to do it."[3]

The colleges for women followed much the same lines as

[1] *Newcastle Commission*, vol. IV, p. 408.
[2] Committee of Council, Minutes, 1848–49–50, vol. II, p. 729.
[3] *Newcastle Commission*, vol. I, p. 140.

those for men. The direction of a women's college was generally vested in a clergyman who combined the function of chaplain with secretarial duties and the general organisation and supervision of the work of the institution. It was usual for the domestic life of the place to be under the direction of a resident lady superintendent, who was generally the widow of a clergyman or professional man. The instruction was carried out by governesses who were recruited in the same way as the tutors of the men's colleges. It is only comparatively recently that it has been considered anomalous for the head of a place of education for women to be a man. Only with the development of the higher education of women has it been possible for women to occupy high academic and administrative positions.

One peculiarity of the women's college was the attention given to training in "domestic economy". This subject was stressed because an important part of the elementary schoolmistress's work was training her pupils for home duties, and because it was felt that the schoolmistress needed such training herself, seeing that she would in all probability have to set up a house of her own, which she would have to manage generally single-handed, in addition to conducting her school. The provision made for this part of training varied from college to college, and often it was made a convenient excuse for making the students do most of the housework, which might be a severe imposition, since the academic and professional work of the training was very heavy and arduous in itself.

The provision made for training in domestic economy at Salisbury may be taken as an example of a systematic attempt to deal with the problem. Every Saturday night four students were detailed to undertake housework for the following week. They were presented with an inventory of the crockery and utensils, all of which were to be handed over *whole* to the party that succeeded them in their duties. The domestic work of the students was under the supervision of the chief kitchen servant. They were on duty for six hours a day for five days in the week, and for the whole of Saturday. There was a small kitchen set apart for their use on Saturdays, equipped with such utensils as they would need for themselves when they started housekeeping on their own, or as would commonly be found in a labouring man's cottage. On Saturday they chose their own dinners, and carried through the whole preparation and cooking of them themselves. In addition they were expected to bake bread for their own use throughout the week, the rest of the time on ordinary days being given up to helping in the domestic work of the college as a whole.

In addition to this routine, from time to time parties of eight or ten students were sent down to the kitchen to observe and assist in the making of puddings, pies, and sundry other things. Laundry work had to be undertaken at intervals during the year. The cleaning of bedrooms and schoolrooms was a regular part of the student's daily life, and the lighting and tending of fires also fell to her lot.

On an average 58 hours a quarter were spent in domestic work—$44\frac{1}{2}$ hours in housework, cooking and baking, $5\frac{1}{4}$ hours in washing and $8\frac{1}{4}$ hours in ironing.[1]

Here we see again the way in which the colleges suffered from being called upon to fulfil too many functions. No doubt, the training given in housecraft was valuable, particularly when it was systematically organised as in this instance. In many cases, however, "domestic economy" was made an excuse for economy of college expenses, and became a mere drudgery. And even granted that it might be valuable, in an organised system of education it is no part of the work of the training college for teachers to give training in the scrubbing of floors and the cooking of dinners. But until such an organised system was evolved, multiplicity of

Committee of Council, Minutes, 1858–9, pp. 318, 319.

function was bound to characterise the work of the training colleges.

In the matter of practical training in the business of the teacher, each college was largely left to work out its own methods. This side of the work was little controlled by the Education Committee, apart from the visits of inspectors. For the certificate examination the candidate had to answer a paper on general school method, and give a lesson, but there was no uniformity of syllabus, and no prescribed minimum of time to be devoted to teaching practice. As a result, this supremely important part of the work of the training college was in many colleges comparatively neglected. The keen student was anxious to gain a good certificate, which depended almost entirely on the standard reached in academic subjects, and so he paid little attention to the professional side of the course. The training college authorities took up a similar attitude only too often, since they measured the success of the colleges by the results of the examinations.

Nearly every college had its own practising school or schools, although in some places use was made of ordinary schools in the locality. A school largely given over to practising students is bound to be a somewhat eccentric place, and the inspectors were frequently pressing for the establishment of model schools in addition to practising schools, so that the students might see a school doing normal work after the best methods. The Home and Colonial College in the Gray's Inn Road had schools of both types, but it stood alone in this respect, and the other colleges did not take up the suggestion.

The amount of time spent in teaching practice varied considerably in different colleges, but it was usually short. This is shown by a comparative table drawn up by the Rev. F. C. Cook, the inspector of women's training colleges, in 1855, indicating the average time in hours given to practice

in a number of women's colleges by students of at least
fifteen months' standing:

	Hours		Hours
Bishop's Stortford	240	Norwich	148
Brighton	178	Salisbury	70
Bristol	No returns	Warrington	90
Cheltenham	80	Whitelands	340
Derby	No returns	York and Ripon	245
Home and Colonial	340[1]		

The practice was often poorly organised, and little effort
was made to use it to the full as an instrument of professional
training. The students came up with considerable skill in the
management of children and the imparting of information in
a mechanical manner. They were generally well pleased with
their teaching powers, and the college authorities did little
to disillusion them and point the way to better things. Help
and advice in the preparation of lessons were rare. The care
the students received when actually teaching varied much
from college to college, but sometimes supervision was
"systematically neglected".[2]

The "criticism lesson" loomed large in every college, and
this piece of solemn training college ritual was as little useful
then as it is to-day. Its dangers were perhaps more marked
with students lacking in breadth of education and the humour
that it should breed, for the nervous were more prone to be
cast down by the strictures of their critics, and the successful
more elated by praise of their pedagogic ability, than is the
case with the students of to-day. But it was an institution
that suited well with the prevailing formalism in education,
and so it remained the great standby of the normal master
or mistress. Often the performance lost what little value it
might have through lack of direction of the criticism of the
audience, although the better of the normal masters insisted

[1] Committee of Council, Minutes, 1855–6, p. 741.
[2] *Ibid.* 1854–5, p. 337.

that the criticisms should be made under heads such as "Matter", "Manner", "Illustration" and "Language".[1]

The custom of the colleges in respect of lectures in "method" was by no means standardised. Some devoted no time at all to the subject. In others there was no person on the staff whose particular work it was to give such lectures, but odd people were called upon to enlighten the students on the theory of what was, after all, to be their life work. In others there was a specially appointed lecturer for the subject, although he would in most cases give other lectures as well, and it was in these colleges that the subject was best taught. It was done, perhaps, best of all at the Home and Colonial College, where there was a tradition of carefully organised instruction on school methods. In some places the difficulties were enhanced by the fact that the normal master and the master of the practising school were openly opposed to each other over the question of method, so that the student never saw the theories of the normal master put into practice, and saw the practice of the school unadorned by appropriate theory. Such a difficulty was likely to arise when the colleges thought it their business to teach specific methods, a relic of monitorial days, instead of giving their students a broad background of theory which might give direction and meaning to their practice. There will always be the contrast between what the student is told in the lecture room and what he sees in the schools, and it would be an unhealthy thing if it were not so, but the conflict should be between the ideal and the real, rather than between one method and another.

The problem of instruction in method was rendered all the more difficult in that there was no accepted "canon" of educational thought, nor were there any very suitable textbooks. If this had merely meant that there was considerable diversity in the theories presented by the various colleges, it

[1] Committee of Council, Minutes, 1856–7, p. 696.

would have been a good thing, but unfortunately it meant in most instances that each individual college gave no organised and rounded account of educational theory and method, but served up a syllabus which was "a thing of shreds and patches", composed of borrowings from "systems" of all kinds. Possibly a common syllabus, worked out by lecturers in the colleges and generally accepted by them, as recommended by one of the inspectors,[1] would have improved matters, at the price of some standardisation, but the defect really arose from the lack on the part of most of the lecturers of any real philosophical approach to the problem of educational theory.

The possibility of introducing a more philosophic element into the lectures on education was a subject upon which official opinion was sharply divided. Cook, an inspector who was acutely aware of the shortcomings of the colleges in this respect, feared that the introduction of moral philosophy and physiology would make confusion worse confounded, since there were no books sufficiently simple and concise, and it was doubtful if the lecturers were capable of carrying out satisfactorily the necessary simplification and avoidance of controversial topics.[2] This opinion was shared by Temple, who made a significant report on the subject in 1856.[3] He maintained that theoretical lectures were not successful, that it was best to limit lectures on education as far as possible to talks on the teaching of special subjects, and that this should form part of the work of the lecturers in each subject. The normal master should be concerned with the work of a school as a whole, and in order to improve the qualifications of normal masters for this work, he recommended that "Method" should be added to the subjects for which "lecturers' grants" were paid. He had circularised principals of training colleges to ask for their opinions as

[1] Committee of Council, Minutes, 1855–6, p. 739.
[2] *Ibid.* 1854–5, p. 338.   [3] *Ibid.* 1856–7, pp. 700–7.

to what branches of knowledge should form the equipment of the normal master, and the resultant list included the science of education, a knowledge of different systems and methods of education, the history of education, and an acquaintance with the state of contemporary education. Temple's own view was that the "science of education" should be limited to logic, and he quoted the remarks of one principal:

"I much doubt whether good would result from giving any direct encouragement to the study of modern systematic works on mental science. Not only is the matter which they contain bearing on education meagre and unpractical, but, if I am not mistaken, it is generally false. I must indeed state that the works in question seem to me more likely to be mischievous than beneficial in reference to the end proposed: I have not known a single practical teacher who has given himself up to the study of them who has not appeared to be the worse—not the better—for his pains".[1]

Possibly this distrust of a study of mental and moral philosophy on the part of an Anglican clergyman was not altogether untouched by religious considerations, and a vigorous reply was made by another inspector, Morell, who expressed the complete disagreement on this point of the principals of the Borough Road and Westminster Colleges, and added: "As the *principles* of all education lie really in the proper application of our knowledge of the human faculties to the means of their development, it is thought to be a conclusion both hasty in itself and ill-sustained either by fact or by reason, that a man should become a *worse teacher* for studying the scientific principles on which all teaching virtually rests. Even admitting that the works on mental science, as applied to education, are at present meagre and unsatisfactory, we must not forget that a *demand* for better digested books on such a subject is pretty sure to create a supply".[2]

[1] Committee of Council, Minutes, 1856–7, p. 706.
[2] *Ibid.* 1857–8, pp. 782, 783.

The truth of this last comment has been abundantly confirmed by the development of a systematic educational theory during the present century and the last years of the nineteenth. As the provision of instruction in the subjects of the curriculum for teachers has improved, the need for presenting them during their years of training with a broad outlook on the whole question of education has become apparent. The development of educational theory has received a great impetus from the raising of education to the status of a university study, and the institution of Chairs of Education in universities and university colleges. It is improbable that education can ever be placed upon a completely scientific basis, or that a systematically organised body of universally adopted educational theory will be evolved, but an enormous advance has been made on the state of affairs in the fifties of the last century. There has been a widespread realisation of the bearing upon educational thought and practice of the work of the physiologist, the biologist, the psychologist and the sociologist, as well as that of the logician and the philosopher, and the educational theory of to-day draws its material from many sources. But whilst this is recognised, experience in training colleges and university training departments has not altogether allayed the misgivings expressed by Temple.

Although there is to-day a very respectable body of simply expressed works on different aspects of educational theory, it is by no means certain that the systematic study of the subject is of great value to the teacher, under the conditions which at present characterise the work of training. In the training college, where the antiquated effort is still being made to combine professional and academic work in a short course, the study of educational theory cannot be otherwise than superficial. In the university, the post-graduate year of training is very crowded, with much time taken up by the demands of teaching practice, and it is a real question whether it is better to make a thorough study of one aspect of educational theory, e.g. the logical, the ethical, the psychological or the historical, than to attempt to give a conspectus of the subject as a whole. Probably it is better to attempt the general survey, honestly recognising its necessary superficiality, in the hope that some general background may be created, against which the young teacher may envisage his work and its particular problems, and that some may be led to undertake serious work on some special educational question. In this connection the institution of post-graduate degrees in education has been a distinct contribution to educational development. Certainly, to limit the training of the teacher to a mere training in methods of teaching would be to set back the clock. The problem of the future is the education of the teacher as a teacher after his academic education is completed, and this can be achieved only by making him in some way cognisant of the rationale of his profession.

The volumes of evidence published by the Newcastle Commission give a clear picture of the teachers produced by the training colleges during the period under discussion. There was general, although by no means universal, agreement that the new teachers from the colleges were superior to the old untrained teachers. One of the inspectors, Brookfield, who was "not at all disposed to overvalue the effects of training", drew up statistics as a result of examining 686 schools, of which 470 were under trained, and 215 under untrained teachers,[1] 0·24 per cent. of the schools under trained teachers enjoyed "good" teaching as compared with 3 per cent. of those in the other category. "Fair" teaching was found in 49 per cent. of those under trained teachers, and in 39 per cent. of those under untrained. In 27 per cent. of those with trained teachers the teaching was classified as "inferior", as compared with 58 per cent. of those with un-

[1] Brookfield's arithmetic seems slightly at fault.

trained teachers.[1] But whilst it was admitted that training had improved the teaching in the schools, there were many faults to find, and it is significant that the official Report of the Commission says that these defects were faults of disinclination rather than of inefficiency.

Two quotations will make clear the two prevailing attitudes towards the teachers. Kay-Shuttleworth, virtually their creator, and still their champion, wrote in the concluding portion of his great survey of the development of popular education under his guidance: "This corps of teachers has been like the raw recruits of an army suddenly raised— brought into the field in successive battalions, on the verge of an immature manhood, and placed, as soon as drilled, in the front of difficulties and dangers. They have had to take up everywhere the work of the untrained masters. They have been the pioneers of civilisation. Fourteen years have barely elapsed since their first companions took up their position, and their ranks are still full of the last batches of raw recruits".[2] As against this we may turn to the summing-up by the *Quarterly Review* of the general impression conveyed by the findings of the Commission: "The Privy Council have been long manufacturing razors for the purpose of cutting blocks, and in future the instrument must be better adapted for its purpose".[3]

The system of pretentious cram which passed muster for training bore evil fruit. It had throughout been a matter of giving mere information instead of a cultivation of the intellect and character, with the result that students left the colleges "with full, but comparatively languid and unbraced minds",[4] and in the majority of cases with an engrained hatred of further study. Even the information they had

[1] *Newcastle Commission*, vol. I, pp. 149, 150.
[2] J. Kay-Shuttleworth, *Four Periods of Public Education*, p. 583.
[3] *Quarterly Review*, No. 220, p. 506.
[4] *Newcastle Commission*, vol. I, p. 135.

172 of Stabilisation, 1846–1860

172 *The Period of Stabilisation, 1846–1860*

received was of doubtful relevance to their future work. The
principal of the college at York, who was one of the sanest
critics of the system and its products, asked pertinently: "In
what village school is it likely that lessons will ever be given
on the history of the Christian Church during the fifteenth
century? To what generation of labourers' children will it
ever be expedient to discourse on the Schism of the Papacy,
the Council of Basle, the Pragmatic Sanction or the Wars of
the Hussites?"[1] This criticism was equally true of moral instruction, as the same critic pointed out, when he discussed
the worth of the trained teacher as an instrument of moral
training in the schools. "The children will, perhaps, show
themselves well versed in Jewish history, able to trace accurately Israel's wanderings from Pi-hahiroth to the banks of
Jordan, to canvass the merits of Hezekiah and the demerits
of Jeroboam the son of Nebat, to give the dates of any
number of Old Testament events, while at the same time
they will exhibit a very superficial acquaintance with the
Gospels and the Acts of the Apostles, and will soon betray
the fact that the lessons they have received have not been
given with any very direct reference to the formation of a
moral and religious character in them."[2] Here is obvious
exaggeration for the sake of effect, but the bulk of the evidence to the Commission corroborates its general intention.
The teachers had too much irrelevant information in their
heads, and this caused their teaching to be over-elaborate,
whilst they tended to neglect the dull routine work in the lower
classes of their schools. The Revised Code throws its shadow
before in a sinister passage in the General Report of the Commission: "The teachers sent out from the training colleges
are quite good enough.... The object is to find some constant
and stringent motive to induce them to do that part of their
duty which is at once most unpleasant and most important".[3]

---

[1] *Newcastle Commission*, vol. I, p. 135.   [2] *Ibid.* vol. IV, p. 414.
[3] *Ibid.* vol. I, p. 157.

Combined with this dislike of solid work was often found a kind of conceit which was particularly galling to managers, who were not always the most tactful of people, and who often saw in the school teacher a fit object of condescension. One lady complained bitterly that the trained teachers refused to submit to authority, and attempted to introduce outrageous subjects like French and fancywork into the schools. "One teacher brought a piano with her, and though she had little knowledge of music, and neither voice nor ear for singing, much time was spent in practising upon it, which would have been better bestowed in preparation for her school duties."[1] They had no ideas of how to teach needlework. "On one occasion a gentleman's shirt was sent home with the long flap in front, the mistress having never even discovered that there was anything wrong about it."[2] Similar evidence was given by a clergyman: "In one instance a trained mistress engaged to a school in one of our most desirable parishes, but having then but a temporary schoolroom till those of a better description were finished, on coming and seeing the school, bade the carman who had driven her to wait till she had inspected the rooms and accommodation as she did not think they would suit her; and being dissatisfied, bade him drive her back to the station. In the case of a master of a school, I found him questioning little boys on the most abstruse parts of grammar, on which subject the boys were most profoundly ignorant. He would scarcely allow me to inspect his school, though I was extra civil and conciliatory in manner, and on leaving, he said, with the greatest air, although one of the most inferior of his kind, and displaying a gold ring whilst he ran his fingers through his hair, 'This place will not do for me', and he was much disappointed, as he expected to find a school of a very superior description, where a very superior education was

[1] *Newcastle Commission*, vol. V, p. 231.
[2] *Ibid.* p. 232.

required, but he could teach those children nothing. I endeavoured to persuade him to stay and do good among the poor and ignorant, but I heard that he left in a few days".[1]

The dissatisfaction with the teachers expressed by various types of external critics was paralleled by a widespread dissatisfaction with the conditions of their work on the part of the teachers themselves. This was aroused, not so much by the standard of payment received, although the teachers would have been scarcely human had they been perfectly content in this respect, but by the lack of social regard which was keenly felt by men who had received what they thought a considerable education, and who looked upon themselves as having attained a definitely professional status. The aspirations of the teachers in this direction found scanty sympathy from the world in general, and this lack of sympathy was a constant irritation. This is well illustrated by the evidence of a schoolmaster to the Commission in answer to a question on the alleged dissatisfaction of the teachers with their lot.

"As far as I know, trained teachers do not dislike their work; there is no reason why they should: it is honourable, intellectual and benevolent, but society has not yet learned how to value them. This they feel with all the sensitiveness that belongs to educated and professional men. The man who studies human laws, he who understands the human frame and the healing art, the artist who can produce a picture, each has a recognised position, and is esteemed; but the man who labours for the elevation of his fellow, who deals with the human intellect, who is entrusted to cut and polish the most precious jewel in creation, is a mere social nonentity. The lawyer is ignorant of his existence, for he is without means, the parson takes the same notice of him as he does of the parish beadle, and the doctor only knows him as he knows all other poor souls, or rather *poor bodies*. The Government, by assisting us to larger incomes and to better

[1] *Newcastle Commission*, vol. II, p. 310.

educations, has done very much to elevate our position, and we are thankful; still we conceive ourselves not holding that place in public estimation we may justly expect to hold."[1]

No doubt many of the defects in the attitude of the teachers which have already been noted were attributable to the influence of this social "inferiority complex", and in some ways the unmannerliness and conceit of the teachers were not to be deplored. They were manifestations of an upward urge in the very heart of the schoolmaster and schoolmistress, signs that they were beginning to honour their work, and to expect that they themselves should receive honour for the work's sake. Such aspiration is the inevitable accompaniment of education. We see it at work in the wider sphere of national education. It is impossible to educate and at the same time to keep in subjection. Even the arid education of the training colleges was enough to fill the teachers with a desire for a fuller realisation of self, which in a great many cases manifested itself in a somewhat crude longing for superior social amenities than had previously been their lot.

It might be an unpleasant thing, it was often an inconvenient thing, but it was by no means a bad thing for English popular education. Professional status carries with it duties as well as privileges, and in their advance to that status the teachers have made great contributions to education by insisting on adequate qualifications, the reform of teaching conditions, and the maintenance of a good standard of work without the constant urge of examination and close supervision. Even yet, to use the convenient jargon of the psychoanalyst, the inferiority complex has not been completely "sublimated", but much of the vigour of social discontent has been redirected towards the promotion of professional societies which, whilst they are not altogether forgetful of the need still to press for material advantages, devote much energy to widening the scope and raising the standard of the

[1] *Newcastle Commission,* vol. v, p. 400.

teacher's work, realising that in the last resort any profession receives the public recognition that it deserves.

There was one grievance, which still exists to some extent, although largely remedied by the institution of salary scales. From the financial point of view, the work of teaching was quite attractive for the youngster, but for many the standard of remuneration would remain practically fixed, the only way of advance being to obtain posts in larger schools. This was no doubt a good thing in that it acted as a stimulus to the more able teachers, but it created a definite hardship for the unambitious who were content to do satisfactory work in subordinate positions, and found themselves in middle age drawing the same salaries as they had as raw recruits from college. The fact that the "augmentations" due on account of their certificates were paid, not direct to them, but to their managers, was a small thing, but a definite annoyance, since it tended to emphasise their subordinate position.

These complaints of the teachers were treated in summary fashion in the Report of the Commission. Having shown how the teachers had been educated as the result of the generosity of the State, it continued: "After receiving these advantages at the public expense, they seem to complain that they are not provided with still further advantages on a progressive scale throughout the rest of their lives".[1] Such criticism was hardly fair. The State had made payments in order to secure a supply of recruits for a national service, but that was no reason for the teachers to be precluded from seeking better conditions. Such a difficulty arises out of a system of State subsidies for a particular kind of professional training, which modifies the intrinsic attractions of that profession. Possibly it would be more satisfactory to replace subsidies for teachers' education by general scholarships, trusting to the profession to gain recruits as a result of its

[1] *Newcastle Commission*, vol. I, p. 160.

natural attractiveness, but even yet this is hardly a practicable proposition, since the State must recognise as a paramount duty the provision of an adequate and regular supply of teachers for the nation's schools, and this might be jeopardised by discontinuing the present specific subsidy.

Another grievance was in the matter of the appointment of inspectors. These were recruited from graduates of Oxford and Cambridge who usually started their work with little or no knowledge of the work of the schools which they were to inspect. A quotation from the evidence of the eloquent schoolmaster before cited will make the grievance clear.

"This, like every other branch of the public service, is appropriated not to the deserving, but to the needy. How many of our inspectors are from the ranks of the clergy? And why? How many of them knew anything of the education of the poor prior to their engagement as inspectors? I verily believe that there be some who were never inside a public school till the day they entered it to decide and report on its character. Of all the inspectors, I do not know one who has obtained the appointment because of his experience, his love of the work, or of his peculiar fitness for it. I do not find fault with the men: I have before spoken in their praise. I do not however consider that they are so well qualified for the situations as zealous, experienced teachers would be; neither is it fair to the profession that its honourable and lucrative posts should be seized by clergymen and lawyers, or young gents born to be squires. But it is idle to attempt to reason in a matter in which reason is set aside, and naught but privilege and patronage prevails."[1]

To this complaint the Report of the Commission made reply that no schoolmaster in a primary school, however good at his work, had the necessary qualifications for the inspectorate, seeing that he would not be able to meet school managers on their own ground. The Commissioners were

[1] *Newcastle Commission*, vol. v, p. 397.

in the main right, although the specific reason they gave was a poor one. Breadth of vision and a wide culture were necessary in the inspectors of a developing educational system, and not mere professional skill.

England was fortunate in the majority of her early inspectors, and owes a great debt of gratitude to men like Moseley, who did valuable service in guiding the policy of the Education Committee. It is interesting to notice that the teachers on the whole had respect, if not liking, for the inspectors, a strong contrast to their attitude after the institution of "payment by results", which degraded the offices of teacher and inspector alike. As the status of the profession was raised, the avenues to higher forms of educational service were opened up, and this particular grievance tended to disappear, although "patronage and privilege" still live on in some departments of educational life.

The way in which the findings of the Newcastle Commission appealed to the general public is shown by the following extracts from an article in the *Edinburgh Review*.

"To justify these grants (i.e. for pupil teachers and Queen's Scholars) it must be assumed that in this matter of public education all the natural laws of demand and supply are to be inverted, and that there is one calling in life, of essential utility to the well-being of society, to which young men and women will not devote themselves in sufficient numbers without a large encouragement or bounty from the nation. It would further appear that although this calling is by no means repulsive or unremunerative, these young persons so trained to it at the public expense are only to be retained in it by an addition of about 20 per cent. to their salaries from the public Treasury."[1]

The article expatiates on the high standard of education given to the teachers, and continues: "But is this class of highly accomplished schoolmasters, fresh from training col-

[1] *Edinburgh Review*, No. 231, pp. 22, 23.

leges, which certainly surpass in many practical respects our highest public schools, exactly the class of men best adapted to the instruction of children under ten years of age in the first steps of human knowledge? The Commissioners reply in the negative. They are perfect in all respects *except that of teaching the junior classes,* including 75 per cent. of the scholars, those rudiments which are most needed. So that the whole system of the Committee of Council on Education lands us in this absurd result—that we have created at a vast expense a body of men and women so superior to their station in life and to their humble work that they cannot subsist without a vote in aid of their incomes from Parliament and the Privy Council, and that they do not perform with effect the drudgery of teaching very young children to spell and to cypher".[1]

The growing pains of English elementary education were mistaken for a chronic disease, and a drastic remedy was applied. The Revised Code restored efficiency in the drudgery of teaching the "three R's", but it ruthlessly destroyed the culture which was slowly creeping into the schools of the people. On the work of the training colleges its results were disastrous. In spite of all their deficiencies, they had been reaching out towards a liberal cultivation of the teacher. For the next twenty years they were sullenly to restrict themselves to mechanical taskwork, narrow in scope and low in standard.

BIBLIOGRAPHY

COMMITTEE OF COUNCIL ON EDUCATION. Minutes and Inspectors' Reports.
Newcastle Commission. General Report, Reports of Assistant Commissioners, Digest of Evidence, Answers to Questions, 1861.

[1] *Edinburgh Review*, No. 231, p. 24.

J. KAY-SHUTTLEWORTH. *Public Education as affected by the Minutes of the Committee of Privy Council from* 1846 *to* 1852, London, 1853.
—— *Four Periods of Public Education.*

DERWENT COLERIDGE. *The Education of the People* (A letter to the Hon. Sir John Coleridge), London, 1861.
—— *The Teachers of the People: a Tract for the Times*, London, 1862.

T. ADKINS. *History of St John's College, Battersea.*

T. H. WARD (ed.). *The Reign of Queen Victoria,* 2 vols., London, 1887.

CONGREGATIONAL BOARD OF EDUCATION. *Crosby Hall Lectures on Education*, London, 1848 (especially Lecture 4).
—— *Tracts on Popular Education*, London, n.d.

E. BAINES. *Address at Breakfast of Congregational Union of England and Wales at Manchester, October* 11th, 1862, London, 1867.

W. F. RICHARDS. *Manual of Method*, London, 1854.

SOCIETY OF ARTS, MANUFACTURES AND COMMERCE. Lectures in connection with Educational Exhibition, 1854. *The Necessity of an Extended Education for the Educator*, by G. E. L. Cotton, London, 1855.

H. S. SKEATS. *Results of Government Education*, London, 1857.
—— *Popular Education in England*, London, 1861.

A. JONES. *The Principles of Privy Council Legislation*, Edinburgh and London, 1859.

NASSAU W. SENIOR. *Suggestions on Popular Education*, London, 1861.

Edinburgh Review, No. 231, 1861.

Quarterly Review, No. 220, 1861.

CHAPTER VII

THE WORK OF THE TRAINING
COLLEGES, 1860–1900

THE Revised Code of 1861, which followed upon the Report of the Newcastle Commission, brought about an almost complete change in the regulations governing the work of the training colleges and the certification of teachers, and it will be convenient to devote the first portion of this chapter to a summary account of the administrative changes brought about by that measure.

Schools were to suffer a loss of grant if there was not a pupil teacher for every forty scholars after the first fifty, but the old indenture, which bound the apprentice directly to the teacher, was to be abolished. In future the managers were to make their own agreements with pupil teachers, neither the teacher nor the Education Department being a party to the transaction. The agreement was to be terminable by either party at six months' notice, and the pupil teacher's wages were to be settled in the agreement, and not laid down by a regulation from the central authority. The pupil teacher was not to teach for more than six hours on any day, or thirty hours a week.[1] At the end of his apprenticeship he was to be free to choose his profession, and entitled to a testimonial from the Committee of Council to assist him in getting any sort of employment he pleased. If he elected to become a teacher, there were three courses open. He could take up a position as assistant in a school, or become a Queen's Scholar at a normal school; or become provisionally certificated for work in a small rural school.[2] This provi-

---

[1] Committee of Council, Circular 573, p. 5.
[2] Committee of Council, Minutes, 1861–2, Revised Code, 90 (the references are to paragraphs in the Code).

sional certificate was to be cancelled when the teacher attained the age of twenty-five unless it had been confirmed by the passing of the regular certificate examination.[1]

A "normal school" was to include "a college for boarding, lodging and instructing candidates for the office of teacher in schools for the labouring classes", and "a practising department, in which they may learn the exercise of their profession".[2] The only grants that would be paid by the State were to be annual, no more money being paid for the building, enlarging, improving or fitting up of training college premises.[3] These annual grants were to be paid in respect of certificated teachers on the staff, lecturers qualified for special grant by examination, and Queen's Scholars.[4] The grants in respect of Queen's Scholars, which formed the chief source of income of most of the colleges, were henceforth to be administered on a "payment by results" system, according to the standard attained in annual examinations, which were to be held at the end of one year and two years of residence. No student was to be eligible for examination unless he had completed a year's residence, and every Queen's Scholar was to be presented. For the first-year examination the grants varied between £20 and £13 per student, according to the class obtained, and for the second-year examination between £24 and £16.[5] Practising schools were to receive grants on exactly the same conditions as any other schools (i.e. payment according to results of individual examination).[6] No grants would be paid to a training college unless the Committee of Council were satisfied with its premises, management and staff.[7]

The Queen's Scholarships were thrown open to other candidates than those who passed the appropriate examination. Assistants of three years' standing were eligible for

[1] Committee of Council, Minutes, 1861–2, Revised Code, 132.
[2] *Ibid.* 94.   [3] *Ibid.* 95.   [4] *Ibid.* 96.
[5] *Ibid.* 119–23.   [6] *Ibid.* 96.   [7] *Ibid.* 97.

such scholarships without examination, as well as certificated teachers who had received not more than a year of training.[1] Training college students who had completed their first year, whether they held scholarships or not, could receive Queen's Scholarships for a further year provided they passed well enough in the first-year examination.[2] Special scholarships were available to pupil teachers, and to young women over eighteen years of age, for the purpose of training as teachers of infants. Such scholarships were available for a year, and might be obtained by pupil teachers without examination.[3]

The certificates were to be of four classes, and no certificates were to be issued above the fourth class, which was to include the special certificate for infants' teachers.[4] The certificate examination was to be open to training college students of at least a year's standing, and to acting teachers who were over twenty-two years of age, and who had either been pupil teachers or had been favourably reported upon twice by the inspector.[5] The certificated teacher was to be upon probation for two years after obtaining the certificate, and after this period was over, the class of the certificate might be raised at intervals of five years on recommendation by the inspectors. In order to check the roaming tendencies of teachers, which formed a frequent cause of complaint, there was to be no revision if more than one move had been made during the five years.[6] The certificates were no longer to carry "augmentations of salary", and the teachers had to make their own bargains with managers. Since the grants to the managers were now dependent on examination results, it meant in practice that the teacher's salary was largely determined by his success in cramming pupils for the annual inspector's examination.

[1] Committee of Council, Minutes, 1861–2, Revised Code, 108.
[2] *Ibid.* 115. [3] *Ibid.* 116. [4] *Ibid.* 67.
[5] *Ibid.* 72. [6] *Ibid.* 73–77.

The syllabus for the certificate examination was simplified. To quote an official statement, "The main features of the alterations are these: excision of the more ambitious parts of the original scheme, and the insertion of some particulars which will more specially require cultivation of the power of memory, facility in mental calculation, a close attention to English composition, and some knowledge of economy, political, social and sanitary".[1] In the syllabus for the first year Church history was excluded, and mathematics was lightened by the exclusion of algebra and the reduction of the number of books of Euclid to be studied from four to two. Additions to the syllabus were repetition from memory, mental arithmetic, exercises in writing English and more fully examined English grammar, the working of geometrical "riders", some knowledge of social economy, sanitary precautions and the "science of common things". The syllabus for the second year was drastically cut down by the omission of physical science, mechanics, higher mathematics, English literature, and Latin. The second-year examination demanded a higher standard in the subjects studied in the first year, rather than the study of new subjects.[2]

The new regulations for grant came as a blow to the training college authorities, but worse was to follow. By Minutes of March 21st, 1863, the whole scheme of payment of grant to training colleges, as set out in the Code of 1861, was swept away. The new scheme was complicated by provisions intended to mitigate the hardships of a transition period, but its essence was that the payment of grant to the colleges was to be retrospective, and was to depend, not upon the results of the annual examinations, but upon the number of certificated teachers in the schools who had been trained in the colleges. The scheme was designed to work in its full simplicity in 1868, when a college would receive as

[1] Committee of Council, Minutes, 1862–3, p. 203.
[2] *Ibid.* pp. 203–4.

grant £20 for each man, or £14 for each woman, who had received two years of training in the college, and had, since 1863, completed probation and become a certificated teacher. The annual grant was not to exceed 75 per cent. of the annual expenditure of the college, nor to exceed £50 for each man and £35 for each woman in residence as students. The number of students trained was not to exceed that for which accommodation had been provided in 1862.

By the same set of minutes Queen's Scholarships were abolished. Candidates for admission to the training colleges were to be examined by an inspector. No grant was to be paid for students who did not stay for two years, and the training college authorities were advised to guard themselves against loss by written agreements with the students. An exception was made in the case of students taking infant school training, in respect of whom half the normal grant was payable for one year's training.[1]

The Revised Code meant that the idealism in education that had been developing during the preceding twenty years was replaced by a sordid materialism. It replaced an administration of encouragement by one of threats, and placed reliance upon the lowest motives. The spirit of the Code was well exemplified by an inspector's remarks on the defects in the teaching of arithmetic in the training colleges, and the right way to bring about a remedy. "I am afraid the financial condition of normal schools will scarcely admit of the immediate application of a remedy suggested by the method of dealing with elementary schools. A deduction of one-tenth of the Government subsidy for defective teaching in arithmetic might, however, be looked for in the future, if the standard of proficiency does not rise. If your Lordships were only to intimate the possibility of such a proposal being entertained, I dare say there will not be any opportunity of enforcing it. Difficulties which seem insurmountable some-

[1] Committee of Council, *Report*, 1862–3, pp. xliv–xlvii.

times are overcome."[1] The gentleman finds himself rather in the position of the schoolmaster who has punished to the full for offences already committed, and finds himself in a disciplinary emergency powerless because the screw has eached the limit of its travel. The training colleges having been reduced to dire poverty by the new administration, the only solution he can offer for the remedying of a defect is the threat of a punishment made in the hope that the bluff will not be called. To such depths had English educational administration fallen in the sixties.

The effect of the Revised Code upon the colleges was disastrous. The number of pupil teachers in proportion to the number of pupils in the schools dropped enormously. Where formerly there had been authorisation for one pupil teacher to fifty children, now there was one allowed for ninety. In 1861 the ratio of pupil teachers to scholars actually obtaining was 1:56; in 1866 it was 1:96. During this same period the number of schools under inspection had increased by 1350, whilst the pupil teachers had diminished in number by 4423.[2] The situation was put into a nutshell by Tufnell giving evidence to Sir John Pakington's Committee: "The whole pupil teacher system is now in danger of being upset, and with it that of the training schools; and if you upset those two things you bring back education to the state in which it was 25 years ago, and all the labour which has been undergone, and the four millions of money which has been expended on that office during the last quarter of a century will be rendered useless".[3]

There was, moreover, a high proportion of wastage among pupil teachers, especially boys, during the apprenticeship period. Other occupations offered better inducements, with the result that the schools often lost the most valuable years

[1] Committee of Council, *Report*, 1865–6, p. 412.
[2] British and Foreign School Society, *Annual Report*, 1867, p. 3.
[3] *Ibid.*

of the pupil teachers' services. An attempt was made to check this by a Minute of February 20th, 1867, which established extra grants for schools in respect of pupil teachers who passed on to training colleges. "The extra grant offered by the Minute", it was stated in the Blue Book, "comes in aid of the increasing expense of the later years of a pupil teacher's service, and we entertain a confident hope that the prospect of obtaining a share of it will help to retain apprentices in their schools, and to stimulate both them and their masters in vigorously applying themselves to the lessons out of school hours whereby these prizes are to be earned."[1]

The basis of the Code was frankly economic rather than educational. Education, like industry, was to be stimulated by free competition. The laws of supply and demand were to be allowed to operate freely. The salary of the teacher was to represent his market value. The college-trained teacher had to prove his superior ability in competition with all others in the field, and thus the value of a college training might be gauged. Unfortunately free competition may favour the cheapest instead of the best, and in a small school an untrained teacher might prove a better business proposition for the managers than a trained teacher, and many managers were forced now to look at the question of staffing mainly from this standpoint. There were some who demanded the abolition of certification of the teacher as an essential qualification for the earning of grant, but that suggestion was resisted even by the officials who supported the Revised Code, since such a measure would soon throw back very many small schools to the "dame-school" stage.[2]

The immediate effect of the Revised Code on the colleges was a marked decrease in the number of entrants, as is

---

[1] Committee of Council, *Report*, 1866–7, pp. ix–xi.
[2] *Ibid.* 1864–5, p. xix.

shown by the following table relating to fourteen training colleges:

Year	Number of applicants for admission	Number admitted
1860	617	529
1861	650	509
1862	650	489
1863	632	542
1864	427	370
1865	341	316
1866	371	340[1]

In 1862 the total number of students in training colleges was 2972; in 1866 it was 2403.[2] In 1862 there were 2513 candidates for admission to all the training colleges; in 1866 the number was 1584.[3] In every college the numbers dropped. In 1866 there were only sixty-eight students at the Borough Road, where there was accommodation for 100,[4] and in 1867 they fell to sixty-three.[5] Some colleges, Highbury and Chichester, for instance, were forced to close.

This decrease in the number of applicants for the training colleges was partly due to the reduction in the number of pupil teachers, partly to the fact that ex-pupil teachers of ability could often do as well for themselves without college training as those who had been thus trained, and partly in the diminution of the attractiveness of the teaching profession as a result of the Revised Code. It was felt that the teacher had definitely lost status under the new administration, having become the servant of the managers instead of a servant of the State. Quite erroneously the teachers had tended to regard themselves as belonging to a branch of the Civil Service, and now any pretence to such a status was

[1] Committee of Council, *Report*, 1865–6, p. 399.

[2] J. Kay-Shuttleworth, *Memorandum on Popular Education*, 1868, pp. 26–7.   [3] *Ibid.*

[4] British and Foreign School Society, *Annual Report*, 1866, p. 2.

[5] *Ibid.* 1867, p. 2.

out of the question. The teachers rightly felt that the Committee of Council had broken trust with them in the matter of augmentations to salary following certification, and their "lachrymose and peevish tone"[1] acted as a deterrent to those who contemplated taking up the work. Salaries were distinctly lower for a number of years after 1861. In that year the average salary of a schoolmaster was £94. 4s. 7d., in addition to which about 50 per cent. of the masters were provided with houses or lodgings. In 1864 the corresponding figure was £88. 19s. 5d., the same proportion being provided with residence.[2]

Financially the training colleges were very hard hit. In 1859 more than 80 per cent. of the expenses of some of the colleges had been met by Government grant (at Cheltenham 94 per cent. were so met).[3] Under the new *régime* the grant could not exceed 75 per cent., and might be less. The whole of the financial risk was thrown on the colleges, whose authorities were placed at the mercy of the students, who might refuse to take up schools except on their own terms, thus causing their colleges to lose grant until they eventually became settled. There was a real danger that the training colleges might be turned from their true function. Under such economic pressure there was a temptation to take in paying students to the exclusion of better qualified candidates, not troubling whether they intended to teach at all, the colleges thus becoming boarding schools with occasional prospective teachers earning grant.[4] Financial hardship of this kind, coupled with a dearth of entrants, and those of a low standard, meant a period of reaction and retrogression in the work of the training colleges throughout the country.

Kay-Shuttleworth, who saw in the Revised Code the destruction of much that he had striven for during the

[1] Committee of Council, *Report*, 1863–4, p. 310.
[2] *Ibid.* 1864–5, p. xviii.   [3] *Ibid.* 1859–60, p. 289.
[4] See Appendix.

previous quarter-century, summarised its effects on the supply and training of teachers thus:

"The whole system of public aid has been shaken to its very centre and the Managers of Schools have been discouraged—the emoluments of the teacher have been lessened, and his hopes disappointed. Pupil teachers are therefore scarce, and are easily attracted to other employment. Their education is not well cared for, because it has ceased to be the interest of the principal teacher; their qualifications at the end of their five years' engagement are much lower than formerly. The Training Colleges have an insufficient supply of inferior students, who pass a lower examination for their certificates, but even though thus imperfectly qualified, they are not trained in greater numbers than are required to supply the annual waste. The extension even of a deteriorated system of instruction is impeded by the effect of the Revised Code in discouraging the apprenticeship, and the supply of Students to Training Colleges".[1]

The system laid down in 1863 proved impracticable, and there was another set of administrative changes in the "New Code" of 1871. The original four classes of certificate were now reduced to three, with a scale for changing the classification of the old certificates to fit in with the new arrangement. No certificate was to be given originally above Class 2, which was awarded to those placed in the first three divisions in the examination, and certificates were eligible for revision only at intervals of ten years, when the teacher's record was taken into account. The Third Class Certificate was reserved for those who only obtained a pass in the fourth division. Holders of such certificates were not eligible to be in charge of pupil teachers, and the class of the certificate could only be raised by re-examination.[2]

[1] J. Kay-Shuttleworth, *Memorandum on Popular Education*, pp. 29–30.
[2] Committee of Council, *Report*, 1871–2, New Code, 53–58.

The Minutes of 1863 had restricted grant to the training colleges to students who had been two years in training, but even yet it was found impossible to induce enough students to stay for more than a year. As a concession, by the New Code of 1871 the colleges were to receive half grant for one-year students until 1873,[1] and in a circular sent to the principals of the colleges it was stated that the Education Department made the concession with great reluctance, and only to help the colleges to cope with the great demand for teachers which had resulted from the establishment of School Boards by the Act of 1870. The system of deferred grants was abolished, and the term "Queen's Scholar" was revived to apply to any student passing the entrance examination and gaining admittance to a training college.

The "New Code" mitigated a number of evils of the "Revised Code", and the colleges settled down to the humdrum business of gaining passes at the annual examinations. The concession with regard to one-year students was welcomed, and when the "boom" caused by the growth of Board Schools subsided, the principle of two years' training became gradually established. So great was the demand for teachers that the standard for a pass in the certificate examination was reduced still further, and the admission of acting teachers to certificate was made still easier, so that in 1874 any efficient acting schoolmaster over thirty-five, and any schoolmistress over thirty, could be certificated without examination.[2] Pupil teachers received more encouragement, and failure to employ a certain proportion of pupil teachers to scholars resulted in loss of grant,[3] whilst in 1877 the period of apprenticeship was reduced to four years.[4] On the other hand a higher standard of adult assistance in the schools was insisted upon. In 1877 there were to be not more than

[1] New Code, 1871, 87, 88.   [2] New Code, 1874, 59.
[3] New Code, 1871, 32 (c).
[4] New Code, 1877, 70 footnote.

three pupil teachers to each adult certificated teacher in a school,[1] and in 1880 the proportion was reduced to 2:1.[2]

The maintenance of the standard of the certificate examination was rendered difficult by the Government's insistence upon certification as a condition of grant, and certification to a large degree became a mere matter of administration instead of an instrument for raising the status of the teaching profession. The situation was clearly put in the Education Committee's Blue Book of 1866, in a report by Cowie, one of the inspectors. "As it is said the Revised Code enabled the present system of State aid to voluntary effort to continue some years longer, so I believe the reduction of the examination for teachers' certificates has permitted the maintenance of certificate qualification for Government aid. This certificate question seems to slumber for a while, but it will assuredly come up again. As the keystone of the training system, I hope it will be maintained, but I cannot conceal from myself that the failure in the supply of trained masters is a very great blow to it; for the increasing difficulty of finding suitable persons to fill vacancies in schools will add to the number of those who are opposed to the condition of the certificate."[3]

Unfortunately the reduction in the demands of the examination did not mean that more enlightened methods were followed in the colleges, and that the little demanded was better known. The narrowness of the scope of the examination merely emphasised the narrowness of the training college "grind". In the examinations rote work was done well, but questions demanding thought and the application of intelligence were generally answered badly. Coaching for the examinations was barefaced. In 1874 the examiners in English reported: "The favourite questions selected to be

[1] New Code, 1877, 70 footnote.
[2] New Code, 1880, 70 (*g*).
[3] Committee of Council, *Report*, 1866–7, pp. 394, 395.

answered are those which refer to the life or writings of the poet studied. This gives the opportunity for the insertion of some essay which really may have nothing whatever of the student's own about it. The students of one college, almost without exception, wrote out an essay which they must all have evidently learnt off by heart. The students of another college did, many of them, the same thing".[1] In geography the tale was the same. "The chief defects in all the answers from all colleges is their mechanical character. Indeed, so very close is the similarity in the answering of the students of each college, and so distinct generally is that answering from that of the other colleges, that I would hesitate much before I could charge any two students with copying. The students slavishly reproduce their knowledge in the mechanical way in which it is fashionable to give it at their college. I should say that there is much geography taught at our colleges, but not much intelligently."[2] Thus the Revised Code brought about its logical result. By exalting "payment by results" as the supreme principle in national education, it lowered the standard of the education of the teacher, it paralysed the earlier enthusiasm of the training colleges, it restricted their curricula, and put a premium on mechanical methods of defeating the examiner.

There were some who preferred the cramming of a text-book to the previously more prevalent lecture system. In 1864 one of the inspectors noted that lecturing and note-taking were being widely replaced by study from text-books, treated largely in a catechetical manner, and commended the change. "A well-read text-book, and frequent oral and written examinations on different portions of it, will be a much more efficient means of imparting knowledge than the 'segnior irritatio' of the lecture, doled out in mournful slowness, and imperfectly registered in a note-book, which when full was

[1] Committee of Council, *Report*, 1874–5, p. 233.
[2] *Ibid.* p. 234.

sometimes carefully put away for ever, sometimes consulted, if legible, but seldom was more than a crude outline distorted and disjointed."[1]

Be that as it may, the picture presented of the methods of instruction in the reminiscences of former training college students in the *Report* of the Board of Education for 1912–13 is one of almost unbroken aridity and sterility, although here and there grateful reference is made to the illuminating and stimulating teaching of an occasional tutor. The "text-book-cum-catechism" method appealed less to the student than to the inspector. The following is a description of the method in action given by a man who was trained in a provincial college about 1871.

"I use the term 'lectures', for thus was the teaching described, but I must take exception to it altogether, for with two exceptions... the instruction was entirely the text-book with notes dictated to and copied by each student. The Principal's Holy Scripture, Liturgy and English were simply the text and notes often gathered together then and there, and with, I am sure, little or no preparation.... The Third Master's Geography was purely the getting up of several pages of the textbook, and being questioned upon them. We drew what maps we thought most useful. The only Geography lecture he ever gave us was on 'the tides' at the annual inspection of H.M. Inspector. So good was it that I took copious notes, and was afterwards reprimanded for my inattention. Like little boys we were expected to 'look at teacher.'"[2]

James Runciman, in a book of scholastic reminiscences, describes the work of his history tutor when he was a student at a training college. "He took his seat with a determined air: indeed he always began his work as though he were about to engage in a prize-fight. The men squatted in the

[1] Committee of Council, *Report*, 1864–5, pp. 324, 325.
[2] Board of Education, *Report*, 1912–13, p. 58.

dingy theatre like a set of charity-boys and awaited the first question. Then the tutor began with a resolute monotonous snuffle, 'What event happened on September 25th, 1066? Hands up those who know'. Then the 'men' held up their hands in a childish way." This mode of direct questioning was varied by asking for words omitted to be supplied, and written tests on slips of paper. "Repetez sans cesse" was the tutor's avowed motto. And yet "the man who organised the silly torture was a sound historical student, and no one knew better than he did the exact lines which an intelligent teacher should follow. His voice would tremble with pleasure when he praised a man who dared to strike out boldly and write an original answer, but he was cramped; the precious departmental system crippled him, and he passed the best years of his life in starving the minds of some of the cleverest young men in England".[1]

Dr MacNamara had a good tale to tell of the same tutor. "We had got to the last page (of the text-book of dates) and one after the other we were repeating to Mr Curtis events chronicled as happening upon the given dates on that page. The book wound up with its final date something like this: '1870. May 1st. Outbreak of Franco-German War'. The man who had successfully recited this very last date upon this very last page had barely sat down when up sprang his next neighbour quite mechanically with 'Printed and published for C. J. Curtis, B.A., by Smith and Son, Stamford Street, S.E.'"[2]

It was the Golden Age of the writer of "potted" text-books which contained much matter compressed into small space, and which might serve conveniently as the basis of constant questioning. As another reminiscence records, "Students were considered well grounded in English, history, grammar, etc., if they were word perfect in dates, facts

[1] James Runciman, *Schools and Scholars*, 1887, pp. 142 et seq.
[2] T. J. MacNamara, *New Liberal Review*, September, 1903.

or definitions laid down in the small textbooks which had been compiled with unflagging industry by their teacher. There was absolutely no encouragement towards wider reading, and only the boldest students dared to venture for themselves. 'Literature' was practically confined to memorising the lines for recitation demanded by the Government syllabus and examined by the Government Inspectors".[1]

In the training colleges, as in the schools, the effect of the Science and Art Department's grants was by no means all to the good. The college authorities saw in these grants a help towards the solution of their financial difficulties, and often time was spent in a very arid study of science, quite unconnected with experimentation by the students, which might have been expended more profitably on subjects of more direct use to the teacher in his profession. The sort of work done in chemistry is thus described by a student: "No student ever did any practical work. Certain operations were performed before a large class, the members of which were assured by the teacher that the results were of such-and-such a nature; all of which had to be verified later from cheap text-books and memorised for after use by the students themselves....For several days before the Science Examinations became due, the teacher, with characteristic energy and persistence, prepared a number of questions covering the Government syllabus and requiring short answers (equations, sketches of apparatus, etc., etc.) which were written on slates and corrected red-hot. When the results were issued it was no uncommon thing to find that there were no failures, and that nearly every candidate was credited with a 'First Class' Certificate (!) for Chemistry".[2]

The Science and Art Department's grants offered a temptation that is inherent in any system of "payment by results". In some colleges it was the custom to pay the lecturers in science no fixed salaries, but to leave them free to choose

[1] Board of Education, *Report*, 1912–13, p. 53.   [2] *Ibid.*

the subjects they would teach, letting them draw as their stipends the grants thus earned. The result was that the lecturers became expert at "spotting winners" among the science subjects, and their syllabuses were not based on educational considerations, but were composed of the subjects in which it was easiest to obtain passes in the examinations of the Science and Art Department.[1] This abuse was aggravated by the fact that many of the lecturers had no scientific qualifications. Some colleges were much better than others in this respect, and the best work was done in London, where it was possible for lecturers to attend the courses at South Kensington.

The bookish training of most of the lecturers made them slow to appreciate the true scientific attitude. T. H. Huxley described as typical his experience with a training college lecturer who came to study at South Kensington. "One most admirable and worthy man, a clergyman, who came up for the sole purpose of qualifying himself to be the teacher of a class, when he was put to look through the microscope for the first time and saw the corpuscles of blood through the microscope, said to my demonstrator, 'Why, these are exactly like the things in Professor Huxley's book'; that there should be in reality before him what he had seen in the book appeared to be a revelation to him."[2]

The Royal Commission on Technical Education in 1884 gave some attention to the teaching of science and art in the training colleges, and the verdict was one of thorough condemnation. "The teaching of art and science subjects in the training colleges of Great Britain for elementary school teachers is very defective.... The answers received by the examiners to such questions as the following—'Write out the heads of a lecture to an elementary class on the chemical and physical qualities of water, mentioning the experiments

[1] Royal Commission on Technical Education, vol. III, p. 384.
[2] *Ibid.* p. 331.

which you would show, and your object in showing them', prove conclusively that the students have no idea as to how such a simple matter ought to be brought before a class."[1]

The trouble was partly due to the lack of qualified lecturers, and partly to the inefficiency of the supervision exercised by the Science and Art Department, which worked independently of the Education Department. By the end of the century things had improved considerably, largely through the steady increase in the number of better qualified lecturers in science. The influence of the work of the Normal School of Science at South Kensington and of the rapidly developing modern university colleges was more and more felt, and it was from institutions such as these that the training college lecturers in science came to be recruited.

The actual training in teaching given by the colleges continued to be unsatisfactory in many ways. In general they still clung to the "practising" or "model" school system, which suffered from the inherent failing that a practising school could never be a model, and a real "model school" was a static thing, often little related to the reality that the teacher would have to face when he left college. It was this consideration which gave point to a "suggestion" put forward by an inspector. "I might perhaps offer the following suggestion of an ideal model school, which would be a great advantage to any training school. Let a number of children be collected together in an inconvenient room, payments and attendance uncertain, cleanliness disregarded at first, discipline bad, ignorance total. Let this by some model process be transformed, so that in a short time the payments and attendance become regular, cleanliness of person and clothing be enforced till they become the rule, discipline exact, kind but strict, and real progress made in elementary religious knowledge, reading, writing and arithmetic."[2]

[1] Royal Commission on Technical Education, vol. I, p. 526.
[2] Committee of Council, *Report*, 1861–2, p. 310.

Educational institutions are slow to give up traditional methods, and it was only gradually that practice in special schools gave way to practice in ordinary schools under everyday conditions. It is recognised to-day that whilst the "demonstration school" has its place in a system of training, and an experimental school is an important institution in connection with a developing pedagogy, the best practical training that can be given is directed teaching experience in an ordinary school. The movement away from the exclusive use of the model school starts in the period under consideration in this chapter. Some of the smaller provincial colleges were forced to resort to using local schools for practice through lack of model school accommodation, whilst Edge Hill adopted this system from the outset with gratifying results. The British and Foreign School Society made a habit of using students from Stockwell as "supply" teachers in their schools, but this practice was not looked upon with favour by the Education Department.[1] It was the advent of the day training college which did more than anything else to modify the old model school system. Unequipped with model schools, indeed often without any accommodation peculiarly their own, they were forced to look to surrounding schools for their practising grounds, and so another barrier between the training college and the world was gradually broken down.

The practical work of the colleges had never been characterised by any great breadth of vision, but in the years following the institution of the Revised Code training in teaching was often little more than training in obtaining passes at the inspector's examination. In 1864 teaching practice at Liverpool was unblushingly arranged to this end, earning inspectoral commendation rather than blame. When the annual inspection of the practising schools took place, all the students were present to familiarise them with the

[1] Committee of Council, *Report*, 1871–2, vol. I, p. 205.

ordeal. In her practice, each student began in the infant schools, instructing a class in one subject for three weeks. She then passed on to Standard 1 or 2 in the girls' school, and taught another subject for three weeks. After this came preparation for a half-yearly trial examination, in which each student was held responsible for the success of twenty or thirty pupils in two subjects. Whenever a student passed from one class to another, the children were formally examined by the mistress of method. Once a year there was a complete reproduction of an inspector's examination, and the students had to carry through all the formalities of the business. In order to prepare them for the non-teaching duties of a schoolmistress, each student in her second year was served out with a set of registers—admission book, "summary", and two class-rolls—and she had to keep the necessary records of two classes. Each student kept her own log book.[1]

Such very elaborate organisation for training in "Revised Code teaching" was uncommon, but every college manifested the same spirit and purpose in its professional training. The Liverpool scheme had the merit of being intimately connected with the realities of the teacher's life, and its ingenuity and thoroughness were deserving of a better object; but there was no justification for the barefaced cramming for the lesson to be given before the inspector, which was common in most of the colleges. Such a lesson is bound to be somewhat strained in its atmosphere, under the most favourable circumstances, but the carefully "got-up" lessons were a constant source of annoyance to the inspectors whose hard lot it was to listen to them. The typical "inspector's lesson" was thus described by one of the inquisitors:

"A class of children suddenly confronted with elaborate diagrams and illustrations of the pump or the barometer (two favourite subjects with students) can hardly be expected

[1] Committee of Council, *Report*, 1864–5, pp. 403, 404.

to do more than sit and listen and admire, while the teacher, like the blessed Glendoveer, has the talking all to himself. With the exception of one or two sharp scholars, they act as dummies. It is not to them, so much as to the Government Inspector, that the lesson is addressed, upon whose mind the student-teacher is naturally anxious to produce the most favourable impression. For him, more than for the children, the lesson with its scheme, evolution, illustrations and recapitulations is intended. But this gives a painful air of unreality to the performance, because a lesson in which the class drops, as it were, out of view, is very much like the play of Hamlet with the part of Hamlet omitted".[1]

Often the notes of the "show" lessons were in effect prepared by the normal master or mistress, and it was no uncommon thing to find that the actual delivery of the lesson had been carefully rehearsed beforehand. The result was that there was no correlation between the results in the test lesson and the teaching power manifested later in the regular routine of school. "Date and Fact" teaching naturally became the order of the day, since it was that type of teaching alone which could be measured by the inspector's measuring rod when he entered a school to test its "results". Enlightened inspectors might raise a voice in protest, but they rarely had the courage to attack the system whose slaves they were. Sharpe wrote in 1879: "Just as surely as the term 'opaque' used to appear in an object lesson applied equally to an elephant and a thin sheet of paper, so will Pedro-talla-galla appear in a lesson on Ceylon; it is as good a word to conjure with as Mesopotamia; but I have never found that either this mountain, whose mere name takes half a minute to spell out on the blackboard, or a list of the tributaries of the Thames to a Devonshire boy, or the capes of England to a Worcestershire boy, created a very lively interest".[2] All of which is

[1] Committee of Council, *Report*, 1869–70, p. 470.
[2] *Ibid.* 1880–1, p. 495.

very true and very amusing. But there is a law known as
the law of supply and demand which holds good in the
economics of education, as well as in commerce. Where had
the demand for Pedro-talla-galla and the capes of England
originated, unless with one of Her Majesty's inspectors?

The attitude of the student to the professional part of his
training at college is well expressed in one of the reminiscences in the Report of the Board of Education previously
mentioned. "I think we looked on them (i.e. professional
activities) all as a nuisance, as an interruption into the main
business of our life there, which was—to us—to do decently
in the Christmas class-lists. The time in the practising schools
we *had* to take seriously, for those schools were conducted
strenuously by their masters, and we 'students' had to take
up the class work just like a permanent Assistant would have
had to do—all the machinery of the place was arranged on
that assumption—and if anyone 'slacked' the master made
himself very nasty to us, and in those days there was an
aloofness in Masters and Tutors which could make their re-
proofs stinging. I don't think that from this we gained anything of what I might call, now, a philosophical character—
I mean, we were never made to think about boys, or subjects
or methods. We were expected 'to fill a class-teacher's
place', to go on from where the last man left off, to go
on in the prescribed way, and to go on at top pressure—
and as that is what we had been doing for five years before
we went there, we didn't think it unnatural; we just didn't
think at all—unless it was to think that the out-of-practising-
school life was much pleasanter."[1]

Undoubtedly most of the ex-pupil teachers came to college
feeling that they knew all that was necessary about practical
teaching, and unfortunately the formality and conventionality
of the pupil teacher training was continued in the colleges.
Notes of lessons were carefully prepared, and then criticised

[1] Board of Education, *Report*, 1912–13, pp. 68, 69.

and cut up by the tutors, whilst in the practising school there was constant close supervision. This pernicious system still lives on in some places where teachers are "trained". Only gradually is it becoming realised that the training of the teacher must be mainly self-training if it is to be successful, and that the young teacher must be allowed to make his own mistakes (and not his tutor's) by teaching his own uncensored lessons. The editing of teaching notes is not merely an irritant to the student; in many cases it kills initiative. In a way it was too much "training" which was responsible for the production of so much mechanical teaching during the latter years of the nineteenth century. No doubt there was more justification for "safety-first" methods then, because of the lower standard of attainment of the students, but "safety first" is a principle that never obtains the highest results in any branch of educational work.

The love of the formal was shown by the way in which the "criticism lesson" lived on as one of the mainstays of training college routine. Students and inspectors alike recognised its inherent weaknesses, yet it continued to flourish, and still lingers on, a hearty nonagenarian. Let us hear what the last-quoted student critic had to say about it. "The 'crit' we took *very* seriously when we had to give it; it was an ordeal, and a nervous man would think of it for days ahead. Our subsequent criticism on him you can easily imagine— about the whole performance there was so much *unreality*, such pompousness, such magnifying of trifles, such missing of the *big* things."[1]

The following is an inspector's opinion. "Something is to be gained, no doubt, from the dissection, under skilful guidance, of a specimen lesson: but I question whether the benefit is not attended with mischievous effects. The tendency of criticism lessons seems to me this,—to fix the student's attention too much on the mere machinery of

[1] Board of Education, *Report*, 1912–13, p. 69.

teaching, and too little on its object and end. They stimulate a finical and pedantic anxiety to be correct in method and form; whereas the grand aim of a teacher should be to penetrate the learner's mind, anyhow, and compared with this, the mechanism of a lesson is a matter of very secondary importance. Let me give an illustration from one of the papers worked in the last Christmas examination. A candidate is asked how a certain subject should be explained to a class of children: her reply is, 'I should make use of the catechetical, picturing-out, exhibitory explanation!' I think that the teaching in after life of this young person would probably be more efficacious if she brought to the task of a village schoolmistress a mind and memory less encumbered with this technical jargon. The characteristic weakness of certificated teachers (a most useful and efficient body) seems to me to be their fanatical belief in machinery. So long as their methods are irreproachable, and their arrangements modelled on the newest and most approved patterns, they have a comfortable assurance that all must go on well; not realising until perhaps some serious breakdown comes to enlighten them, that instruction may be very scientifically organised and yet fail to reach and impress the scholars' minds; in a word, that a thing may be very well taught and yet very ill learnt."[1]

A considerable body of evidence could be brought forward to show that matters were not much improved even at the end of the century, but one further inspector's criticism must suffice. "It (i.e. the criticism lesson) is very like teaching people to use paper and string to make very neat parcels which contain nothing. One would pardon many faults of detail of method if only there were evident the presence of the educative spirit with its vivifying touch on the mind of the learner."[2]

Formalism was the curse of the lectures on "method".

[1] Committee of Council, *Report*, 1869–70, p. 466.
[2] *Ibid.* 1895–6, p. 170.

At the instigation of their lecturers, students gave themselves up to an orgy of pretentious terminology. Great play was made with the necessity to "educe", "deduce", "elicit", "obtain or abstract" knowledge and information from the pupils, and there seemed a living faith in the unfathomable depth of children's knowledge. "The fault lies with the college staff", said one inspector, "and it is high time that they should be told that we may as reasonably expect the Sahara to refresh the parched throat of the traveller at the option of the latter, as expect to get a child to supply *all* the matter of an oral lesson by means of 'Socratic', 'tentative', 'preliminary', 'introductory', 'deductive', 'inductive', 'educive', 'educational', 'recapitulatory' and 'artistic' questions."[1] Other terms bandied about were "mechanical", "experimental", "synthetic", "analytical", "elliptical", "incidental", and "diacritical".

It was in the lectures on education that the lack of broad culture on the part of the average training college lecturer manifested itself. The pretentious always has an attraction for the half-educated, and "education" as a subject of lectures suffered from this plague of terms borrowed from psychology, logic and philosophy, with little understanding and no criticism. Note-taking was as prominent in method lectures as in any other subject, and instruction tended, as elsewhere, to centre around the text-book. Nor was the text-book commonly a full and scholarly one; more often it was a small compendium of undigested psychology and logic mixed with copy-book maxims for budding teachers. Often these petty text-books were committed piecemeal to memory, the tutor turning his lecture periods into "recitations". "The text-book was the Gospel of truth, the compendium of all knowledge, the only complete and infallible guide to the intellectual Valhalla."[2] "Conscientious conventionality"[3]

---

[1] Committee of Council, *Report*, 1881–2, p. 523.
[2] Board of Education, *Report*, 1912–13, p. 60.   [3] *Ibid.*

was the keynote of the lectures on school management, which kept religiously to well-worn paths, uninterested in educational adventure and experiment.

The following are reminiscences of three students, the two first illustrating the common type of school management lectures, the third indicating the good work that might be done by an unpretentious and efficient master of method.

"The 'lectures' were very thin stuff—they were served up every year to successive students, and when men of my time meet now, we can say bits of copy-book headings on 'School Management' which a Monitor could follow with ease,—they *were* poor stuff. As for the Psychology, it was just silly, but it never did us any harm."[1]

"The Method Master's School Management 'took the cake', for it consisted solely of notes lifted bodily from two or three text books and dictated. This was an absolute waste of time, for some of us had read much of this during our apprenticeship, and had the books by us. The Master was also Head of the Practising School, and it was fortunate that most of us had had serious practice in teaching previously, for we learnt none here."[2]

"The Master of Method was, in his day, regarded as at the head of his class. His personality counted for much—every student respected him, and perhaps feared him a little, though his efforts were conspicuous in the sincere desire to uplift the children through the teacher—the teacher, high-minded, well equipped and expert. His lectures were welcomed by the classes and dealt mainly with the practical work in the everyday Elementary School, methods of teaching each subject, plans for organisation, hints on discipline, and the like. Although Psychology was not dealt with *as a subject*, the master was full of suggestion as to mental processes and their development in the Elementary School, from his

[1] Board of Education, *Report*, 1912–13, p. 69.
[2] *Ibid.* p. 59.

own reading and more so from his own intelligent observation and his more than usually fruitful experience."[1]

More amenities were gradually introduced into the general life of the colleges towards the end of the century, but on the whole the life of the training college student continued narrow, strenuous and rather drab. Whilst outside most of the colleges presented a good appearance, poverty and bleakness were the outstanding characteristics within, in spite of what jealous critics might say concerning their "always handsome and usually superfluous accommodation".[2] In the majority of cases there was neither comfort nor privacy. The students slept in dormitories and cubicles. A bathroom was a rare luxury. Interference by inspectors in domestic matters was resented, as is witnessed by the complaint of the Venerable Archdeacon of Bristol to the Cross Commission of the outrageous conduct of an inspector in regard to a women's training college: "He has ordered complete sets of baths for all the students. Now these girls will never see a bath when they leave their training colleges in their future life. It is accustoming them to luxuries and creating a taste which they will not be able to gratify afterwards".[3]

Common rooms, reading rooms and libraries were either absent or very defective. In 1885 only two of the colleges for women had recreation rooms, although by 1893 they were nearly all so provided.[4] Where libraries existed, they rarely contained anything like a reasonable collection of educational works, nor did they provide light reading for leisure moments. More often they were filled with old and "improving" books presented by patrons who saw in the training college an alternative to the jumble sale or the rubbish

[1] Board of Education, *Report*, 1912–13, p. 54.
[2] Lord Fortescue, *Public Schools for the Middle Classes*, 1864, p. 31.
[3] *Cross Commission*, vol. III, p. 183.
[4] Committee of Council, *Report*, 1893–4, p. 156.

heap.[1] In many colleges spare time indoors had to be spent in the classrooms, where reading and letter-writing might struggle on in the midst of a miscellaneous uproar. In some colleges, however, some pains were taken to provide for the students' leisure within the college walls. Concerts and debates were encouraged and flourished. There were a number of excellent college musical societies, and one college was blessed with a "Second Year Brass Band" conducted by the third master.[2] Occasionally a carpenter's shop was provided, but there was rarely any instruction in handicraft.

Often little was done to provide facilities for recreation out-of-doors, although matters improved greatly during the last quarter of the century. Drill was common, generally of a military kind. Occasionally a college had a few odd pieces of gymnastic apparatus, but there was no systematic gymnastic training. Cricket and football were played at most colleges, but playing fields were commonly rough and unsatisfactory. Gardening was almost universal. Some colleges had volunteer companies. In this respect Saltley led the way, followed closely by York, and in time many colleges imitated the example thus set. In women's colleges the chief outdoor recreation was the compulsory daily walk in "crocodile", unsupervised walking being strictly forbidden. On Saturday afternoons, in one college, a number of students were allowed out in the town accompanied by a governess, and they were expected to make purchases for those condemned to remain within the four walls of the college. Dancing and croquet were legitimate occupations. Physical education for women students was limited to military drill of a modified kind under the direction of a sergeant.

Discipline in both men's and women's colleges was strict. A certain amount of self-government was common, monitors

[1] See, for instance, G. A. Christian, *English Education from Within*, 1922, p. 7.
[2] Board of Education, *Report*, 1912–13, p. 57.

being made responsible for good order in dormitories, lecture rooms, during private study periods, and so on. This was an inheritance from early Battersea days. Often there were monitors for special tasks—gas, garden, bell, dining-room monitors. The general disciplinary tone was that of a somewhat inferior boarding school, and certainly was not conducive to the highest type of self-control. The division into "years" which is still so characteristic of training college life manifested itself early as the two-year course became common. Smoking was an offence within college walls—sometimes anywhere within a three-mile limit—but often the practice was indulged in with what was suspiciously like connivance on the part of the authorities. Sunday was generally a free day, and students could visit friends. Generally this freedom was carefully controlled. A common practice was to make the student exercising the privilege write out a solemn statement of the way in which he had spent the Sunday away from college. But more important than official rules and regulations is the inevitable discipline which is inherent in community life. What was said of the Borough Road might have been applied to any of the colleges. "Two years at the Old Borough Road was a fine chastening for any man."[1]

In the women's colleges the strictest propriety was observed. Plainness in dress was insisted upon. A typical regulation reads: "The Ladies' Committee wish it to be distinctly understood by all candidates for admission that they consider neatness and plainness of dress incumbent on those who undertake the instruction and training of the young; and it is the express wish of the Committee that no flowers, ornaments, or other finery should be worn".[2] Bonnets were the regulation headgear for Sunday wear.

Very gradually the "old-maidish" type of discipline in

[1] T. J. MacNamara, *New Liberal Review*, September, 1903.
[2] British and Foreign School Society, *Annual Report*, 1871, p. 9.

the women's colleges gave way to something more rational, as the movement towards feminine independence progressed and the element of patronage disappeared in the attitude of college authorities towards the students. Writing towards the end of the century, Fitch commented on the change. "I have pleasure in recording a distinct gain to the students during the last few years in regard to their own personal freedom, and the cultivation among them of the art of self-government. I found prevalent in some of the colleges petty and unwise rules regulating the dress of the students, requiring them when walking out to march two and two, in procession, as if they were in a girls' boarding school or an asylum, and imposing upon them a needless amount of domestic service. Some of these usages seemed to me to have been deliberately designed many years ago to give to the young people a humble view of their office and to check undue ambition. It may well be doubted whether this intended purpose was ever fulfilled. But it is now generally admitted that, since these young people will ere long be thrown on their own resources, and will be entrusted with the responsibility of managing their own life and disposing of their leisure, they should while at college be trained and accustomed to use as much freedom as is compatible with reasonable discipline. The guarded and sheltered life contemplated for them by the Lady Bountiful of a college committee, a life in which every duty is prescribed, every hour appropriated, and the whole responsibility for thought and for action is taken out of the students' hands, is not altogether a healthy life for young people at the age of 20, who have to be trained for self-government and for the duties of a liberal profession."[1]

The college day became much reduced compared with the heroic days of the forties. The Borough Road had always been a place noted for working its students hard, but the

[1] Committee of Council, *Report*, 1893–4, p. 159.

following "daily round" of 1878 shows some mitigation of pressure, though still a sufficiently heavy routine: 8.0, breakfast; 8.30, prayers; 9–12, classes; 12–1.15, outdoor exercise; 1.15, dinner; 2–5, classes; 5.5, tea; 5.30–6, outdoor exercise; 6–8.30, classes; 8.35, supper; 9.45, prayers.[1]

The question of food always looms large in any residential institution. In general the food in the training colleges seems to have been reasonably good, but often ruined by the carelessness with which it was cooked and served. The authorities of one large training college asked an expert to report on the dietary, and in his report there were these significant remarks: "One may generally judge from the faces round a dining table as well as from the plates when dinner is over, whether the dinner has possessed these essential qualities (i.e. variation, good cooking and good service). May I venture to say that neither the faces nor the plates in the dining hall were suggestive of 'a good dinner'".[2] One college was reported to the Cross Commission as spending no more than sixpence a day per head on food for its students.[3] Beer survived for a long time as the normal beverage both in men's and women's colleges, although it was gradually ousted by tea, milk, and cocoa.

The quality of the students improved only very gradually after the set-back following the institution of the Revised Code. As late as 1876 the average qualifications of students on entry to a training college were thus described: "The average candidate can work the ordinary rules of Arithmetic, but not problems involving rules; he can write out a proposition of Euclid by memory, but cannot employ it intelligently; he knows just enough Algebra to be confused; he can parse an English sentence fairly, and has a very fair knowledge of the bare facts of geography and history; he

[1] British and Foreign School Society, *Annual Report*, 1878, p. 33.
[2] Committee of Council, *Report*, 1881–2, p. 536.
[3] Cross Commission, vol. I, p. 289.

has a slight smattering of a French or Latin vocabulary; he knows the ordinary forms of schoolkeeping".[1] In the same year it was found out by means of a questionnaire that 25 per cent. of training college students had received less than the legal minimum of instruction during apprenticeship.[2] The pupil teachers came up to the colleges with weak bodies and relaxed minds. An inspector said of them: "Their bodily health is often enfeebled, and their answers, especially in a searching viva-voce examination, show that they have been crammed with a vast amount of mental food which they have been utterly unable to assimilate. A pupil teacher of the fourth year told me that one of the reasons which made Magna Charta necessary was 'the increasing deposition of succeeding kings'. She could not the least explain what she meant, and it was some time before I perceived that 'deposition' was put for 'despotism', and 'succeeding' for 'preceding', the amended phrase having evidently been taken from some cram-book. And this is just the complaint made by the principals of our training colleges, that candidates come to them professing to know almost everything, and knowing nothing well. It would be better that half the number of subjects should be thoroughly mastered even if the other half were altogether dropped, rather than they should come with dim, hazy, vague and almost always inaccurate notions of the whole".

The preceding quotation is taken from a book published in 1878 called *The Education Craze*, an attack on popular education in general, and the Board Schools in particular, with special reference to the attainments of the teachers. A number of "awful examples" are given, drawn from authoritative sources, to prove how low was the standard of education of the teacher, and amongst others the following

[1] Committee of Council, *Report*, 1876–7, pp. 685–6.
[2] *Ibid.* p. 686.

answer by a pupil teacher at the end of apprenticeship to a question on "the state of England under the Heptarchy". "People had three meals a day, breakfast, dinner and supper. They retired to rest in a state of nudity and laid on a bed of straw. The Saxons were eminently social, when they drank they would put their tumblers together, very often accompanying it with a kiss, and tell of great exploits of going to the theatres to see the dancing bears."[1] We must not be misled by extreme examples of this type, but there is copious evidence that the average was lamentably low. One training college principal bitterly remarked that the pupil teacher "comes up telling us that he has passed in acoustics, light and heat, and he spells acoustics with two c's".[2] The principal of Bishop Otter's Training College, Chichester, had good opportunities of comparing ex-pupil teachers with students who had followed a more "ladylike" preliminary education, since a special feature of the college was the admission of a number of students of the latter class. Her opinion was that the pupil teachers were not so good as the "ladies". "It is difficult to find the right word, they are less receptive....We cannot do so much with them; they go out nearly as they came in, beyond having learnt a little more by cram."[3]

The teachers that were produced did not come in for quite the same storm of criticism as was levelled against them in the days preceding the Newcastle Commission, but the old accusations of "priggishness" and conceit recur. In the evidence given before the Cross Commission, however, there was only one really eloquent diatribe delivered against the trained teachers, and that was by Mrs Fielden, a friend of education, but a woman with a living faith in her own powers and a conviction of the inefficiency of others. She preferred

[1] "D.C.L." *op. cit.* p. 128.
[2] Cross Commission, vol. I, p. 440.
[3] *Ibid.* vol. I, p. 500.

to bring up under her own eye teachers for the schools established by her husband, a benevolent manufacturer, and to carry out their training in the schools themselves. The ordinary practising or model school was held to be a poor place in comparison, because of the floating staff, and the fact that the children "snapped their fingers" at students. The trained teachers were not desirable persons. They thought themselves "ladies and gentlemen", and as a result were extremely improvident in their manner of living. "A girl leaves the board school a very poor inferior creature, knowing very little indeed. She goes up to a training college, and she comes back, and she knows a lot of grammar; she knows the names of kings and queens; she knows a good deal about analysis, and that is all that she does know, and she comes back exceedingly conceited, so that you cannot manage her. She says, 'Well, I have got my so-and-so from my college; I am a college girl and I want £20 more than anybody else'. That is my experience of a training college."[1]

Such an outburst, however, is exceptional. Probably the trained teachers had less of the irritating self-respect that had marked them before the blight of "payment by results" fell. Certainly they were less enthusiastic, and the energies of the more active were increasingly devoted to the promotion of professional societies and the devising of plans to frustrate Her Majesty's Inspectors of Schools. For the most part the students went out into the schools with a sound technique of managing large numbers of children, with an acquaintance with a few "methods" of teaching various subjects, with a mass of undigested and miscellaneous knowledge, and no ideas at all on the general significance of education, and the true principles underlying it.

The Cross Commission of 1886 was concerned mainly with the national educational system as a whole, with particular reference to the working of the Education Act of 1870,

[1] Cross Commission, vol. II, p. 381.

but some attention was paid to the quality and training of
the teachers. The verdict on the work of the training colleges
was on the whole good. Warburton's description of them as
"an admirable bargain for the country" was endorsed, and
it was pointed out in the report that by means of a denominational training system the country saved 25 per cent.
of the cost of training teachers, and also saved through a
system of private local management.[1] This economic justification of a sectarian system of training teachers is a significant
thing, when it is compared with the religious and moral
justifications that loomed large in earlier discussions. There
is no doubt that the Education Act of 1870 had accustomed
an increasing number of people to think of education as a
secular matter, and this was an important factor in the later
developments of the training system. Just as the Board
Schools stood for secular education, so the day training
colleges came to stand for the secular training of teachers.

Most of the criticisms directed against the colleges were
commonplace. The hours of study were too long. There was
need for a supply of better candidates. The training college
students were not so good at teaching as they should be,
owing to the artificiality of the conditions under which they
practised, but they improved greatly when they started work
in the schools as full-blown teachers. There was too much
"spoon-feeding" of students. It was stated that there were
too many denominations at work in the training college field,
but it is difficult to see how such a criticism could be maintained. Once a system of denominational training of teachers
is recognised, surely any denomination has a perfect right to
establish training colleges. As a matter of fact, the number
of denominations directly concerned with training colleges
was not large. The Church of England had the vast majority
of colleges, the Roman Catholics had several, the Wesleyans
one, the Congregationalists one. There were numerous

[1] Cross Commission, *Final Report*, p. 94.

flourishing sects unrepresented, although many nonconformist bodies were staunch supporters of the British and
Foreign School Society, which had several training colleges.
Actually nonconforming principles were a distinct handicap
to an aspirant to the teaching profession, and it was stated in
the report that there was need for an extension of training
facilities, and that in future grants should be given to any
undenominational colleges that were established.[1]

From the Cross Commission to the end of the century
there is little to record of the work of the residential colleges,
the chief developments being in connection with the day
training colleges, which are considered in the following
chapter. The position was summed up by an inspector in
the Blue Book of 1894–5: "The Education Act of 1870 did
not touch them. While it reacted with much and increasingly
energetic effect upon the buildings and curriculum of the
schools of the country, the training colleges remained outside the influence of the current that was bearing onwards
the elementary schools, and, except in so far as the higher
life of these latter reacted on them by stimulating them into
a higher intellectual activity, they remained quiet, or moved
only very slowly on their own lines".[2]

This does not mean that the training colleges were not
doing highly valuable work along their traditional lines.
They remained the chief instrument of training, and the
quality of their staffs and accommodation improved steadily.
In 1893 provision was made for especially able students to
spend a third year abroad, and a number of such students
spent a year as assistants in foreign normal schools, but the
two-year course was the norm of training college activity.

For some years after the Newcastle Commission it had
been difficult to fill the training colleges with students. The
Act of 1870 had filled the colleges again, and the growth of

[1] Cross Commission, *Final Report*, pp. 94–8.
[2] Committee of Council, *Report*, 1894–5, p. 131.

the Board School system created a steady and increasing demand for teachers. The raising of the school age coupled with the movement for the reduction of numbers in classes enhanced this demand, so that by the end of the century the accommodation afforded by the colleges was inadequate. In 1898 it was stated that the number of candidates passing the Queen's Scholarship examinations was three times as great as the number of vacant places in the colleges,[1] and the disadvantage under which the nonconformist candidate suffered was enhanced. Many who failed to get into college managed to obtain the "acting teacher's certificate", and some obtained sufficient marks in the examination to qualify them to take pupil teachers. Such teachers were, however, deficient in many ways, and, "though strenuous and sincere, failed in fulness and depth, because there was wanting in them the substructure of a sound mental habit and well-developed intellectual attainments".[2]

The whole training system came under the review of a Departmental Committee on the Pupil Teacher System in 1898, although that committee was mainly concerned with the pre-training college stage. It frankly recognised the lack of adequate training college accommodation, and realised that there was little hope that new training colleges would be established through voluntary effort ("only another word for the efforts of the very few").[3] The committee expressed its belief in the residential training college as the best institution for the training of the teacher, whilst admitting that the day training colleges were doing good work, and that it was to the latter that it was necessary to look for any large extension of training college facilities.

In actual fact the main extension of accommodation has taken place in the University Training Departments which grew out of the day training colleges, although a number of

---

[1] Departmental Committee on the Pupil Teacher System, 1898, *Report*, p. 21.   [2] *Ibid.* p. 22.   [3] *Ibid.*

local authorities in the early years of the present century established training colleges of their own, sometimes completely residential, such as Neville's Cross, the women's training college of the Durham County Council, sometimes day colleges with some hostel accommodation, such as the Cheshire County Training College at Crewe.

BIBLIOGRAPHY. See end of next chapter.

APPENDIX

The Training Colleges and Proposals for the Establishment of Public Schools and a University for the Middle Classes

(a) *The "County School" and "County College" Scheme.* In 1864 Earl Fortescue published a book with the title *Public Schools for the Middle Classes*, which embodied a proposal for the establishment of "County Schools" for the sons of farmers and other rural residents, after the model of the great public schools, but with a curriculum more related to the realities of rural life, and "County Colleges" for higher education of a similar type. The author commented on the "notorious unpopularity" of the training colleges (nicknamed "Protestant Maynooths") among the middle classes, and hoped that some of them might be turned into places of general higher education for those classes, one of their functions being the supply of teachers for the "County Schools", which could not look for satisfactory masters either to Oxford or Cambridge, or to the ordinary training colleges.

See also J. L. Brereton: *County Education,* 1874.

(b) *Derwent Coleridge on the Possible Future of the Training Colleges* (1862). "If hereafter the training colleges should be collectively incorporated; should be combined into one, or perhaps into more than one aggregate, each with a central authority, and common organisation for corporate purposes, while the several colleges should be separately, and to a great extent independently administered; and if, having obtained this character, they were thrown open for the purposes of general education, real education, of a liberal yet practical kind, dealing as at present with the

lower rather than the upper branches of learning, with the elements rather than the higher combinations of knowledge, yet so
as to provide, not a school, but something analogous to an university training, for the sons of yeomen, tradesmen, artizans of
the higher, and professional persons of the lower grade; while the
training of the schoolmaster, no longer limited to a particular class
of schools, though not the sole, continued to be the leading object,
and characteristic feature of the system...so, and I believe so
only, might these colleges obtain general and adequate support
from independent sources, when the aid and control of the State
might be gradually, though never perhaps wholly, withdrawn, and
the elementary schoolmaster be trained, if not at his own expense,
yet with the help of some comparatively small exhibition."

Such a scheme "would fill up the space downwards in the
social scale, which the elder universities and public schools have
long left vacant, and which I do not think it desirable that they
should attempt to resume; a space which no institution not
offering the advantages of collegiate residence can adequately fill".

The Teachers of the People, 1862, pp. 58–9.

(c) *A Proposal for a Teachers' University* (in an address by
Harry Chester to the United Association of Schoolmasters of
Great Britain, 1861). The speaker commented on certain defects
of the existing training system: the fact that teachers were drawn
too exclusively from a single class; the danger of an overstocked
supply of certificated teachers; and the doubtful value of "Parliamentary Protection" for elementary teachers—and urged the
desirability of transferring the power to grant certificates from
the State to a University. "Now if your degrees and licences to
teach, which we call certificates, were granted by a University,
the graduates would have naturally a share in its government.
But this is, of course, impossible, when the degrees are issued
by one of the political departments of the State; and I need hardly
ask you which system is the more likely to produce a robust,
masculine character, that which cannot confer, or that which
naturally confers, upon its subjects a power of self-government."
Whilst recognising that the Education Department was doing

valuable work, he felt "convinced that every one of its measures should be so shaped as to prepare for the time when its powers, being no longer needed, might be safely surrendered to another authority more in harmony with our constitutional traditions". "I conceive", he said, "that the great want of popular education is a University which may do for the middle and lower classes what Oxford and Cambridge, apart from the collegiate life which is in them, but not essentially of them, have done and do for the higher classes." They had seen the foundation of the Universities of Durham and London. Why should there not be, say, a University of South Kensington? All training colleges might be incorporated colleges of the University, which would grant degrees and licences to teach. Such institutions as the Royal Academy of Art, the Royal Academy of Music, the School of Mines, the College of Preceptors, and Schools of Science and Art might also be incorporated in the University.

"When you (i.e. the schoolmasters in the audience) or your successors became graduates of the University, teachers would no longer be a protected class, artificially raised, and necessarily subject to numerous restrictions; they would have before them a far wider career; they would find in their ranks men drawn from a much greater variety of social origin than at present; they would become a part, not separate, but blended with the other parts, of the great scholastic profession of the country; and they would be associated with other graduates, not teachers, but most successful students, the very elite of the working-class, and middle-class, and not a few of the higher class, having special attainments which the University had tested and recorded. Thus circumstanced, the elementary teachers would be a more liberal body than can ever be created by a Government; and would be free from the reproach which is now sometimes directed against them, that they are too much penetrated by a class feeling, too much given to talk and to think in the grooves of the Council Office, too narrow and confined in their views."

   H. Chester: *The Proper Limits of the State's Interference in Education*, 1861.

CHAPTER VIII

NEW DEPARTURES IN TRAINING:
(a) THE DAY TRAINING COLLEGE,
(b) THE PUPIL-TEACHER CENTRE

THERE was a sharp division of opinion among the Cross Commissioners upon certain proposals to establish "Day Training Colleges", which received considerable support as a solution of the two outstanding difficulties in the field of teachers' training at the time, viz. the need for undenominational colleges, and the need for increased facilities for training. The idea of the day training college was by no means a new one. Witnesses before the Select Committee of 1834 had suggested a scheme of such colleges before the residential college became the norm in England. In Scotland the residential college had never found favour, the only residential institution at the time of the Commission being the Episcopalian College at Edinburgh. Stow's Glasgow Seminary and Woods' Edinburgh Sessional School had been the prototypes of the Scottish training college. The renewed demand for training colleges of a non-residential type came mainly from the great urban School Boards, where commonly the secularist and the nonconformist elements were strongly represented. As the system of Board Schools developed, there was an increasing demand for trained teachers, and it was felt that the products of the denominational colleges were by no means the best for the work. The steady development during recent years of provincial university colleges added point to the demand for day training colleges, for here were institutions ready and willing to undertake the work of teachers' training. The

Yorkshire College, Leeds, was already conducting numerous evening classes for acting teachers, and Professor Bodington had devised a scheme for the institution of a training department in the college. The Welsh University Colleges at Aberystwyth, Bangor and Cardiff were also anxious to establish training departments, since in Wales the lack of accommodation, particularly for nonconformists, was acute.[1]

The most elaborate of the schemes brought forward was that of the Birmingham School Board, sponsored by the Rev. E. F. MacCarthy.[2] In Birmingham an attempt had been made to train ex-pupil teachers under Article 110 of the Code, which authorised grant for the training of assistant teachers. The grant from the Education Department for this purpose, however, was dependent upon the student having been a teacher for three years in schools under the same management, and hence the scheme was very unpopular, since teachers could elsewhere obtain their certificates in two years by studying on their own. The scheme was commenced in 1884, and classes were established under a Director of Training Classes, to be carried on in connection with central classes for the instruction of pupil teachers. The scheme was abandoned in 1886, but out of the experiment grew the scheme which was suggested in a memorial presented to the Education Department in December, 1885.

The new scheme was justified on four grounds. (*a*) The existing training colleges were providing an inadequate supply of trained teachers. (*b*) The denominational character of existing training colleges made it difficult for some candidates to get training. (*c*) Many eligible candidates would rather live at home than go into residence. (*d*) Finally there was pressing need for the provision of a course less expensive than the one in existence.

The day training college envisaged in the scheme had

[1] Cross Commission, *Final Report*, pp. 100, 101.
[2] Cross Commission, vol. II, pp. 657–62.

been in part suggested by the normal school at Worcester, Massachusetts. Ten or twelve colleges, each with 250 students, were to be established about the country in large towns, preferably those where university colleges were already at work. Students of both sexes were to be admitted at the age of sixteen for a period of five years' training. For two years they were to be full-time students at the college, attending practising schools when required. They were to spend one year as half-time teachers on half-pay in schools within a three-miles radius. The last two years they would spend as probationary teachers on full pay, but still under supervision from the college. The gap between leaving the elementary school and entering the day training college was to be bridged by the giving of maintenance grants and the provision of facilities for instruction, if possible in secondary schools, but failing that, in classes set up by the School Boards for the purpose.

This was one of a number of schemes brought before the Cross Commission, and it is noteworthy as tackling the whole question of training from the school-leaving point, and boldly suggesting an alternative to the pupil-teacher system. Other schemes were more concerned with the training college stage only, and suggested that part or all of the instruction of students in training might be carried out by the staffs of university colleges. Such a system was already in operation in Glasgow, where students at the training college who were sufficiently highly qualified on admission were allowed to attend one or two university classes, the subjects most commonly taken being mathematics, Latin, Greek, and English literature. In 1884 thirty-six out of seventy-four men attended, and in 1885 forty-one out of seventy-four, and in 1886 forty-six out of seventy-two. It was found that the training college students did well in the university classes, and also occupied the top places in the certificate lists.[1]

[1] Cross Commission, vol. II, pp. 836, 837.

The idea of the day training college came in for much criticism. It was pointed out that all the valuable training that followed from life in a residential college would be lost, and with it all religious influence. The result of this would be that, although the "day"-trained teacher might be intellectually in advance of the products of the older training colleges, there was no guarantee that his character had been rightly moulded for the important task of teaching the youth of the nation. Even Matthew Arnold, who bluntly stated that he did not like the existing system of denominational training colleges, and approved of the day training college system of Germany, did not feel favourably disposed towards the association of the training of teachers with the university colleges. He thought that there was no harm in the "seminary spirit", and preferred a "good training college", although he would like to see the control of the training colleges pass into the hands of the State or the local authorities.[1] A training college devoted to purely professional training would be "a very curious thing, with no real teaching in it, and nothing but a talking about educational principles".[2] The superiority of the German training colleges lay in the higher standard of ability of their staffs. "It is more as if you had in men like Professor Huxley or Professor Seeley to teach physiology and history."[3]

The training colleges on the whole were well pleased with their teaching, and saw no need for bringing university teachers into the business. "I do not like to say anything offensive about university professors," said the principal of Battersea to the Commissioners, "but I have not a very high opinion of them, I am bound to say, as teachers. I can conceive scarcely that they could teach more efficiently than we do."[4] Another training college officer pointed out, by comparing the annual cost of living of a Scottish student with

---

[1] Cross Commission, vol. I, p. 201.   [2] *Ibid.* p. 194.
[3] *Ibid.* p. 221.   [4] *Ibid.* p. 445.

that of an English student in a residential college, that the latter was very little greater, and that in return for the very small additional cost, better board and lodging were provided, meals were taken under better conditions, and both associates and surroundings were much more desirable. The Scottish student was often forced to take very poor and inadequate lodgings, and lost the advantages of college discipline and religious instruction.[1] The success of Scottish training college students, he said, at the university, was due to their superior previous education. In the Queen's Scholarship examination twice as many "first classes" were gained by Scottish candidates as by English, 72 per cent. of the former entering for Latin as against 12 per cent. of the latter. Moreover, it was important to remember that the standard of the Scottish university was lower than that of the English.[1]

The majority of the Commissioners gave little encouragement to these day training college schemes. It was felt that such colleges would lack force in moral training, and, considering home conditions, it was very desirable that the student should reside in college during his period of training. If day training colleges were to be established, it should be through private liberality. Residential colleges, however, might take "day" students if they wished.[2]

In the vigorous minority report drawn up by Lyulph Stanley, Dr Dale, Sir John Lubbock and others, it was stated that they did not consider that the official report had done sufficient justice to the need for more facilities for training. The Church of England was in a disproportionately privileged position in the matter of training colleges, the ratio of denominational colleges to others being much greater than the ratio of denominational schools to others. It was felt also that the majority report was "too grudging"

[1] Cross Commission, vol. I, pp. 481–2.
[2] Cross Commission, *Final Report*, pp. 101–2.

to new schemes like that of the Birmingham School Board.[1]

Yet another minority report, representing the opinions of a smaller minority led by Lyulph Stanley and Dr Dale, not merely supported the day training college suggestion, but passed severe strictures on the existing training colleges. Their denominational character was condemned, and the contention that this character was essential in order to foster and preserve the right tone of college life was refuted by reference to the undenominational colleges of the British and Foreign School Society, and women's colleges like Girton, Newnham and Royal Holloway. The work of the residential training colleges was poor. The principals were often inexperienced in educational work, the staffs were certificated elementary teachers, often with insufficient experience. Their moral influence was admitted to be good. The subscribers to the minority report agreed with the sentiments of an inspector of women's training colleges when he said: "My predominant feeling is one of admiration for the zeal and energy with which the work is being carried on, mingled with a certain sense of disappointment with the intellectual acquirements and technical skill obtained as the result of so much forethought, self-denial, watchfulness and ungrudging labour on the part of all concerned in the work of the colleges".[2]

In the matter of day training colleges, the enthusiasm of the minority was to prevail over the faint encouragement of the majority, and in 1890 the Education Department drew up regulations for the administration of grant to "day training colleges" in connection with universities and university colleges.[3] The number of day students who were Queen's Scholars was first of all limited to 200, but that limit was

[1] Cross Commission, *Final Report*, pp. 242–3.
[2] *Ibid.* pp. 285–91.
[3] New Code, 1890, Part 2.

removed in the following year. The students were to receive their general education in the ordinary classes of the university institution, their professional training being the work of a special department of the college.[1] Sanction was given to students to remain for three years if they wished, in order to take a degree. A number of university institutions seized the opportunity, and day training colleges were established in 1890 in connection with King's College, London, Mason's College, Birmingham, the Durham College of Science (now Armstrong College, Newcastle-on-Tyne), Owens College, Manchester, University College, Nottingham and University College, Cardiff. Others rapidly came into being: in 1891 Cambridge, Leeds, Liverpool and Sheffield; in 1892 Oxford, Bristol and Aberystwyth; in 1894 Bangor; and in 1899 Reading and Southampton. The day training college established at University College, London in 1892 was shortly afterwards given up.

For some time the number of students in the day training colleges was not large, the residential colleges being more popular, and attracting the better students. At Firth College, when the training department was opened, there were nine applicants for admission, but "unfortunately they all failed in the Queen's Scholarship examination".[2] In the first year there were twenty-five students at Manchester, and twenty at Newcastle, the Board Schools being used for practice in each case. King's College, London, made use of three voluntary schools for the students' teaching.[3]

The institution of the day training college is one of the most important points in the history of teachers' training in England. Certain immediate practical advantages accrued. The problem of staffing was largely solved, since all the non-professional work was carried out by the regular university

[1] Committee of Council, *Report*, 1889–90, p. 206 (Circular 287).
[2] *Ibid.* 1890–1, p. 421.
[3] *Ibid.* p. 420.

teachers, the only special staff needed being those concerned with lectures on education and the arrangement and supervision of teaching practice. Even the education lectures might be taken over by members of the academic staff, as at Liverpool, where they were in the hands of the warden and the professor of philosophy.[1] Indeed, there was a danger lest, in the attempt to provide lecturers of good academic standing, the importance of school experience might be forgotten. "A proper leaven of teachers of higher academical standing", wrote an inspector, "is most salutary, but there is reason to think that some colleges, and especially some day training colleges, need reminding that there are details and habits which can never be so well understood or communicated as by those who have been in continuous and close personal contact with the work of primary education as it is in actual working."[2]

From the start the examination of day training college students in academic subjects was left in the hands of the college teachers, so that they might cover all or some of the syllabus for a degree. Here began that policy of delegation in the matter of examinations for certificate which has steadily proceeded until the latest act of the Board of Education in handing over the duties of conducting the certificate examinations to local boards on which are represented the various interests concerned in the matter—the training college authorities, the universities, and the local education authorities. It was a token of the advance made by education, that it was felt by the responsible national authority that a centralised and rigid control of the certification of teachers was no longer necessary.

There were a number of immediate practical disadvantages which were only gradually remedied. Undoubtedly the day training college was no place for the weak student. Instead

[1] Committee of Council, *Report*, 1893–4, p. 149.
[2] *Ibid.* 1894–5, p. 174.

of the stuffy atmosphere of thorough-going coaching that prevailed in the residential training college, the student found himself in the more bracing atmosphere of the university, a place where commonly the very indifference of the teaching is a challenge to the initiative and ability of the student. The student who needed to be taught, instead of teaching himself, was better off in the ordinary training college. On the other hand the rigour of the university college meant that fewer really inept students were able to struggle through to certification, and thus a number of weak teachers were kept out of the schools. A more serious disadvantage was that the nature of the lectures attended by the students was often unsuitable. Commonly they attended the ordinary degree lectures, and as these were fitted into a three-year course, they were in most cases badly suited for a course of two years. There were certain practical difficulties in arranging for academic and professional activities to go on together without clashing, and there was always the danger of overwork. Because of the demands of the professional part of the course, there was often a considerable segregation of the education students from the other students of the college, so that one of the alleged benefits of the day training college, that of mixing teachers in training with men and women preparing for other professions, was lost.

No doubt a number of students were encouraged to embark on degree courses who were not really equipped for such an undertaking, although the number each year that obtained degrees was not large. In the year 1897–8, whilst 122 students matriculated, only seventeen passed intermediate examinations, and only six graduated.[1] A widely held doubt, however, was expressed by an inspector, after the day training colleges had been at work for seven or eight years. "I am more than doubtful myself of the good to the education of the country of degrees thus obtained (i.e. by inordinate

[1] Committee of Council, *Report*, 1898–9, p. 313.

pressure and study), and feel assured that more of the students who are pushed by main force through a degree course would have done better by following the more suitable, if less showy, curriculum, prescribed by the Department. I am far from saying that there are not students who have taken degrees and been greatly benefited by the discipline of their preparation; but they are, as far as I know, quite exceptional. We are running before we can walk."[1]

But apart from matters of detail, the institution of the day training colleges opened a new era in the training of the teacher. It meant that the "seminary" idea, popularised by Kay-Shuttleworth, was challenged after it had held the field in England unopposed for half a century. No longer were the residential training colleges to have the monopoly. No longer could their authorities prate, without fear of contradiction, of the inestimable advantages for moral growth and social development of herding together young men and young women, all preparing for the same work, in institutions where narrowness of outlook and meanness of administration were too often the rule. Their claims were now to be brought to the test of experience, and if those claims were to be justified, the justification must arise from a comparison of the qualities of the teachers coming from the residential colleges with those manifested by the products of the new training institutions, where the benefit of residential life was lacking. Thus it came about that the older colleges responded to the challenge of the day training colleges by increased activity and an expansion of outlook.

Certainly the day student lost a great deal through the lack of experience of collegiate life, but it was not all loss. He escaped the repressive, and often pettifogging restrictions of the training college, and enjoyed instead the educational opportunities of freedom. He escaped the petty intellectual atmosphere, where *ad hoc* instruction prevailed. He had the

[1] Committee of Council, *Report*, 1898–9, p. 322.

chance of mixing with students preparing for all kinds of professions, and stood a chance of avoiding that professional self-satisfaction which was one of the characteristics of the teachers sent out by the training colleges.

But the greatest significance of the development of the day training colleges lies not so much in the mere technique of teachers' training, as in the status of the study of education in popular estimation. The training college was never likely to produce an organised body of educational theory or history. The training college existed to train, that was its business, and that is what it claimed to do. In the broader aspects of education it was uninterested. The day training college, also, set out simply to train, but it proceeded to establish the systematic study of education as appropriate work for a university, and the progress which has been made in the formulation of educational principles, in the evolution and testing of new methods, and in investigation into the history of education, has very largely been due to the work of men and women connected with the education departments of universities and university colleges. A true university is loth to include purely professional studies in its activities unless it can carry them beyond the purely professional stage. Accordingly the universities refused to look upon education merely as the training of the teacher, or the study of the art of school-keeping. They saw in it a subject of vast significance and with great possibilities, a subject susceptible of scientific, philosophical and historical treatment, which they had neglected in the past, and they proceeded to render it worthy of university status. In time the day training college became the university department of education, and the change in nomenclature was highly significant. Professors of education were expected to "advance their subject" as well as train teachers; research degrees were instituted; centres of experimental study of educational problems came into being.

It was the university training departments that made the

training of teachers for secondary schools a matter of practical politics. The reputation of the colleges, and the reputed characteristics of the trained elementary teachers, made the training colleges proper distasteful to the secondary schoolmaster. But the same ill odour did not cling round the education departments of the universities, and after the institution of University Diplomas in Education, these departments began to undertake secondary as well as elementary training. In many cases, as time went on, the secondary element came more and more to predominate, and, with the gradual elimination of the non-degree student, there was some fear lest elementary training might disappear from the universities. Since the War, however, owing to the large numbers of students in training at the universities, which coincided with the check to educational development caused by the demand for economy, a great many graduates from the university training departments have taken up work in elementary schools.

Much adverse criticism is directed against the university-trained elementary school teacher, particularly by the older teachers in the schools who themselves went through the pupil teacher and training college treadmill. It has to be admitted that, so far as the actual technique of elementary teaching is concerned, the university sends out teachers less well qualified than the training colleges. But it is to be hoped that their longer academic training, and their broader and more philosophic treatment of educational principles and method, will render them capable of working out their own methods, which, because individual, should be more fruitful and significant than "cut-and-dried" methods acquired during training. Head teachers and the officials of local education authorities should not be too anxious for "quick returns" from their young teachers, in whose work potentialities of development are more important than immediate efficiency of a somewhat pedestrian kind.

It is interesting to speculate as to the possible future of the training colleges. Some critics maintain that as institutions they are obsolescent, but this, in the writer's opinion, is an erroneous point of view. It is too early yet to predict the result of their rapprochement towards the universities. Perhaps some of the smaller and more remote colleges will be found in time to have reached the limit of their usefulness, and will be turned to other uses, but there remains a place for an institution which definitely specialises in the technique of elementary education. The training colleges in university towns will possibly develop into halls of residence where all students will take degree courses and be trained in the university department of education, the training college retaining some autonomy in the matter of arrangements for the practical side of the training course. But there will remain a class of teachers for whom the university degree as it now exists is of doubtful value, especially the teachers of infants and the younger pupils in primary schools. There is, indeed, much to be said for the development of special degrees for such teachers which should involve a certain study of general cultural subjects together with a thorough scientific and historical study of some particular branch of educational technique. For work of this nature the training colleges might well be adapted.

The second new departure in connection with the training of teachers which became of importance during the latter years of the nineteenth century, was the growth of central instruction for pupil teachers, which aroused considerable discussion by the Cross Commission. At the time the Commission was sitting, whilst the day training college was yet only a project, the pupil-teacher centre was already in existence.

The whole pupil-teacher system came in for considerable debate. There was an increasing body of opinion which regarded it as obsolete, and definitely detrimental to the best interests of the teacher, although the conclusion reached by the majority of the Commission was that it remained the only possible means of supply, in spite of its disadvantages. Even the minority reports did not condemn it root and branch, although they expressed a more vigorous dissatisfaction than the official report with the working of "that specially English contrivance"[1] which had been intended by its founder, Kay-Shuttleworth, as a merely temporary measure, maintaining that the teaching of the pupil teachers was bad, and their own instruction inefficient. Some critics were in favour of the complete abolition of the system. The Rev. Dr Crosskey, of the Birmingham School Board, for example, said roundly: "I do not think that it is right to sacrifice the education of the working classes to an indifferent mode of preparing teachers". He pointed out the steady growth of facilities for secondary education, and quoted statistics to show that in 1886, 67 per cent. of the boys and 43 per cent. of the girls had entered their pupil-teacher apprenticeship from secondary schools. His recommendation was that "intending teachers" should proceed straight from the secondary school to the training college, half-time teaching being introduced during the last years of the school course.[2] He believed that the pupil-teacher system was "at once the cheapest and the very worst possible means of supply"[3] for the training colleges.

Matthew Arnold represented the commonest attitude towards the question, although one Commissioner was unkind enough to remark that "his affection seemed almost too strong for his judgment in the matter".[4] When asked whether it was his opinion that the pupil-teacher system had done its work, and that it was time to supersede it, he replied: "I have such an affection for it that I should be very sorry

[1] Cross Commission, *Final Report*, p. 267.
[2] Cross Commission, vol. II, pp. 556–7.   [3] *Ibid.* p. 637.
Ibid. vol. I, p. 197.

to speak ill of it; but the number of pupil teachers is diminishing, and I think one feels that a higher order of teaching has come in, and will come in more and more, than can be given by them; but it has specially suited England. The discipline, the relation of the boys to the teachers, I think, in the good cases was excellent, and prepared them better than any other mode".[1]

Excellent as had been the relations between master and apprentice in the best cases, for the most part the instruction of the pupil teacher had been, and remained, poor, and it was to remedy this that the centre system was devised. The development of centres is commonly associated with the great city school boards, but they were not alone in the effort to improve the education of the pupil teacher. Perhaps the earliest attempt at central instruction was not in a city at all, but in a completely rural district. As early as 1859 there was established at Wantage a residential institution for the training of pupil teachers and monitors, all girls, who resided together with their mistresses. There they received instruction, and were sent out into local schools to carry on their practical work. By 1898 sixty pupil teachers had completed their apprenticeship in this way, and of these, forty-five had passed on to a training college.[2] Such an institution was an isolated case, however, and was due to private enterprise and benevolence.

Amongst the religious bodies it was the Roman Catholics who made the first move. The Sisters of Notre Dame carried on a training college at Liverpool, attached to their convent at Mount Pleasant. Ten or twelve years before the Cross Commission, they had started the practice of boarding a number of pupil teachers in the institution. These girls taught during the day in the schools conducted by the sisters, and

[1] Cross Commission, vol. I, p. 186.
[2] Departmental Committee on the Pupil Teacher System, 1898, pp. 452–3.

were instructed together in the evening and on Saturday in the convent. The experiment proved very successful, and in 1886 there were fifty pupil teachers in residence, and arrangements were being made to receive a further forty in a branch convent in Everton Valley. Impressed by the superior results obtained in the examinations by these Roman Catholic pupil teachers, the Liverpool School Board instituted in 1878 half-time classes for first-year stipendiary monitors, and in 1884 made all their first-year pupil teachers into half-timers, and established special central classes for them.[1]

The most extensive experiments in central instruction were made by the School Boards of London and Birmingham. As early as 1874 the London Board had been concerned at the glaring defects in their pupil-teacher system, the chief being that the apprentices in their early years were really useless as teachers, whilst the apprentices at all stages were not receiving adequate instruction. In 1875 a scheme was devised whereby arrangements were made for more efficient instruction of pupil teachers out of school hours. This scheme, however, brought the Board into conflict with the Education Department, because the Code stipulated that the instruction of apprentices was to be given by the headmasters of the schools in which they worked. In spite of representations by the London Board, the department declined to alter the Code, but a modification was introduced in 1876, whereby certificated assistants were allowed to instruct pupil teachers belonging to the schools in which they were employed. In 1878 the London Board drew up another scheme, which was submitted to counsel for opinion, and declared to be illegal. By the Code of 1880 central instruction received official recognition, and a class of probationers was recognised. These were girls and boys between the ages of thirteen and fourteen who spent a year previous to apprenticeship in a school, receiving instruction and doing a certain amount of teaching.

[1] Cross Commission, vol. I, p. 333, and *Final Report*, pp. 90–91.

The London Board accordingly drew up a new scheme in 1882, which was not entirely satisfactory, and in 1884 a more radical reform was effected.[1]

Pupil teachers and probationers were divided into two sections. The junior section consisted of those who had not passed beyond the status of second-year pupil teacher; the senior section of pupil teachers in the third and fourth years. Juniors were not counted on the staffs of the schools, whilst seniors were distributed in the ratio of one to every forty children. The juniors spent half of every school day and Saturday mornings at centres. The only excuse which a teacher with apprentices might plead for keeping them from a centre was the visit of an inspector. Whilst in the school, they were not to be treated as menial assistants, but were to be engaged in learning school management, both in theory and practice, in examining home lessons, and preparing lessons on simple subjects, some of which might actually be delivered to a class under superintendence. The head teacher was to examine once a week the entries in the pupil teachers' report books, and to add his own comments. Managers were requested to examine the report books also.

The seniors spent a good deal more time in teaching, and attended the centres only on two half-days a week and on Saturday mornings.[2]

By 1887 there were eleven centres at work, giving instruction to 1636 pupil teachers.[3] Accommodation of every type was utilised to house the centres—"disused voluntary schools, private houses, one floor of a board school"[4]—and for the most part the accommodation was very poor. In a book of reminiscences one of these early London centres is eloquently described as a "rat-hole".[5] Each centre was put

---

[1] Board of Education, Circular 573, 1907, pp. 8, 9.
[2] Cross Commission, *Final Report*, pp. 88, 89.   [3] *Ibid.*
[4] G. A. Christian, *English Education from Within*, p. 23.
[5] *Ibid.* p. 4.

in the charge of a responsible teacher, and in 1887 there were forty-one permanent assistants employed, of whom nine were peripatetic, whilst there was a panel of thirty-six teachers available for occasional assistance on Saturdays.[1] The time-tables were complicated because of the various types of attendance, and work lasted for three hours morning and afternoon. Attempts were made to do something for the social life of the pupil teachers in the better of the centres, and Saturday afternoons were often devoted to social and athletic activities, carried out generally in the face of enor-mous difficulties. Various associations were formed. The social and athletic activities were organised by the London Pupil Teachers' Association, which introduced the majority of the pupil teachers to organised games for the first time. Non-professional interest was aroused. Toynbee Hall, for example, became a "sort of unofficial headquarters".[2] Within three months of the formation of the centres, the Rev. (later Canon) S. A. Barnett invited the heads of the centres to a dinner and a conference, and that was the beginning of a close co-operation between the hall and the centres. Every Saturday evening the pupil teachers would assemble for de-bates and similar activities, whilst in the summer excursions of various kinds were arranged. A resident at Toynbee Hall described vividly to the Cross Commissioners how difficult it was at first to arouse any interest or enthusiasm on the part of the pupil teachers. "I had for some time", he said, "a voluntary class of four pupil teachers who did the play of *As You Like It* with me. I was struck with their want of interest in reading generally, and the way in which all knowledge was valued according to its bearings on examination. ...When a party of thirty pupil teachers visited Cam-bridge...to look over the colleges and see the college boat races, it was frequently remarked by the men who entertained

[1] Cross Commission, *Final Report*, pp. 88, 89.
[2] G. A. Christian, *op. cit.* p. 35.

them how unenthusiastic they were, and how difficult it was to make them laugh."[1]

At Birmingham the pupil teachers were not allowed so much time away from their school work in order to attend the centres for instruction. Each pupil teacher was allowed only half a day away from school each week, and had to attend for two and a half hours for instruction at the offices of the School Board. In addition, three hours every Saturday morning were spent in central instruction in one of the Board Schools, and two and a quarter hours on two evenings in the week. Each of the centres was provided with a full-time organising director and an assistant, a science demonstrator and assistants who gave one lesson a week to each class, and an art master, whilst there was a panel of head and assistant teachers from elementary schools who might be called in to teach special subjects on Saturdays and at the evening classes. The scheme was put into operation in 1884 and met with considerable success.[2]

Undoubtedly the centre system made for more efficient instruction, although it was by no means universally successful. It appeared difficult of application in rural districts, and even in some towns (Sheffield for instance) its results were not good. A system instituted at Leeds, whereby pupil teachers were farmed out in groups to selected masters, but allowed no time off from school, was condemned by the inspectors. In London, however, the effect of the introduction of centres was gratifying, and the results in the Queen's Scholarship examination showed the centrally trained candidates to be distinctly the best. The Birmingham School Board, also, was very well pleased with the working of its system.[3]

There was not the same sharp division of opinion on the Commission over the centres as over the proposal to institute

[1] Cross Commission, vol. III, p. 464.
[2] Cross Commission, *Final Report*, p. 90.   [3] *Ibid.* pp. 91, 92.

day training colleges. Most of the witnesses were favourably disposed towards the new departure, although Matthew Arnold, whilst confessing that he had had no experience of the working of the system, condemned the centres, averring that they were adapted only to the most brilliant apprentices, a remark which had singularly little reason behind it.[1] There were, nevertheless, certain disadvantages about the centre system. It was felt by many that it would destroy or weaken what might, under favourable circumstances, be the most attractive part of the pupil-teacher system as a whole—viz. the personal relationship obtaining between master and apprentice. It was feared that the teaching power of the pupil teachers might be sacrificed to their more effective instruction, especially as the centre system, if it was to be successful, seemed to demand that a certain amount of central instruction should be given during school hours. There was the danger that the centres might develop into mere secondary schools and that boys and girls would become pupil teachers with no intention of taking up teaching as a career, in order to benefit from the secondary instruction given by the centres. In this connection one witness told the Commissioners of one father who regarded the pupil-teacher centre as the best institution for preparing for the Civil Service.[2]

Various suggestions were brought forward to provide for the elimination of the unsatisfactory pupil teacher. The simple solution of increasing the stringency of the annual examinations found considerable support. Another proposal is indicative of the way in which the problem was in effect tackled in later years, although it did not receive the official sanction of the Commission. Manchester already had a scheme whereby apprenticeship was delayed until the age of sixteen, the years intervening after the candidate's leaving the elementary school being spent at a secondary or "higher-grade" school, and it was suggested that similar schemes

[1] Cross Commission, vol. I, p. 200.   [2] *Ibid.* p. 482.

might become general. The suggestion which received the official blessing was the somewhat insignificant one that the apprenticeship period should be in two parts, and that unsuitable pupil teachers should be dismissed at the end of the first period.[1]

In its recommendations the Commission showed definite approval of the principle of central instruction, and advised financial encouragement by the Education Department. It was suggested that pupil teachers, especially those in their first year, should have more time allowed in school hours for private study. The institution of central classes should be encouraged by grants to the managers of voluntary schools and school boards, and that where central classes were impossible, grants should be made for the provision of some other means of special instruction.[2]

From 1886 to the end of the century, pupil-teacher centres came into being all over the country, although naturally the system was most developed in the great cities, where the rough and ready accommodation of the pioneer years was replaced by buildings specially designed for the purpose, the best being equipped with assembly halls, laboratories and art rooms, becoming, in fact, secondary schools for "intending teachers". This development of the centre system marked another stage in the downfall of the pupil-teacher system. It emphasised again the fact that the whole question of teachers' training centred round that of popular secondary education, and the whole trend of pupil-teacher legislation since 1890 has been to emphasise the aspect of education at the expense of that of apprenticeship, with the result that soon the voice of the pupil teacher will no longer be heard in the land. The centres were the precursors of the county and municipal secondary schools which came into being as a result of the Education Act of 1902, and in a great many cases they proved to be readily convertible. There were

[1] Cross Commission, *Final Report*, p. 92. [2] *Ibid.* p. 93.

many who stood out for the maintenance of distinctive institutions for the education of pupil teachers, but the struggle was a vain one, and as time progressed, centre after centre either closed its doors, or opened them to pupils of all kinds, irrespective of the professions they proposed to follow.

The general position of the pupil-teacher system and the training colleges was reviewed by a Departmental Committee in 1898. In its report this committee stated that the pupil-teacher system did not deserve all the adverse criticism that was directed against it, the deficiencies of pupil teachers being due more to their previous schooling than to shortcomings of the system. It was felt that the greatest defect was the low level of attainment expected in the pupil teacher and training college syllabus, and that the time was ripe for bringing all "intending teachers" on a level with "the best scholars of secondary schools".[1]

The supply of boy apprentices was very deficient, chiefly because of the relatively poor prospects offered by the profession in consideration of the years of preparation necessary. Whilst the elementary schools were bound to remain the chief source of supply, it was considered that all pupil teachers should complete their education in secondary schools, whilst it was desirable to get more candidates direct from the secondary schools, in order to broaden the outlook of the profession. The pupil-teacher centres were looked upon merely as "substitutes and supplements in an imperfect system", and it was recommended that the Queen's Scholarships should be extended to secondary school pupils who might fill in the time intervening between taking the examination and entering the training college by gaining some practical experience in elementary schools.[2]

The provision made for the education of the pupil teacher varied greatly in different parts of the country. Centres were

[1] Departmental Committee on the Pupil Teacher System, 1898, p. 5.
[2] *Ibid.* pp. 6–9.

mostly located in the large towns and were carried on by School Boards, generally in specially equipped buildings with special staffs. Central classes in the evenings were common in connection with voluntary schools, where the services of the pupil teachers could not be dispensed with so easily as in the Board Schools. Such classes were a severe strain both upon teachers and pupils. Correspondence classes, carried on as a business for private profit, were very flourishing, and many were very efficient within the inevitable limitations of the method. In some parts of Wales two out of the four years of apprenticeship were spent in a secondary school, when no teaching at all was demanded. Such a system was made possible by the enthusiasm of the Welsh for secondary education, which had resulted in the development of intermediate schools throughout the Principality, eighty of them being at work at that time. The rural pupil teacher presented a difficult problem, as is still the case. Correspondence classes and peripatetic teachers were suggested remedies which were considered by the committee to be unsatisfactory, and the best solution seemed to be the institution of small central classes.[1]

The centres suffered from many defects. They manifested a "professional and social narrowness of aim", and were liable "to subordinate educational aims to pressure of examinations".[2] The attitude of a certain section of the middle class to the centres is well illustrated by the evidence given to the committee by the headmistress of a London secondary school for girls.[3] She disliked the whole pupil-teacher system, and girls at her school who wished to become teachers were persuaded to remain at school until they were eighteen or nineteen, and then to go for six months as "volunteers" in good elementary schools. Some, however, became pupil teachers after passing the junior local examinations, and of

[1] Departmental Committee on the Pupil Teacher System, pp. 18–20.
[2] *Ibid.* p. 8.   [3] *Ibid.* pp. 250–2.

such the headmistress said, "I would sooner send them to a poor church school without a centre than I would send them to the best board school in London". The centres did nothing but drive their pupils for examination results. There was no moral control, and the talk was most objectionable. Girls who attended centres altered for the worse, "blossomed out a good deal in the matter of dress", and became rougher in manner.

There was a good deal of truth in some of the criticisms directed against the centres, quite apart from the somewhat snobbish suspicion shown in the criticism just quoted. Nevertheless they were doing a most valuable work, and in 1899, when a Committee on the Pupil Teacher System appointed by the National School Society reported, it recommended that pupil teachers from voluntary schools should be allowed to attend the Board centres.[1]

The Report of the Departmental Committee did not lead immediately to many reforms. Certain provisions in the Code of 1899 (e.g. the reduction of the number of pupil teachers per head teacher, and the prohibition of pupil teachers in schools with less than three adult teachers) were met unfavourably, and they were withdrawn by a Minute of June 29th, 1899. The Code, however, recognised probationers without examination, made certain changes in the curriculum for pupil teachers, and sanctioned the admission direct to training colleges of pupil teachers who had passed Senior Local or Matriculation examinations. The Code of 1900 reduced the ordinary period of pupil teachership (except in rural districts) from four years to three, and in 1902 the annual examination of pupil teachers was abolished. Centres developed steadily. A Report by the Federation of Teachers in Central Classes made in 1902 stated that of a total of 32,000 pupil teachers and probationers, 17,000 were receiving

[1] National School Society, Committee on Pupil Teacher System, 1899, p. ix.

their instruction in centres, whilst in the 1902 examination ninety-one out of the first 100 came from large centres.

The new regulations which came into force in 1903 initiated an era of real reform. They were based on two main principles—the deferring of the employment of pupil teachers in schools until a late age, and the continuance of preliminary education during pupil teachership. The minimum age for pupil teachers was raised to sixteen years (fifteen in rural areas). Their employment in school was limited to half-time, the rest of the time being devoted to the pursuit of approved courses of instruction, if possible in fully organised centres, otherwise in central classes.[1]

BIBLIOGRAPHY

COMMITTEE OF COUNCIL ON EDUCATION. Minutes and *Reports.*

BOARD OF EDUCATION. *Annual Report,* 1912–13 (contains sketch of development of teachers' training, and a set of reminiscences of training college life).

DEPARTMENTAL COMMITTEE ON THE PUPIL TEACHER SYSTEM. 1898. *Report* and Minutes of Evidence.

BOARD OF EDUCATION. Memorandum on the History and Prospects of the Pupil Teacher System (Circular 573) (being the Introduction to Board of Education: *General Report on the Instruction and Training of Pupil Teachers,* 1903–7).

ROYAL COMMISSION ON TECHNICAL INSTRUCTION. 1882–4, *Reports.*

ROYAL COMMISSION ON THE WORKING OF THE ELEMENTARY EDUCATION ACTS (CROSS COMMISSION), 1886–8.

SELECT COMMITTEE ON EDUCATION (PAKINGTON'S), 1865 and 1866. *Report* and Minutes of Evidence.

NATIONAL SCHOOL SOCIETY. *Annual Reports.*

—— Committee on the Pupil Teacher System. *Report,* etc., London, 1899.

[1] Board of Education, *General Report on the Instruction and Training of Pupil Teachers,* 1903–7, pp. 13–16.

J. P. Kay-Shuttleworth. Two Letters to Earl Granville, 1861 (included in *Four Periods of Public Education*, 1862).
—— *Memorandum on Popular Education*, London, 1868.
—— "Memorandum in recapitulation of the Facts and Suggestions discussed at the Conference on Training Colleges, March 21, 1872" (included in *Thoughts and Suggestions on certain Social Problems*, London, 1873).
Derwent Coleridge. *The Education of the People: a Letter to the Right Hon. Sir John Coleridge*, London, 1861.
—— *The Teachers of the People: a Tract for the Times*, London, 1862.
H. Chester. *The Proper Limits of the State's Interference in Education*, London, 1861.
British and Foreign School Society. *Annual Reports*.
Earl Fortescue. *Public Schools for the Middle Classes*, 1864.
T. Twining. *Technical Training*, London, 1874.
Birmingham and Midland Society of Teachers. Report of Deputation to Geo. Dixon, M.P. on the Position and Prospects of Certificated Teachers, 1872.
"D.C.L." *The Education Craze*, London, 1878.
University of Manchester. *The Department of Education in the University of Manchester*, Manchester, 1911. (See article by M. E. Sadler: "University Day Training Colleges: Their Origin, Growth and Influence in English Education".)
J. Thompson. *The Owens College: its Foundation and Growth*, Manchester, 1886.
J. Runciman. *Schools and Scholars*, London, 1887.
G. A. Christian. *English Education from Within*, London, 1922.
T. J. MacNamara. "Training College Student Days" (article in *New Liberal Review*, September, 1903).
A. Park. "The Higher Education of the Elementary Teachers" (reprinted from the *Manchester Guardian*), Ashton-under-Lyme, 1889.
S. Pryce. "The Pupil Teacher System: Its Abolition or Its Improvement" (paper read at St Asaph's Diocesan Conference), Lampeter, 1899.

H. MACAN. "Secondary Education for Pupil Teachers" (an abstract of recommendations and evidence of Departmental Committee), Kingston-on-Thames, 1898.

S. R. EVANS. *The Abuse of the Pupil Teachers' System and a Remedy*, Bristol, 1900.

NATIONAL FEDERATION OF TEACHERS IN PUPIL-TEACHER CENTRAL CLASSES. *The Pupil-Teacher Problem: the Latest Phase*, 1907.

CHAPTER IX

THE TRAINING OF TEACHERS FOR SECONDARY SCHOOLS

THE battle for the principle of training for teachers for schools other than elementary developed considerably later than in the field of primary education, and is not yet over. The great public schools are still sceptical of the value of professional training, although in many cases the lip-service continues which was given by the Headmasters' Conference fifty years ago. In the lower grades of secondary schools the majority of teachers are still untrained, but it is becoming increasingly difficult for the untrained graduate to obtain a post in such schools, which is clear evidence that the principle of training is now widely recognised in this sphere of education. All students who propose to become teachers in secondary schools and who accept Board of Education grants to assist them through a university course with this end in view, have to include professional training in their work at the university, and this usually consists of a post-graduate year spent in a university training department. Nevertheless, even yet, much less emphasis is placed in the secondary school upon training than in the elementary school, and the reason for this is in part historical. In the case of the elementary teacher the question of training involved the preparation of the teacher for his work both on the academic and the professional sides. With the secondary teacher, so far as men were concerned at any rate, the need for academic training was less pressing. Early in the nineteenth century the universities gave a fairly sound preparation in this respect for teaching the narrow curriculum of the secondary schools of the day, and as that curriculum gradually broadened the universities extended their work to meet the new demands.

Thus it came about that professional training, as such, had to stand or fall on its own merits.

This was true only for teachers in the better type of schools. There was dire need for both academic and professional preparation of teachers in private schools, and for women teachers, who were debarred (until the last quarter of the century) from the privileges of university education. It was in connection with these two classes that the movement for the training of secondary teachers began.

The pioneer was the College of Preceptors, which still continues a somewhat anomalous existence, but which has rendered signal services to the cause of education in the past. This body was founded in 1846, largely as the result of the efforts of Henry Stein Turrell of Brighton, and its object was to raise the status and efficiency of the teacher in the private school, who belonged to a particularly despised, and to some extent despicable, educational class. It was realised by the founders of the College of Preceptors that their status and respectability could be raised only by improving their qualifications and instituting a professional register of those recognised as efficient practitioners. Thus it may be said that the long and rather dreary battle over teachers' registration begins at this point.

The original membership included sixty names, and the aims of the new body were clearly embodied in two resolutions adopted at the opening meeting. The first stated that proof of qualification "both as to the amount of knowledge and the art of conveying it to others" should be required of all entrants to the teaching profession, the second, that the eligibility of candidates for recognition should be judged by a legally authorised body of people engaged in tuition. Accordingly in 1847 an Examining Board was set up, and twenty candidates were awarded diplomas.[1]

[1] College of Preceptors, *Fifty Years of Progress in Education*, 1896, p. 4.

The foundation of the College of Preceptors was a very significant event. It meant the introduction of a principle diametrically opposed to that holding in the State-aided elementary schools. Teachers themselves were to be responsible for maintaining the standard of their profession, and from the start it was hoped that the college might provide facilities for rendering members efficient, as well as setting up a bar to the inefficient. In other words, what was envisaged was a kind of Teachers' University, and with this purpose in mind, the college was incorporated by charter, in which it was provided that surplus funds might be devoted to "the founding or endowing of normal or training schools or instituting Lectureships on any subject connected with the Theory or Practice of Education".[1]

The ideal was lofty and admirably conceived, but the practical difficulties were enormous. The teachers concerned were mostly unmoved by any desire to improve their efficiency, and there was no means whereby an effective barrier might be erected against inefficiency. The establishment of such a bar was clearly the first thing to be fought for. Until 1860 little further was done, but in that year began a vigorous agitation for teachers' registration which continued, without any striking success, until the close of the century.

With the slender resources at its command, the college could do little in the way of provision for training. However, in 1861 a series of monthly evening meetings for lectures and discussions was commenced, and the services of distinguished lecturers were secured. The introductory address was given by Dr Jacob, and other lectures given included such topics as "Corporal Punishment" (by Joseph Payne, who was later to play a leading part in the activities of the college), "The Teaching of Euclid", "Heraldry as an Auxiliary to the Study of History", "The Best Means of Registering the Progress of Pupils", "Public Examina-

[1] College of Preceptors, *op. cit.* p. 9.

tions", "Physical Education", "The Teaching of the Classics", "The Education of the Eye", and "The Teaching of Geography". Some of these lectures were subsequently published.[1]

Meanwhile part of the growing interest in female education had been focussed on the question of training of women teachers in girls' schools. The Governesses' Benevolent Institution was founded in 1843 for the purpose of improving the status of the woman teacher in the school and the private family, and soon after its establishment the Rev. David Layng, the secretary of the institution, suggested that it might issue certificates of knowledge and of teaching capacity.[2] Most emphasis was laid, however, on academic training, for the need in that connection was the more insistent, and so we find that Queen's College and Bedford College, founded in 1848 and 1849 respectively, gave none of their attention to actual training in teaching. On the other hand a notable lead was given by Miss Buss, headmistress of the North London Collegiate School, who took a course of training at the Home and Colonial Training College, where, largely as a result of her enterprise, a "governess class" for non-Government teachers was set up. Miss Beale followed up this good example by establishing a "training department" at the Cheltenham Ladies' College for girls who proposed taking up the teaching profession, the training being little more than an informal pupil teachership.

The Schools Enquiry Commission, which reported in 1868, gave some attention to the training of teachers for endowed schools, and considerable interest was shown by witnesses in the question. There was fairly general agreement on the need for measures to be taken to increase the efficiency of teachers in schools of this type, but considerable variance as to the right method to adopt to attain this end. The

[1] College of Preceptors, *op. cit.* pp. 17, 18.
[2] Board of Education, Educational Pamphlet 23, p. 1.

actual report of the Commission was non-committal. It re-cognised that there was much to be said for the institution of a normal school for masters in endowed schools, after the pattern of the elementary training colleges. The improve-ment in the elementary schools was regarded as largely due to the work of the training colleges, whose success was owing, not so much to actual lectures in method and teaching practice, as to the continuous presence of the purpose of such institutions in the minds of teachers and students.[1]

John Stuart Mill was a strong advocate of the normal college scheme, pointing out that the worst products of the training colleges were better than many of the masters in endowed schools, since teachers dismissed from elementary schools regularly found posts as ushers in such schools. He considered that training colleges should be established both to teach subjects and to train in method, and should be provided with practising schools.[2]

The need for a wider academic, as well as professional, training was emphasised by W. C. Lake, who deplored the exclusively classical attainments of teachers drawn from the older universities. A training college giving a high, but broad, academic training in addition to professional work would be very valuable. Such a college would need to be financed by the Government, since it would make no appeal to charity like the elementary training colleges, and it should not be regarded as the only training college for secondary teachers, but as "a means of beginning the kind of teaching which will be found most suitable for the average of schools of this description".[3]

Earl Fortescue and the Rev. J. L. Brereton, who were the leaders of a movement for setting up "County Schools" and "County Colleges" analogous with the public schools and

[1] Schools Enquiry Commission, *Report*, p. 612.
[2] Schools Enquiry Commission, vol. II, p. 65.
[3] *Ibid.* vol. II, pp. 45, 46.

universities, found an excellent opportunity for pushing forward their scheme. The idea was that "county colleges" should be established, and federated after the manner of the University of London. Many of the existing training colleges might well become "county colleges", since they were in a transition stage and the number of "independent students" was steadily decreasing. Training would be retained as one function of the county colleges, which would be recruited largely from the "county schools", and thus both elementary and secondary teachers might be drawn from the ranks of the middle classes.[1]

Attempts to maintain a connection between ordinary training colleges and schools other than elementary had met with scant success. The most interesting instance was at York. Originally the middle-class "Yeomen's School" had been attached to the training college, but later it was transferred to Archbishop Holgate's Grammar School, and a model school was established. This was intended as an elementary school, but its pupils were mostly drawn from middle-class families. When eventually the Government grant was withdrawn because of the excessively high fees charged, the school became completely middle class, and the activity of the students was limited to observation. The principal of the York Training College recommended the institution of "middle" training colleges and practising schools, to work in combination with some scheme of apprenticeship.[2]

On the whole there appeared scant enthusiasm for the institution of "higher" training colleges. It was pointed out in the Report that in Prussia, where there was no normal training for secondary schoolmasters, in some respects they were better than their colleagues in France, being more concerned with "character and control" than mere teaching. It was felt that training colleges had a cramping influence on

[1] Schools Enquiry Commission, vol. v, pp. 134 and 302.
[2] *Ibid.* vol. iv, pp. 602, 603, 618, 619.

the mind, and there was a prevalent feeling that even elementary teachers would be the better for being trained with students destined for other professions. Moreover, a training college for secondary teachers would perforce be a Government institution, with the result that the State would lay its deadening hand on secondary education as well as primary, and methods would become stereotyped. Money available for such a purpose might be better spent in other ways.[1] Typical opponents of the secondary training college idea were T. Southeron Estcourt, who said "I am entirely opposed to normal training in Government schools or institutions as a means of supplying teachers. Open the trade, and the demand will ensure the supply required";[2] and the Bishop of Peterborough, who denied the need for higher training colleges, since the headmasters and senior assistants of endowed schools should be graduates from Oxford and Cambridge, and would not need training, whilst the lower assistant masters could be recruited from the diocesan training colleges.[3]

The Report had no suggestion as to the possibility of making the training of secondary teachers a university concern, which was to prove the key to the situation. One or two witnesses, however, raised their voices in favour of this plan. The veteran R. J. Bryce, who had given similar evidence to the Select Committee in the thirties, claimed that teachers should receive a philosophical training at the universities, and that an attempt should be made to place education upon a scientific basis. His whole life had been devoted to preaching this cause, and he had made numerous practical experiments in training in Belfast, where he had been principal of the academy for many years. This was the only vigorous plea for that form of training.[4]

---

[1] Schools Enquiry Commission, *Report*, pp. 613, 614.
[2] *Ibid.* vol. II, p. 6.   [3] *Ibid.* vol. II, p. 40.
[4] *Ibid.* vol. V, pp. 862–70.

The only point of almost general agreement was the desirability of setting up some machinery for testing and registering the qualifications of teachers in endowed schools. The Report recommended a "well-devised system of certificates" to be awarded on an examination not necessarily difficult, but "precise and strict", and opined that the institution of such a system of certificates would go far to solve the vexed question of teachers' registration.[1]

Following on the Report of the Commission, Forster introduced, together with his Endowed Schools Bill, a Bill for the organisation of secondary education and the registration of teachers other than elementary. This measure, known as the Forster No. 2 Bill, provided for the setting up of an educational council for the examination and registration of teachers. No unregistered teacher was to practise as head or assistant in a school. This was the first of a number of Bills dealing with registration, and the fate that befell it was to come upon several of its successors. It was vigorously opposed on the grounds of unwarranted interference with the liberty of the subject, and was discreetly dropped by the Government.

Foiled in the attempt to procure compulsory registration, the College of Preceptors concentrated for a time on developing its own training facilities, having widened its scope in 1869 by the admission of women to its Council, a noteworthy step forward, the first woman member being Miss Buss. In 1871 a Lectureship in Education was established, and Joseph Payne was appointed to deliver a course of three lectures at the house of the Society of Arts during the July of that year. The lectures dealt respectively with the Theory or Science of Education, the Practice or Art of Education, and Educational Methods, or special applications of the Science and Art of Education. Encouraged by the success of this venture, the college established a Professorship of

[1] Schools Enquiry Commission, *Report*, pp. 614, 615.

Education in 1873, in the hope that the Chair might be permanently maintained. Joseph Payne was appointed to the new position, and thus it may be claimed for him that he was the first Professor of Education in the United Kingdom. The post was little more than titular, however, and the first real Chairs of Education were those established in 1876 in the universities of Edinburgh and St Andrews.[1]

The scheme of Payne's course was as follows: (1) The Science of Education, based upon the study of the individual. (2) Application in the Art of Education. (3) History of Education, including an account of the theories and methods of most of the eminent writers on education from Aristotle, Plato and Quintilian down to Jacotot, Froebel and Herbert Spencer. In this way the first Professor of Education set out to cover the ground which still forms the field of work for the University Education Department—Principles, Method and History of Education.[2]

When the class started in February, 1873, only seventeen teachers had registered for the course, but fifty-one eventually put in an appearance, and this number was soon increased to eighty. The students attending were "mainly young teachers, unskilled in the art of teaching, and perhaps even more unskilled in the art of thinking".[3]

That Payne was aware of the criticisms which might be directed against a course of lectures on education divorced from organised practice, was shown by some of his remarks in his Inaugural Address given at the opening of the Second Year's Course in 1874. He agreed that it might fairly be asked what was the good of such a course, and admitted the justice of the criticism that without the co-operation of a training school it was bound to result in nothing but words. His not too convincing reply was that the students were

[1] *Vide infra*, p. 258.
[2] J. Payne, *Lectures on the Science and Art of Education*, 1880, pp. 163, 164.　　　　　　　　　[3] *Ibid.* p. 168.

practising teachers, who would gain experience by trying to put into effect the principles expounded in the lectures.[1] The realisation by the college of the inadequacy of such a course was made manifest by their later attempt to establish a thoroughly organised training college, which was definitely stated to be the ultimate goal in a "Proposal for the Endowment of a Professorship in the Science and Art of Education", an appeal for funds made public in 1874, in which it was said that the college looked forward to the day when it would have its training college with model and practising schools, library, educational museum and students' reading room.

The appeal complained of the indifference of the Government to the training of secondary teachers: "While Parliament has been liberal, not to say lavish, in its expenditure of public money in promoting the training of teachers for primary schools, and while the claims of our Universities, as well as those of science, literature and art have been fully recognised by the Legislature, as is shown by the ample Parliamentary grants annually voted for their support, the important class of teachers engaged in our public and private schools, to whom so large a part of the higher education of the country is entrusted, have hitherto had no means provided for them by which they could obtain any professional training". The college had approached the Privy Council in 1872 suggesting that Chairs of Education should be set up in the universities, but their representations had met with no result, and so the college was taking upon itself to supply the need.[2]

The appeal met with little response, and the professorship was suspended after the second year's course, but three lectureships were established in the following year: one on Psychology, held by Croom Robertson, one on the History

---

[1] J. Payne, *Lectures on the Science and Art of Education*, 1880, p. 181.   [2] College of Preceptors, *op. cit.* p. 24.

of Education, held by Quick, and one on the Practice of Education, held by Fitch.[1]

About the same time as the College of Preceptors was struggling to establish a settled Chair of Education, two such Chairs were set up in Scotland. Andrew Bell had left much of his large fortune for educational purposes, and he had founded at Edinburgh a lectureship on the principles of teaching and on the monitorial system. The lectureship had been allowed to lapse, but in 1876 the trustees of Bell's bequest decided to establish Professorships of Education at the Universities of Edinburgh and St Andrews. The bulk of the money from the bequest had been distributed amongst Scottish elementary schools, but this distribution was rendered unnecessary by the Scottish Education Act of 1872, and so funds were available for the new venture. S. S. Laurie was appointed to the Chair in Edinburgh and J. M. D. Meiklejohn to that in St Andrews.

Noteworthy inaugural addresses were given by the new professors, each significantly dealing with the position of education as a university subject. The more interesting was Meiklejohn's. He commented on the neglect of education as a subject by the universities. "Neither the English nor the Scottish Universities", he said, "have up to this time thought at all about the education of the people of the country; to them the primary and the secondary education of Great Britain has hitherto stood in the relation of that most-to-be-pitied class of orphans—those whose parents are still alive."[2] Whilst pointing out that the Chairs were in the "Theory, History and Practice of Education", he stressed the importance of the historical approach, which could humanise a subject otherwise merely technical.[3] He also noted

[1] College of Preceptors, *op. cit.* p. 26.
[2] J. M. D. Meiklejohn, Chair of Education, Univ. of St Andrews, Inaugural Address, 1876, p. 2.
[3] *Ibid.* pp. 12, 13.

the need for developing a true professional spirit by breaking down the barriers between the secondary and elementary schools, and the institution of qualifying tests for teachers in higher branches of education.[1]

This question of the training of teachers for higher schools had received some attention at the annual Conferences of Headmasters of Public Schools, and in 1871 a resolution was passed instructing the Committee of the Conference "to press upon the Universities the importance of taking some steps for the purpose of promoting the directly professional training of upper and middle-class schoolmasters". In 1873 it was decided to publish a list of headmasters who were willing to receive graduates as apprentices in their schools. Fourteen headmasters responded to the appeal, but at the 1875 Conference at Clifton it was reported that the scheme had met with little success.[2]

Sir James Kay-Shuttleworth, who had done so much to foster the training of elementary teachers in England, devoted much of his failing strength to an attempt to procure some provision for the training of secondary schoolmasters. With a view to promoting a committee to consider the possibility of making such provision, he called in 1875 a conference at his London house, to which were invited the heads of a number of public schools, the principals of the metropolitan training colleges, some inspectors under the Education Department, and a few other persons interested in the matter. As a result a committee was set up with Lord Lyttelton as chairman and Kay-Shuttleworth as vice-chairman, and, at its first meeting in February, 1875, resolutions were passed asserting the need for the training of teachers in secondary schools, and the desirability of establishing

[1] J. M. D. Meiklejohn, Chair of Education, Univ. of St Andrews, Inaugural Address, 1876, pp. 47 et seq.
[2] Select Committee on Teachers' Registration and Organisation Bills, 1891, *Report*, Appendix 2, p. 329.

normal colleges for the purpose. A Standing Committee was appointed "more particularly to confer with the Charity Commissioners as to the possibility of employing educational endowments in this way, with the Education Department, and with the Universities". Shortly afterwards Lyttelton and Kay-Shuttleworth were asked to prepare a memorial to the Charity Commissioners stating the case, and to draw up a statement for publication. A conference was held with the Committee of the Headmasters' Conference, and a declaration in favour of training was prepared and circulated, which bore the signatures of 200 head and assistant masters in higher schools. In the same year was published a "Sketch of the Reasons" for the establishment of secondary training colleges. Unfortunately after this first burst of activity the committee languished, largely owing to Lyttelton's death and the illness of Kay-Shuttleworth, and nothing more was accomplished.[1]

The interest of the Headmasters' Committee had, however, been revived, and in 1877 memorials were prepared to be forwarded to the universities of Oxford and Cambridge asking their co-operation. A tentative scheme was put before the Oxford Hebdomadal Council in April, 1878, in a letter to the vice-chancellor from the chairman of the committee, Dr Bell, which suggested the institution of a training department under a professor or lecturer. As a consequence of this approach a committee was set up at Oxford to consider the matter, and recommended the establishment of a delegacy to examine candidates in professional subjects and to make provision for lectures. When this committee's report was presented, it was lost by a small majority against the proposals.[2]

Cambridge responded by the establishment of the Cam-

[1] F. Smith, *Life of Kay-Shuttleworth*, pp. 312–15.
[2] Select Committee on Teachers' Registration and Organisation Bills, 1891, *Report*, Appendix 2, pp. 328 et seq.

bridge Teachers' Training Syndicate under the secretaryship of Oscar Browning, which was to arrange for lectures in the history, practice and theory of education, and to conduct an examination on the result of which a certificate was to be awarded. In addition to passing the examination, successful candidates had to give evidence of having taught for at least a year in approved schools. The syndicate also expressed its willingness to inspect places of training for non-elementary teachers, and to award certificates to successful candidates from those centres. The lecturers appointed by the syndicate were R. H. Quick for History of Education, James Ward for Educational Theory, and J. G. Fitch for the Practice of Education.[1]

The chief immediate result of the establishment of the syndicate was to show that the support of the public school headmasters was little more than lip service. Although in 1879, in response to a circular, which was sent out to discover how far the headmasters would support a scheme of university training, thirty-five favourable replies were received, and only eight unfavourable,[2] when it came to the point little was done to foster the scheme, and the lectures had to be discontinued. The syndicate, however, continued its existence as an examining and inspecting body and as such rendered great services in the cause of improving the status of women teachers, who provided the majority of candidates for the examination.

The first successful attempt to establish a training college, in the traditional sense of the term, for secondary teachers was the outcome of the efforts of the Teachers' Training and Registration Society, which was founded in 1877. This society opened, in 1878, the Bishopsgate Training College for Women, which was the first training centre to be

[1] Select Committee on Teachers' Registration and Organisation Bills, 1891, *Report*, Appendix 4, pp. 334, 335.
[2] *Ibid.* Appendix 2, pp. 328 et seq.

inspected and recognised by the Cambridge syndicate. The institution was organised on lines similar to those of the elementary training colleges, and use was made of the Central Foundation School for teaching practice. Five years later, in spite of the efforts of Miss Buss to have the college attached to the North London Collegiate School, it was removed to Brondesbury, and rechristened the Maria Grey Training College. The Maria Grey School had been opened in Brondesbury in 1881, so there was a practising school ready to hand.

The training given at the college included lectures in psychology, physiology, hygiene, logic, history of education, and methods of teaching, in addition to teaching under supervision and the conducting of criticism lessons. Visits of observation were paid to other schools. The school and college staffs were separate, and some lecturers were introduced from outside institutions. Thus Daniel of Battersea assisted with criticism lessons, Sully lectured on psychology, and teachers from schools lectured on the teaching of special subjects.[1] There were several courses available for students. One-year students could study for the Cambridge Higher Local Examination or for the Cambridge Teachers' Certificate. The latter course included teaching practice. The former course was essential for those wishing to become candidates for the Teachers' Certificate. In addition students might spend two years preparing for the certificate in Kindergarten work of the National Froebel Union.[2]

In 1885 the Cambridge Training College for Women was founded, and opened in two small cottages near Newnham, with no funds, but with the enthusiastic support of Miss Buss, Miss Clough and Dr Ward. Miss E. P. Hughes was

[1] Select Committee on Teachers' Registration and Organisation Bills, 1891, *Report*, pp. 103–6.
[2] Maria Grey Training College Prospectus, 1885–6, and Select Committee on Teachers' Registration Bills, pp. 103–6.

the first principal. The work of the college was based on a conception of training differing from that of the Maria Grey Training College. The training college tradition was largely deserted, and an attempt was made to approach education in a scientific and philosophical way. Practice was, however, included in the course, and four schools were willing to admit students for that purpose. The college flourished, and within ten years 283 students had passed through. Of these eighty-six had had a university training, but only ten of them had passed the Cambridge Tripos examinations.[1]

This progressive spirit amongst women teachers was a marked contrast to the prevailing apathy among the men. Undoubtedly it was in part due to the difficulties in the way of women obtaining degree qualifications, with the result that they were keen to qualify themselves in other ways. But probably the most important reason was expressed in the evidence of a witness to the Select Committee on Teachers' Registration and Organisation Bills in 1891: "To a great extent the women's movement was new: they were open to new ideas: they felt that they were fighting a great battle; they were more in earnest and more interested in the matter than the men, who had been going on in the same groove for many years".[2]

Practically nothing had been done so far as men teachers were concerned, the one attempt to establish a secondary training college proving a complete failure. In 1881 the question of training was again discussed at the Headmasters' Conference, and in 1882 a second series of questions was sent out to the headmasters, who returned a second series of discouraging answers. In spite of this rebuff, a number of public school headmasters decided to establish a secondary training college for men. A sum of £500 was subscribed, and in 1883 the Finsbury Training College was opened in

[1] Board of Education, Educational Pamphlet 23, p. 7.
[2] Select Committee, etc., p. 143.

rooms which had been offered free of charge at thē Central
Foundation School, with Courthope Bowen as principal.
Included among the members of the Council were prominent
headmasters such as Butler, Perceval, Bell (of Marlborough),
Thring and Ridding (of Winchester). The college opened
with four students, one of whom, an ex-pupil teacher from
an elementary school, was soon sent away on account of his
defective preliminary education. Assistance was given in the
work of the college by the staff of the Maria Grey College,
by James Sully, Daniel, and Quick. But sufficient students
were not forthcoming. As Courthope Bowen himself said,
prospective students always asked the question "How shall
I be the better off at the end of the practice?" He tried to
get the headmasters to commit themselves to lay stress on
training in making appointments, but without success, and
this he felt was the chief reason for the failure of the college.
"As a body the Headmasters rather admired training than
were anxious to make use of it. That I think was the great
reason why the men did not come."[1] The Finsbury Training
College ended its brief and inglorious career in 1886.

The pressing need for some provision for the training of
secondary teachers is shown in a striking manner by statistics of the Agency of the College of Preceptors. In the
year 1890–91, out of 1418 teachers passing through that
agency, both men and women, none held university certificates in education, twenty-five held the Diploma of the
College of Preceptors, and twelve the Government certificate. Only 113 were graduates, and forty-eight held Higher
Local certificates.[2]

Besides attempts at training in definite training institutions, in one or two places an "apprenticeship" system was
introduced, which found favour with those averse from any-

[1] Select Committee, etc., pp. 142 et seq. and *Education in the Nineteenth Century*, ed. Roberts, 1901, p. 181.
[2] Select Committee, etc., Appendix 2, p. 326.

thing more definitely systematic. The most striking of these
experiments was started at Cheltenham Ladies' College by
Miss Beale in 1885. The college, which was described by its
headmistress as an "aggregate of schools", was registered
as a training college, and in 1891 there were thirty-six students in training, including a number of kindergarten mistresses. Two mistresses of method were employed, one for
high school students, the other for kindergarten students.
Miss Beale expressed a vigorous preference for the school,
as against the training college, as a training agency, emphasising the importance of unbroken tradition between school-
days and training, and laying stress on the value to the
student of living the full life of the school. It is to be feared
that there was an element of lip service about this enthusiasm, for, when pressed by the Select Committee of 1891,
she had to admit that very little practice was done in the
college itself. "We have separate schools because they (i.e.
the students in training) cannot practise in the College much;
it is an expensive school, and we cannot give them much
practice there, and so they practise at an independent school,
a sort of high school."[1]

A somewhat similar training department was instituted in
1888 in connection with the Mary Datchelor Girls' School,
which had been founded in 1877. This department was open
to students from other schools, and was inspected by the
Cambridge syndicate. A mistress of method was in charge
of the department, and courses of lectures were arranged to
supplement the practical work.[2]

There was an apprenticeship system at work also in
the schools of the Society of Friends. In 1848 Benjamin
Flounders of York left £40,000 for the founding of the
"Flounders Institute" for the training of teachers for Quaker
schools. The institute was attached to Ackworth School, and

[1] Select Committee, etc., pp. 311 et seq.
[2] Board of Education, Education Pamphlet 23, p. 40.

provided residence for twelve young men who continued
their academic studies, receiving at the same time instruction
in teaching methods and doing teaching practice in the school
itself. The regular course was for two years, and in 1891
most of the students were taking external London degrees
in arts. By that date 260 men had received training in this
way. A somewhat similar training department had existed
at the Mount, the Friends' School at York, since 1838.[1]

A training by apprenticeship of this type was favoured by
many school authorities who looked askance at anything
more organised, in the belief that training should be kept in
the closest possible connection with actual school work. In
the event the method has largely given way before the
systematic course of the University Education Department,
although the Board of Education at the present time is willing
to give grants to students trained in approved schools. The
number of students so trained is very small, but it is noteworthy that the training departments both of Oxford and
Cambridge lay stress on students putting in continuous full-
time attendance at schools, and delegate a good deal of
responsibility to the schools. Thus the latest proposal of the
Cambridge syndicate suggests that each student should put
in two consecutive terms in a school (generally a boarding
school) during the year's training.[2] The immense advantages of a scheme which centres round the practical work of
the teacher are obvious, provided that the theoretical part
of the course is not neglected, and that provision is made for
adequate supervision and guidance of the student whilst he
is in the school.

The problem of the training of secondary teachers was
intimately bound up with the question of teachers' registration. The College of Preceptors revived its agitation for
compulsory registration, and in 1879 a Bill was introduced

[1] Select Committee on Teachers' Reg. and Org. Bills, pp. 255, 256.
[2] *Cambridge University Reporter*, October 28th, 1930.

into Parliament, mainly at the college's instigation, by Sir Lyon Playfair. This was dropped, but was reintroduced by Sir John Lubbock in 1881 in a debased form which opened the door of registration to all and sundry, did not insist upon training as an essential qualification for registration, and offered no inducements to teachers to put their names on the register. This Bill was also dropped, and for a time Parliament had rest from registration Bills, only to be faced with two in 1890. One of these was simply the Lubbock Bill exhumed, the other, promoted by the Teachers' Guild and the National Union of Teachers, was sponsored by Arthur Acland. This second Bill was designed to include teachers in all grades, and was modelled to some extent on the Medical Registration Act of 1858. Training was insisted upon as an essential qualification for registration, and unregistered teachers were to be excluded from the endowed schools and prevented from recovering fees in a court of law.

The rival Bills were submitted to a Select Committee, which heard evidence from a number of witnesses on the question of registration and training. The Committee's Report was presented in July, 1891. It was a non-committal document which, while manifesting a preference for the Acland Bill, recommended neither to the House, although giving a general approval to the principles both of registration and training. So once again the question of legislative action to enforce registration was shelved.

This was a distinct set-back to the enthusiasts for training. Compulsory registration, with some emphasis upon training as a qualification, though not making it essential, would greatly have furthered their cause. As it was, the situation was well summed up by the headmaster of Marlborough to the Select Committee: "I think that if a Registration Bill was introduced which made the training of teachers a prominent part of its provision, these schemes (i.e. of training) of the Universities might revive in full activity. There has been the want of some impulse (or constraint, if you like,) drawing the headmasters on the one side and the candidates for masterships on the other, into connexion with these schemes".[1]

Public interest was now well aroused on the question of the training of teachers for secondary schools, and the topic received considerable attention at an important Conference on Secondary Education which was held at Oxford in 1893. On the whole the Conference was favourably inclined towards training, although there were differences of opinion as to the right methods to adopt with secondary teachers. The point of view of most of the headmasters of public schools was a fear that legislative action in connection with training would lead to uniformity in the public schools, and a belief that the best method of training was a probationary period of two years in a school coupled with study for a university examination in the theory and practice of teaching. There was a general agreement that the university was the right body to concern itself with secondary training, although the president of the National Union of Teachers put in a strong plea for the common professional training of secondary and elementary teachers.[2] Miss Beale advocated the establishment of "academies"—local grouping of institutions around provincial universities, all of which should have training departments, with central model training colleges established at Oxford and Cambridge.[3]

The College of Preceptors now returned to its project of a training college. In 1887 it had been stated in the report to the general meeting that the Council had decided to double the number of educational lectures, to institute scholarships to assist students proposing to become teachers,

[1] Select Committee on Teachers' Reg. and Org. Bills, p. 64.
[2] Secondary Education Conference, Oxford, 1893, *Report*, pp. 106–8.
[3] *Ibid.* pp. 169, 170.

and to accumulate funds for the establishment of a training college for secondary teachers,[1] and by 1894 the training college fund amounted to £4000. A scheme was drawn up for a college for men only which was to provide a one-year course of professional training. Students must be over eighteen years of age, and must have received a good education, although graduation was not a necessary qualification. Scholarships were to be awarded to Honours Graduates and men who had distinguished themselves in the examinations of the college. Teaching practice was to be carried out in London schools.[2]

The training college was opened in 1895 under the direction of J. J. Findlay. Very little support, however, was received, and the experiment was abandoned in 1897 on the appointment of the principal as headmaster of the Cardiff Intermediate School. So failed still another attempt to provide for the training of men for secondary school teaching.

The question of training was bound to demand the attention of the Bryce Commission in 1895, but the Report of that body did little to further the cause. The rather dreary discussion on registration and training was recapitulated, and a recommendation was made that a register of all teachers was desirable, the qualifications for admission to the register being a certificate of general attainment together with some professional diploma. The sceptics with regard to training found a doughty champion in Bowen of Harrow, who emphasised that secondary, and particularly public school, teaching was quite distinct in kind from elementary teaching, and that character was all-important. "A bad man", he said, "teaching history well is a far worse thing than a good man teaching history badly",[3] a remark which illustrates well a whole body of muddled thinking in connection with the

[1] College of Preceptors, *op. cit.* p. 34.
[2] *Ibid.* p. 38.
[3] Bryce Commission, Minutes of Evidence, vol. III, p. 61.

question under discussion. The most valuable contribution to teachers' training made by the Commission was the publication of three memoranda: "The Training of Teachers", by Sir Joshua Fitch; "The Training of Secondary Teachers in France", by H. Ward; and "The Training of Secondary Teachers in Germany", by J. J. Findlay.[1]

The Commissioners recommended the establishment of an advisory body, the "Educational Council", to be made up of persons interested in and qualified to deal with educational problems and holding independent positions, to assist a Minister of Education, one of the duties of this Council being the establishment and maintenance of a register of teachers. A Bill to give effect to this recommendation, but leaving registration a voluntary matter, was introduced in 1896, but withdrawn half-way through the session.

Whilst the Bill was before Parliament a Conference on Secondary Education, along similar lines to that held at Oxford in 1893, took place at Cambridge. There was considerable discussion of the clauses in the Bill providing for voluntary registration, and a resolution was passed in its favour, although the measure was regarded as quite insufficient by some, and as undesirable by others. It was felt that a move in the right direction had been made, although it was realised that under a system of voluntary registration it would be mainly the doubtfully qualified who would seek the inclusion of their names on the register. "The main difficulty is to get a respectable register at all", said the Rev. J. O. Bevan, voicing the general opinion of the progressive party.[2] A resolution was also passed in favour of training, after a vigorous discussion.

In the spring of 1896 the London Division of the Incorporated Association of Headmasters appointed a subcom-

[1] Bryce Commission, Minutes of Evidence, vol. v.
[2] Cambridge Conference on Secondary Education, 1896, *Report*, p. 103.

mittee to see whether it was possible for steps to be taken to make effective provision for the training of secondary schoolmasters. This subcommittee, having considered the position in London, felt that it was desirable for the Council of the association to deal with the problem as a whole as it had been left by the Bryce Commission and by the Cambridge Conference. Accordingly the whole question was discussed at the Summer Meeting of the association held at Leicester in the same year, and a Training Committee was appointed with the Rev. Dr Flecker as convener. The business of this committee was to gather information as to systems of training of secondary teachers in foreign countries, to make a survey of the provision already made at home both in schools and in separate institutions, and to determine the precise nature of primary training and its relation to secondary training. The evidence thus gathered was incorporated in a series of articles in *Education.*

It was realised that the question was not one for sectional treatment, and a Joint Committee was set up on which were represented, in addition to the Association of Headmasters, the Association of Headmistresses, the College of Preceptors, the Teachers' Guild, the Assistant Masters' Association, the Assistant Mistresses' Association and the Preparatory Schools Association. This was the most representative attempt hitherto made to grapple with the problem. The first meeting of the Joint Committee was held on March 17th, 1897. The Headmasters' Conference had no official representation on the Joint Committee, but a conference was held with a number of heads of public schools in order to discover the reason for their indifference to training.[1]

The conclusions reached were expressed in a very important series of resolutions, which may be taken as summarising the most enlightened opinion of the time, and which accurately foreshadow the form which secondary training

[1] Training of Teachers Joint Committee, *Report*, pp. 3–6.

has actually taken. Preparation for secondary teaching should comprise a course of two separate but consecutive periods of academic and professional training respectively. A study of education should not be included as part of the work for B.A., lest culture should be reduced and education studied apart from practice; but whilst education should definitely be a post-graduate study, there was no objection to be made to the institution of higher degrees in the philosophy of education, analogous to the degrees of B.C.L. and D.C.L. Candidates entering for a professional diploma should be over nineteen years of age and possess a general education not less than that demanded by the other learned professions, including special advanced knowledge, not lower than pass degree standard, of some secondary school subjects. Professional training should include theoretical study of education, including psychology, and if possible ethics, logic and physiology; school organisation; method; and all or some of hygiene, educational administration and the history of education. Practical work should be carried out in some institution for professional training. Connected teaching experience should be gained in some recognised secondary school. The minimum time devoted to training should be one year, and a certificate should be given only after a year's successful experience of teaching. The institutions for training should if possible be associated with universities or university colleges, and should be responsible both for the theoretical and practical parts of the course. A training institution attached to a school should have a separate staff. Secondary training should not become a function of the primary training college. The staff of a training institution should consist of lecturers of university standing with secondary school teaching experience. A demonstration school was a desirable adjunct. The central authority should inspect training departments and decide what bodies were authorised to grant diplomas. The awarding of a diploma was to depend upon the candidate's satisfying public examiners, his lecturers, and the heads of the schools in which practice was carried out.[1]

In 1898 still another Teachers' Registration and Organisation Bill was introduced in Parliament, only to be dropped by the Government owing to pressure of other business. In the next year, however, the Board of Education Act set up the Consultative Committee, one of whose duties was to be the establishing and maintaining of a register of teachers, and in 1902 the Teachers' Registration Council was set up by Orders in Council, the register to come into force in 1906. As registration was not made compulsory the practical results of the institution of the register have not been very striking.

There was a general opinion in the teaching profession that training should be an essential qualification for registration, a resolution being passed by the Headmasters' Conference in 1899, and by the Incorporated Association of Headmasters and the Headmistresses' Association in 1900, "That this Conference (Association) is of opinion that, after the expiration of 5 years from the commencement of the Board of Education Act, no new member of the profession should be qualified for a place on the Register of Secondary Teachers who has not undergone a systematic course of training".[2]

The growing recognition of the university as the right place for the training of secondary teachers was in part due to the efforts of the Universities themselves. It came to be realised that the "day training college" system was very elastic and might easily be extended to include secondary training. Parallel with this extension came the institution of university certificates and diplomas. For some time the certificate of the Cambridge syndicate was not imitated, but in

[1] Training of Teachers Joint Committee, *Report*, pp. 6–15.
[2] *Ibid.* Memorandum on the Relations of Training and Registration, 1900, p. 2.

1883 the University of London instituted a "Diploma in Education" with graduation as a preliminary requirement, thus emphasising the post-graduate nature of professional training in a way not done by Cambridge. The Victoria University instituted a diploma for graduates in 1895, and in the same year a secondary training department was established at Armstrong College, Newcastle-upon-Tyne, to prepare candidates for the "University of Durham Certificate for Teachers in Secondary Schools", which became in 1902 the Diploma in the Theory and Practice of Teaching. At last, in 1896, Oxford followed the lead of her sister university. The Oxford Diploma in Theory, History and Practice of Education was instituted, whilst arrangements for lectures and training were left in the hands of the delegates for Local Examinations. Secondary training departments developed in other universities, until in 1900 there were twenty-one in action.

BIBLIOGRAPHY

SCHOOLS INQUIRY COMMISSION (TAUNTON) 1868. *Report* and Minutes of Evidence.

ROYAL COMMISSION ON SECONDARY EDUCATION (BRYCE) 1895. *Report* and Minutes of Evidence.

SELECT COMMITTEE ON TEACHERS' REGISTRATION AND ORGANISATION BILLS, 1891. *Report* and Minutes of Evidence.

BOARD OF EDUCATION. *The Training of Women Teachers for Secondary Schools* (Educational Pamphlet No. 23).

UNIVERSITY OF OXFORD. *Report of Conference on Secondary Education*, 1893.

UNIVERSITY OF CAMBRIDGE. *Report of Conference on Secondary Education*, 1896.

—— *Report of Conference on Training of Teachers in Secondary Schools for Boys*, 1902.

TRAINING OF TEACHERS JOINT COMMITTEE. *Summary of Report of Proceedings*, 1897.

TRAINING OF TEACHERS JOINT COMMITTEE. *Memorandum on the Relations of Training and Registration,* 1900.

MARIA GREY TRAINING COLLEGE. Prospectuses.

COLLEGE OF PRECEPTORS. *Fifty Years of Progress in Education,* London, 1896.

J. M. D. MEIKLEJOHN. "Chair of Education, University of St Andrews: Inaugural Address", Edinburgh, 1876.

S. S. LAURIE. "Chair of Education, University of Edinburgh: Inaugural Address", Edinburgh, 1876.

H. FORTESCUE. *Public Schools for the Middle Classes,* London, 1864.

J. L. BRERETON. *County Education,* London, 1874.

R. H. QUICK. "The Schoolmaster, Past and Future." (First course of lectures at Cambridge 1879–80.) Cambridge, 1880.

J. PAYNE. *Works,* 2 vols., London, 1880.

A. PEMBER. *Croesus Minor,* London, 1888. (Chap. III, "Those Who Teach Him".)

F. STORR. "The Registration of Teachers." (Paper read before the Brighton Branch of Teachers' Guild.) London, 1887.

—— "The Registration and Training of Secondary Teachers" in *National Education,* ed. Laurie Magnus, London, 1901.

E. LYTTELTON. Essay in *Thirteen Lectures on Education by Members of the XIII,* London, 1891.

A. BREMNER. *The Education of Women and Girls,* London, 1897.

H. HOLMAN. *English National Education,* London, 1898.

E. P. HUGHES. "Training of Teachers", Cambridge, 1901. (Article in *Education in the Nineteenth Century,* ed. Roberts.)

SIR P. MAGNUS. *Educational Aims and Efforts,* London, 1910.

Education, March 20th, 1897.

Educational Review, 1896, 1897, 1898. (Series of articles on teaching Diplomas and Certificates for non-elementary teachers.)

F. C. STEADMAN. *In the Days of Miss Beale,* Cheltenham, 1931 (Chap. XXII).

GENERAL BIBLIOGRAPHY

The following is a list of works having a general bearing upon the history of teachers' training in the nineteenth century. Some have been mentioned previously in connection with particular chapters.

BOARD OF EDUCATION. *Report*, 1912–13, Chapter I, contains a survey of the development of teachers' training, together with a collection of former training college students' reminiscences.

BOARD OF EDUCATION. *General Report on the Instruction and Training of Pupil Teachers*, 1903–7. (Historical Introduction, printed separately as Circular 573.)

BOARD OF EDUCATION. *Report of Departmental Committee on the Training of Teachers for Public Elementary Schools*, 1925.

BOARD OF EDUCATION (Special Reports):

    L. MANLEY and H. L. WITHERS. *English Students in Foreign Training Colleges.*

    J. J. FINDLAY. *The Study of Education.*

    F. J. R. HENDY. *Training of Secondary Teachers and Educational Ideals.*

BOARD OF EDUCATION. *Training of Women Teachers for Secondary Schools*, 1912. (Educational Pamphlet 23.)

COMMITTEE OF COUNCIL ON EDUCATION IN SCOTLAND. *Report*, 1905–6, pp. 595 ff.

G. E. LANCE JONES. *The Training of Teachers in England and Wales*, Oxford, 1924, especially Chapter I ("Historical development"), and Appendix B, 1, i, which contains useful statistics.

C. BIRCHENOUGH. *History of Elementary Education from 1800*, London, 1925, Chapter XII.

F. SMITH. *History of English Elementary Education 1760–1902*, London, 1931.

J. W. ADAMSON. *A Short History of Education*, Cambridge, 1919.
—— *English Education* 1789–1902, Cambridge, 1930, especially Chapter XVII, "The Schoolmaster's Profession".

R. L. ARCHER. *Secondary Education in the Nineteenth Century*, Cambridge, 1921, Chapter XIII.

GRAHAM BALFOUR. *Educational Systems of Great Britain and Ireland*, Oxford, 1903 (2nd ed.).

R. R. RUSK. *The Training of Teachers in Scotland*, Edinburgh, 1928.

R. D. ROBERTS (ed.). *Education in the Nineteenth Century*, Cambridge, 1901, Chapter IX, "The Training of Teachers", by E. P. Hughes.

T. H. WARD (ed.). *The Reign of Queen Victoria*, London, 1887. Article in Vol. II on "Schools" by MATTHEW ARNOLD.

H. B. BINNS. *A Century of Education*, London, 1908. (A history of the activities of the British and Foreign School Society, with numerous references to its work in connection with teachers' training.)

BRITISH AND FOREIGN SCHOOL SOCIETY. *Annual Reports.*

NATIONAL SCHOOL SOCIETY. *Annual Reports.*

P. SANDIFORD. *The Training of Teachers in England and Wales*, New York, 1910, Chapter II.

G. C. T. BARTLEY. *The Schools for the People*, London, 1871.

C. S. BREMNER. *Education of Girls and Women in Great Britain*, London, 1897.

H. CRAIK. *The State in its Relation to Education*, London, 1896 (2nd ed.).

S. S. LAURIE. *The Training of Teachers and Methods of Instruction*, Cambridge, 1901.

J. H. YOXALL. "The Training College Problem" (article in *Contemporary Review*, 1901).

J. E. G. DE MONTMORENCY. *State Intervention in English Education*, Cambridge, 1902.
—— *The Progress of Education in England*, London, 1904.

I. SHARPLESS. *English Education*, New York, 1905, especially Chapter III.

R. GREGORY. *Elementary Education*, London, 1895.

W. C. GRASBY. *Teaching in Three Continents*, London, 1891.

J. H. RIGG. *National Education*, London, 1873.

F. ADAMS. *History of the Elementary School Contest*, London, 1882.

R. E. HUGHES. *The Making of Citizens*, London, 1902.

D. KAY. *Education and Educators*, London, 1883.

C. NORWOOD and A. H. HOPE. *The Higher Education of Boys in England*, London, 1909.

COLLEGE OF PRECEPTORS. *Fifty Years of Progress in Education*, London, 1896.

D. SALMON and W. HINDSHAW. *Infant Schools: Their History and Theory*, London, 1904.

J. KERR. *Scottish Education*, Cambridge, 1910.

INTERNATIONAL HEALTH EXHIBITION. *Literature*, Vol. XVI, pp. 1–168, London, 1884.

ROYAL COMMISSION FOR THE PARIS EXHIBITION 1900: Descriptive Handbook accompanying the British Education Section.

INDEX

Schools Enquiry Commission, *see* Royal Commissions

Science and Art Department, 196 ff.

"Science of everyday things", 159 f.

Science, teaching of in training colleges, 127, 159 f., 196 ff.

Secondary education in relation to training of teachers, 22, 36, 77 ff., 117, 135 f., 141, 157, 234, 240 ff.

Secondary schools, training of teachers for, 23, 232, Chap. IX

Select Committees on Education, 23, 37, 41 ff., 221

Select Committee on Teachers' Registration and Organisation Bills, 263, 265, 267

Sharpe (H.M.I.), Rev. T. W., 201

Sheffield, Pupil Teacher Centres in, 239

Sheffield University, 227

Sierra Leone, 6

"Simultaneous" method, 2, 12, 26, 38 f., 51, 98, 102, 111, 130

Sisters of Notre Dame, 235

Society of Friends, 51, 265 f.

Southampton University College, 227

South Kensington Normal School of Science, 197 f.

Stanley, Lyulph, 225 f.

Stanley Grove, Chelsea, *see* Chelsea Training College

State Normal School, 50 ff., 60, 96, 134, 146

Steinmetz, 27

Stettin Training Seminary, 27

Stipendiary monitors, 122

Stockwell Training College, 199

Stow, David, 2, 12, 26, 31 ff., 51, 148, *see* Glasgow Normal Seminary

Strasbourg Training Seminary, 29

Sully, James, 262, 264

Switzerland, development of teachers' training in, 29 ff.

Syllabuses (Training College, Queen's Scholarship and Pupil Teacher), 120 ff., 127 f., 132 f., 149, 151 ff., 184, 242

"Tapahoe", 6

Tate, Thomas, 62

Teachers' Guild, 267, 271

Teachers' Registration Bills, 266 f., 273

Teachers' Registration Council, 273

Teachers' Training and Registration Society, 261

Teaching practice, 72, 83, 92 f., 100 f., 104, 107, 164 ff., 198 ff., 263, 265

Temple (H.M.I.) Rev. F., 154, 167, 169

Theory of education, 45 f., 112 ff., 157, 166 ff., 232, 255 ff., 258, 261, 272

Thring, Edward, 264

Thurtell (H.M.I.), Rev. Alex., 151

Tolling, Isaac, 6

Toynbee Hall, 238

Trimmer, Sarah, 3

Truro Training College, 147

Tufnell, E. C., 30, 64, 186

Turrell, Henry S., 249

Universities and teachers' training, 48 f., 77, 136, 169 f., 198, 218 ff., 221 ff., 248, 254, 257 ff., 266, 272 ff.

University College, London, 98, 227

University Training Department, 49, 157, 217, 231 ff., 248, 260 f., 266, 268, 273 f.

Unwin, Rev. J., 148

For EU product safety concerns, contact us at Calle de José Abascal, 56–1°, 28003 Madrid, Spain or eugpsr@cambridge.org.

www.ingramcontent.com/pod-product-compliance
Ingram Content Group UK Ltd.
Pitfield, Milton Keynes, MK11 3LW, UK
UKHW010347140625
459647UK00010B/896